OFF
BASE

new insights
into an old game

ANDREW TORREZ

Woodford Press • San Francisco

Printed in the United States.

Book, cover design and photography:
Jim Santore, Woodford Press

Library of Congress Catalog number 99-61897.
ISBN: 0-942627-43-1

Distributed in the United States, Canada and Europe by
Andrews McMeel Universal
4500 Main Street
Kansas City, MO 64111-7701

Woodford Press / Woodford Publishing Inc.
660 Market Street
San Francisco, CA 94104
www.woodfordpub.com

Daniel C. Ross, CEO and Publisher
C. David Burgin, Editor and Publisher
William F. Duane, Senior Vice President

Associate Publishers:
Franklin M. Dumm
William W. Scott, Esq.
William B. McGuire, Esq.

Laurence Hyman, Publisher Emeritus

To my wife, Terri, who's really the much better writer in our family.

ACKNOWLEDGMENTS

Everything about preparing this book has been a first for me, and it simply would not have been possible but for the assistance of a number of people. First and foremost, I would like to thank my editor, Phil Finch, who believed in me from the very beginning. Phil wore two hats during the writing and editing process. He was the man in the trenches, agonizing over every one of my painful comma splices and randomly placed semicolons, but more important, he was my "Morale Officer." Phil's suggestions uniformly improved what I had written, and he was a constant source of support and encouragement.

Most of this book was written during my term as a judicial clerk for Judge Lawrence Rodowsky of the Maryland Court of Appeals. (Well, during my off-hours.) Judge Rodowsky not only served as a sounding board for many of my initial ideas but also allowed me to take in the occasional afternoon Orioles game, or, at least, borrow his radio. All of the really good lawyers I've ever met have been passionate baseball fans, and Judge Rodowsky is first among them.

My ideas about baseball have been shaped over the years by discussion with other thoughtful fans, both in person and (in particular) over the Internet. To me, the best fans by far have been the ones on the unofficial Baltimore Orioles e-mail mailing list. The discussions there have been at a consistently high level, with criticism that is almost always well-founded (and free-flowing!). I can't begin to thank everyone on the O's list individually — you know who you are! — but I do want to highlight David Gerstman, who helped me track down a number of messages to supplement many of the chapters in this book.

Finally, I owe a large debt of gratitude to my friends and family, who provided unconditional support. My parents, Sharon and Gary, read over much of the book and offered their advice, encouragement, criticism and the occasional nagging. My wonderful sister, Carla, steadfastly believed in me, and also invented the word "zorbleen." Carla, I'm sorry I couldn't find a way to work John Locke into the book. My baseball friends — Mark, Rob, Gary, Dusty, Ruh, Steve and Jerry — listened to my ideas and helped me flesh out my arguments. And my non-baseball friends helped me figure out how to make this book more interesting to a wider audience. In particular, I want to thank Lisa Sullivan for all of her help (and occasional admonishments). And, of course, I would not have managed to write a book, move twice and change from one full-time job to another without the patience and loving support of my wife, Terri-Lynn.

CONTENTS

PART ONE

A NEW LOOK
AT AN
OLD GAME

1

Everything you think you know about baseball is wrong

The ace right-hander your favorite team just signed for five years and forty million bucks? He's going to allow five runs per game.

That hot prospect they just called up from Yahoo Falls? He's going to hit .190, get sent back to the Dustbunnies, and eventually discover his true calling, selling auto parts in upstate Iowa.

That outfielder your team just sold to Japan? Too bad; he could have hit thirty home runs here, and now he'll have to settle for being a fan favorite in Yomiuri.

And even though that speedy leadoff hitter is going to steal another fifty bases this year, your team will still somehow have trouble scoring runs.

Everything you think you know about baseball is wrong.

Don't feel bad, though. When I say "you," I'm putting "you" in some pretty good company. "You" includes most major league general managers, guys who get paid seven figures to make baseball decisions. "You" includes nearly all of the sportswriters, guys who spend eight months of the year eating deli sandwiches with the big leaguers and, supposedly, studying every minutia of the game in excruciating detail. "You" includes practically every single person who's ever cast a ballot electing a ballplayer into the Hall of Fame. "You" covers players, coaches, managers, owners, fans, groupies, trainers, rocket scientists, concert violinists, your great-uncle Rupert, and even that annoying know-it-all in the Yankees cap at the bar.

Want proof?

Okay, here's an easy one. Everyone knows that the hallmark of a good team is doing the "little things" effectively, right? Even if you've got Hall of Famers around the infield and enough Cy Young awards to fill a suitcase, if your team doesn't execute the bunt, doesn't pick the right situations in which to steal, or can't pull off the hit-and-run, then they won't win the World Series, right?

Care to guess which team has employed "little ball" most often over the past three years? The one that has laid down the most bunts, put on the most hit-and-run attempts, and swiped the most bases?

The Kansas City Royals.

Over that period, KC has three all-expenses-paid trips to the cellar to show for it.

In 1997, the World Champion Florida Marlins had fewer steal attempts over the full season than the Cincinnati Reds did in half a season under Ray Knight. They ranked near the bottom in steals attempted (173), steal success rate (66.5%), bunts attempted (ninety-one), bunt success rate (84.6%), squeeze bunts (one, dead last in the NL), and hit-and-run attempts (eighty-three).

Their World Series opponents, the Cleveland Indians? Same story. Middle of the pack in steals (177), not an impressive rate of success (66.4%, near the bottom), and in the middle of the pack in terms of bunts attempted (sixty) and hit-and-run rate (ninety-six attempts).

Moreover, for the past ten years, championship teams have had lousy rates of success playing "little ball." They don't just bunt infrequently; when they bunt, they do it poorly. They don't just save up the hit-and-run for close games, they stay away from the hit-and-run because it doesn't work for them.

There is no evidence that good teams play "little ball" against other good teams in order to win; indeed, the evidence is overwhelming to the contrary.

Yet every year the experts drone the same mantra: "A winning team has to do the 'little things'." It's wrong. It has been proven false again and again. Still, almost everyone accepts it as true.

Here's another good bit of conventional wisdom: "pitching and defense win championships."

In reality, a team has to do only one thing to win a game: score more runs than its opponent. Pitching and defense prevent runs. That's exactly half the game. Prevent all the runs you want; if you don't score any, you can't win. It says so right here on Page One of the rule book.

Some championship teams have had really good pitching and an average offense; these teams win a lot of 2-1 games. Some championship teams have had really good hitting and average pitching and defense; these teams win a lot of 6-5 games.

No team has ever won a championship with pitching, defense, and a last-place offense. None. Not even the Hitless Wonders, the 1906 Chicago White Sox.

Want still more? Flip open your newspaper and you'll undoubtedly read how the newly acquired thirty-seven-year-old DH your team just shelled out big bucks for will bring his "veteran leadership" and "post-season experience" to the clubhouse and, presumably, improve the quality of everyone around him.

Care to guess the player with the most post-season experience in the 1990s? Rafael Belliard. Perhaps the single worst player in the history of the sport; certainly the worst active major leaguer. Does anybody really think that this guy is going to help a team?

I realize that this is a radical proposition. After all these years, surely the baseball experts who have been close to the game for decades would have figured out the angles by now, right?

Not necessarily.

Bad ideas are like diseases. The obviously idiotic notions kill their host instantly and die out before they can spread. Like bunting with your cleanup hitter: the stupidity is so clear that nobody does it. Any manager who did do it very often would find himself out of a job.

The most destructive baseball ideas, like the worst viruses, are insidiously bad. They lay dormant for a long time, slowly eating away at your team from inside. They're not so bad as to make you lose instantly and for all time; otherwise they would get pruned out.

But they still kill you, slowly.

If you look around baseball, there are plenty of signs that the people running the game often don't have all the answers. (Or, at least, all the *right* answers.)

When one team can have the largest payroll for more than a decade and have zero championships to show for it, that's probably a sign of a bigger problem than mere bad luck.

When a general manager expresses surprise that his team's star free agent is hitting .250, chances are good that someone's method of evaluating talent could use some fine-tuning.

When an organization trades a future Hall of Famer for one month of a pedestrian left-handed reliever, that's more than just an accident.

When the best catcher in the history of the game goes sixty-three rounds in the amateur draft and is picked up basically as a nepotistic favor, then something is very wrong.

All of the above actually happened. For those of you playing along, that's the 1981-95 Yankees, the White Sox and Albert Belle, the Boston Red Sox trading Jeff Bagwell for Larry Andersen, and Mike Piazza.

How did it get to be this way? What set this virus loose?

It's a combination of multiple factors, but let's look at the three big ones up front:

1. Media coverage

Most fans get their information and ideas about baseball from the opinion leaders in the sport, the sportswriters and sportscasters who are paid to be experts. And most of these individuals have not seriously changed the way they cover and discuss the game in thirty years. Go down to your local library and check out the microfiche copy of any sports page from a major city's newspaper in the summer of 1968. The difference between that story and one written today will be trivial, at best. (And, as I'll discuss later, most of those small differences are misleading rather than informative.)

Think about that for a minute. Since 1968, baseball has undergone a series of drastic changes. They're easy to list, and I'm probably still leaving out a dozen things: the pitching mound has been reduced from a mountain to a molehill; the strike zone has been shrunk to postage-stamp size; half the teams get to replace a pathetic hitter with a powerful one;

baseball is played in Coors Field, and, with lesser effect, in a half-dozen other hitters' havens; the rosters have been expanded to twenty-five men; and so on, and so on. The net effect of all these changes has been to double the average number of runs scored per game.

To put it bluntly: in 1968, if your team scored three runs in a game, you probably won; in 1998, if your team scored three runs, you almost certainly lost.

Despite all this, most sportswriters and broadcasters cover a game today exactly the way they would have covered it thirty years ago, and with the same assumptions about game strategy and talent.

2. Management sloth and disincentives to compete

This isn't really a book about economics, so I won't dwell too long on it, but big league baseball — notwithstanding Commissioner Bud Selig's protests to the contrary — is an amazingly profitable business today.

Baseball really needs a sort of "sunshine" law that prevents any owner from publicly whining that he's losing money hand over fist without first opening his books to an independent public accounting. I'm confident that such an audit — taking into account the massive tax breaks, public subsidies, funding, and other goodies given away by cities — would show that every single team in baseball is making a healthy profit.

Each of these teams is owned by a group of smart business men and women, people who aren't known for throwing money away. And every single franchise that has changed hands recently — even much bemoaned "small market" teams like Pittsburgh — has been sold at a nice profit. In 1989, George W. Bush, Jr. invested $605,000 in the Texas Rangers; nine years later, when the club was sold, Bush's profit was ten million dollars.

The construction of the new Ballpark in Arlington helped to inflate the value of the franchise. Still, that's a 1,650% return on investment for a franchise that played essentially .500 ball, sported a mid-range payroll, and had one division title and playoff appearance.

Why are all these smart business people buying ball clubs if it's such a lousy investment? And how come nobody has had to sell at a loss?

I'll let you ponder those questions. In the meanwhile, I'll say that the easy profit being turned in baseball has resulted in stagnation in the extreme.

What is the most creative promotion you've ever seen from a big league franchise in an attempt to sell more tickets? Wacky Refrigerator Magnet Give Away Day? Three Dollar Bleacher Night? This is innovation? (Okay, maybe "Disco Demolition Night.")

The stagnation extends to the field, too. If a ball club were truly losing money, you'd see the team's management experiment with the game itself, and try some high-risk strategies — after all, what would they have to lose?

What do I mean by high-risk strategies?

Employing a "slugger's shift," in which a team plays with three infielders and four outfielders. (Yes, this is legal.)

Starting the team's best reliever every day for one inning, and then relieving him with the team's would-be "starting" pitcher.

Effectively start two pitchers — one righty and one lefty — by swapping them back and forth between the pitching spot and one defensive position, say, left field. Since a player can move between defensive positions without penalty, the team could then maximize its lefty-righty matchups all game without using more than two pitchers.

Lead off the team's best hitter, hit the second-best hitter second, and so on, in order to get maximum at-bats for the best hitters.

Field a team of nine great-hitting, lousy-fielding DHs and completely ignore defense for a season.

Completely ignore stolen bases. Refuse to hold runners on because of the disadvantage in positioning your fielders.

Tag up from first base on fly balls to right field, rather than go halfway. The Bill Veeck special: DH a midget and lead him off to draw, maybe, 500 walks per season.

Sure, some of these ideas are probably pretty stupid (but they've never been proved wrong, either). How do we really know whether they would work? In more than one hundred years of baseball, is it really plausible that no one has tried anything more radical than sitting down a left-handed batter against a left-handed pitcher or moving the second baseman ten feet to the left?

If Selig's Brewers were losing a hundred grand a day, you can bet that his team would be doing all of these things and more; after all, what would he have to lose?

In reality, though, ball clubs have everything to lose. So they play it conventional and ultraconservative. Take a look at any randomly selected team press release; it will read like a bad *Saturday Night Live* parody of a George Bush campaign address. ("Stay the main course ...") Teams are afraid to deviate from that course, for a variety of reasons that will come up in most of the rest of this book.

3. Business versus baseball interests: the "Name Game"

Take a look at the following numbers, which represent the 1997 seasons of two real big-league players:

	AB	R	H	2B	3B	HR	BB	K	SB	CS	BA	OBP	SLG
Player A	397	71	105	19	3	21	32	73	15	1	.264	.323	.486
Player B	612	76	143	30	4	21	40	105	8	2	.234	.284	.399

Now for a little background information: Player A is twenty-six years old and a good defensive outfielder who can fill in capably in center field. Player B is thirty-seven years old and, while a fair defensive outfielder in his prime, has clearly lost a step or more out in the field. Given all that, is there any logical reason to prefer Player B to Player A?

Not for me, there isn't.

Yet in the 1997-98 offseason, the Baltimore Orioles — a team with the highest payroll in baseball, a team with almost unlimited resources for acquiring talent — deliberately went out and signed Player B (Joe Carter) to replace Player A (Jeffrey Hammonds).

And this isn't an isolated example. The Minnesota Twins brought in Otis Nixon to replace Rich Becker. The Toronto Blue Jays added Jose Canseco and Mike Stanley, knowing that it would take time away from Jose Cruz, Jr. The Boston Red Sox added Mark Lemke instead of turning to, well, anybody.

In every case, the team turned to an older, more expensive, less capable player instead of going with the younger, cheaper, more productive option from within the farm system. Most of these examples — and countless others — involve snubbing not some "unproven rookie" who has yet to taste big league pitching, but a quality young player with two, three, four years of major league experience.

Why?

Name recognition. Add a well-known player whom everyone has heard of, that your fans have seen on SportsCenter, and suddenly the newspaper stories appear with the news that the team is contending, the fans are talking about the new guy in bars and on radio talk shows, and, in general, the customer gets the impression that the team is serious about winning.

Stick with a young guy, or — worse yet! — suggest bringing up a minor leaguer with no name recognition, and the exact opposite happens. Newspaper articles begin fretting about the team's "unsettled" second base spot, and Joe turns to Jim in the bar and says, "I've never heard of half these guys."

What is smart business in terms of marketing and publicity is ultimately poor baseball sense. But just about everybody does it the business way, and not the baseball way.

It doesn't have to be this way.

Baseball is a beautiful game for more reasons than I could list. But I believe there is one reason above all why baseball is the game that binds fathers to sons, that sparks bar-room debates, fantasy leagues, call-in shows, web pages, fan newsletters, conventions, and even research organizations: baseball is accessible. It is a sport that you or I or anyone can understand, completely, just by watching, paying attention and thinking.

In baseball, unlike every other sport, the media opinion leaders and experts are the guys who have paid the most attention. Simply having played the game is not enough. If Bob Costas or Peter Gammons or Gary Huckabay or Pete Palmer or Bill James have played baseball above the pick-up game on the street level, I'd be very surprised.

This is not to say that understanding baseball is easy — far from it! Baseball is like chess; the rules are (relatively) easy, and the game can be learned by anyone, but the strategic possibilities are virtually endless. A chess match is won not by the person with the most chess experience, or the one who knows the most secret inside stuff about chess, but the person who has thought ahead most effectively.

Think of this book as a vaccination against bad baseball ideas.

Armed with the proper knowledge, there is no reason why a team can't be competitive despite a payroll a fraction the size of the biggest clubs.

There is no reason why a first-year manager shouldn't be able to keep his job, and quietly put up Hall of Fame credentials while doing it.

There is no reason why a team's GM couldn't merrily fleece his competitors and have them thank him for doing so.

There is no reason for a beat sportswriter to miss the opportunity to write the kind of insightful columns, full of accurate predictions, which ultimately earn him respectful national attention.

There is no reason for even a casual fan to be surprised when one rookie comes up and plays like a dog while another rookie comes "out of nowhere" to lead the team in runs scored.

Above all, there is no reason why *you* can't be more savvy and knowledgeable about the game than 90% of the "experts" who have made it their career.

Before You Object . . .

I want to offer a preemptive defense against what I anticipate will be three big objections to the ideas in this book. I know these objections by heart because I have heard them so often from friends and acquaintances who happen to be baseball fans.

Objection #1:

There are too many numbers in this book. It's not about Real Baseball, it's about Rotisserie ball or computer games or something. But Real Baseball can't be measured in numbers.

I have played only one season of Rotisserie ball. I enjoyed it, and I have one chapter about it, but this is indeed a book about Real Baseball.

Furthermore, I'm not trying to persuade you to use numbers when you discuss baseball. If you're a baseball fan, you probably already do that. But I do want you to use the *right* numbers. Or use none at all. But understand that if you do, you're never going to know the sport.

Most people who loudly complain about "using too many stats" also use numbers when they're discussing the game. But the numbers they're accustomed to are so deeply ingrained that they don't really seem like numbers anymore: they're more like shorthand.

Here's an actual conversation I had a couple of days before I wrote this chapter.

Fan: Tony Gwynn is the best hitter in baseball.

Me: Really? What makes you say that?

Fan: What do you mean, what makes me say that? What's his lifetime batting average, three-sixty-something?

Me: .339. But isn't it significant to you that he's never hit as many as twenty home runs in a season? Or that he generally draws only about forty walks a year?

Fan: But he's a professional hitter. There's nobody in the game better than Gwynn at getting a hit.

Me: Tony Gwynn is probably the best singles hitter in the game today, I think you're right. But is that important?

Fan: What, are you nuts? He's a three-sixty-something hitter! Of course it's important!

(And so on.)

The Fan in that discussion used statistics in every single sentence! Sure, it looks a lot less mathematical when you gloss over it in vague generalities and write the words out instead of using numerals. But each and every claim that he made was, at its heart, based on a stats. When I asked him why he thought Tony Gwynn was the best hitter in baseball, he immediately responded with a batting average.

The Fan's problem isn't that he wants baseball free of stats; it's that he wants to rely on a stat which isn't very useful. Yes, I know we've had batting average for almost as long as we've had the game of baseball itself. But it isn't an essential part of the game: it's just shorthand that someone invented to help us understand how well a particular player is performing. And today we have other numbers which do that better.

This book isn't about convincing you to believe a number instead of believing something intangible. It's about getting you to use the proper number when you want to make a factual argument.

Numbers can't tell you everything. A stat line won't show whether a player's off-season conditioning regimen is lifting weights or drinking seven vodka tonics a day. Stats can't tell you if a ballplayer is distracted by a divorce or suffering from nicotine withdrawal.

But the statistics *will* show the effect of any of those things. When a pitcher with a career 3.00 ERA starts giving up five or six runs a game, the statistics don't tell us whether he's distracted or incapacitated, but they do suggest that something out of the ordinary is affecting his performance. On the other hand, if a player has been lifting weights and working out, but is still hitting .235 with middling power, we can conclude that maybe he isn't ready to blossom into a big home run threat after all.

Baseball is full of mysteries and imponderables, and numbers can't help us answer them all. But the right numbers, used properly, can help us understand the true value of a player's past performances, and — even more important — help us to predict that player's future performances much more reliably than most "baseball men" who make their living in the game.

I'm not kidding when I say that if you know what numbers to look at, and how to use them, you can be a better judge of baseball talent than most major league general managers.

That brings us to ...

Objection #2:

Come on — coaches and general managers do this for a living. They've played the game at every level, they understand it in a way you and I never will. They're the experts — they must be right, and we can't possibly know more than they do.

Corporate marketing whizzes with seven-figure salaries came up with the idea for "New Coke." Experienced political pros staged a photo opportunity featuring the five-foot-six Michael Dukakis wearing an over-size helmet and sitting in a tank, instantly evoking unflattering comparisons to Rocky, the Flying Squirrel. Hollywood producers, after careful consideration, spent tens of millions of dollars to make "Howard, The Duck."

Experts made all these mistakes, with enthusiasm and with full confidence in their own wisdom.

If mistakes like these don't convince us that experts are fallible, then we have the day-to-day evidence in our own lives. Who hasn't had the experience of one's boss, or one's boss' boss, or some higher-up, promulgating an order that makes absolutely no sense? Ever wondered why the shipping department spends $15 to overnight a package to a location seven blocks away? Have you taken a look at the TV screen and wondered, "What were those people thinking when they made such an idiotic commercial?"

We know that professionals, the people at the top, are capable of horrendous blunders and appalling stupidity.

Why, then, should the actions of major league ball clubs be cloaked with an aura of invincibility? Why do some fans — and virtually all journalists — have such a hard time accepting that professional baseball people make some very dumb mistakes? And that they often make same mistakes, over and over again?

Don't be afraid to second-guess the hometown sportswriters or the front-office professionals. Much of their understanding of the game is based on principles that were out of date before Franklin Roosevelt was elected to his second term. I doubt that most baseball experts have ever bothered to question the assumptions that underlie the decisions they make throughout their professional careers.

But you can. And you should.

Objection #3:

Okay, maybe you're right: maybe a ball club's front office does overrate mediocre players, and maybe the media are just reporting p.r. blather uncritically. But what's wrong with that? Why are you so negative? Can't you be a fan?

I don't believe in fluff pieces and press releases and feel-good journalism about the hometown team, precisely because I *am* a fan — a fan who cares about my favorite baseball team, a fan who wants really to understand what's happening in my favorite sport.

I don't buy into the fantasy that every prospect grows into his abilities at the major league level, that ballplayers stay at their peak until age forty and then retire gracefully, that every player is always as good as his best season. But a lot of people — including many baseball professionals — do seem to reside in this never-never land.

Personally, when I fall for feel-good, warm-and-fuzzy thinking like this, I end up feeling cheated. As you will no doubt discover from these pages, I grew up and have lived most of my life in the Baltimore area, as a lifelong Orioles fan. I cut my sports-analyzing teeth on the likes of Craig Worthington, Ken Gerhart, Billy Ripken, John Stefero, Mississippi Mike Smith, Bob Milacki, Jeff Robinson, Juan Bell, Damon Buford, and Manny Alexander. You've probably heard of half of these guys, and that's my point.

Are the front office and broadcast announcers and the other uncritical media doing a service to the fans when they twist the numbers and try to argue that these guys can play?

I wish one of the experts in the club management or the press had had the courage to admit, "Juan Bell is a stiff. He can't play. He's not going to help this team."

Just once, I would have liked someone to say, "Dammit, the emperor has no clothes."

Also, a critical baseball analysis isn't just about separating out the people who can play from the people who can't. It's about understanding the relative value of players. That Juan Gonzalez, rather than Alex Rodriguez, was the American League MVP in 1996, is a travesty. Not that Gonzalez isn't a great player. He just wasn't quite as great as A-Rod in 1996, and to say otherwise is to confuse fans and cloud the issue.

I also don't believe that criticism of a player means that you no longer like or respect or admire him. I think Tony Gwynn is a great ballplayer, and I enjoy watching him hit. He is one of the most amazing men to ever play the game, given that he hits almost as well with two strikes on him as he does any other time.

Nobody else in baseball can do that. Frank Thomas hits .251 with two strikes. Ken Griffey hits .213 in those situations. Albert Belle, .224. Juan Gonzalez? A paltry .195.

But Gwynn hits .337. That's astonishing, far and away the best in all of baseball.

It doesn't mean that Gwynn is one of the best hitters in the game, though. He's not. He doesn't hit for enough power, nor does he draw enough walks to be ranked up there with the big boys. I know that he has the endorsement of Ted Williams, but, quite frankly, Tony Gwynn isn't even close to Williams as a hitter.

So, this book is critical in a lot of places. Somewhere in here, I'm probably going to suggest that one of your favorite players isn't as good as you think he is. (Particularly if your favorite player is Joe Carter.)

I do that because I'm a fan.

I do it because I want to see as many well-informed fans as possible. I want to see the best possible game of baseball. Read on, and you'll discover how the sport can be better than it is now. And isn't that really what optimism is all about?

3
Misleading Statistics

"Ninety percent of the time I will stick with batting average, homers and RBIs for hitters, and won-loss record and ERA for pitchers, when I use statistics, because the reader can digest those without thinking. I will throw in such things as on-base percentage, slugging percentage and strikeout-walk ratio when it's pertinent to a story. If, for instance, I'm writing about Daryl Hamilton's troubles or success as a leadoff hitter, I pretty much have to delve into his OBP."
— San Francisco Giants beat writer Henry Schulman, in an interview
  with *Baseball Prospectus*, April 27, 1998.

Baseball, for even the most casual fan, is a game of numbers. Ask a friend what he thinks of a particular player, and the answer you get will likely revolve around a number or two. "That guy's a .300 hitter," "a twenty-game winner," "a 100-RBI man," "he stole thirty bases" — we have all heard these phrases, we've all said them.

Moreover, each of those statistics carries a distinct meaning, independent of any actual results. Three years ago, Ken Griffey was hurt for most of the season, and hit .258. But fans watching Griffey in the Kingdome — probably on a night when Junior was 0-for-4 — could turn to each other and say, "Hey, that's Ken Griffey, he's a .300 hitter."

Mike Mussina has never won more than nineteen games. David Cone hasn't won twenty games in a decade. But when somebody says that these guys have "twenty-win stuff," we know exactly what they mean. The numbers no longer simply measure a player's performance; they have become a substitute for describing the ballplayer himself.

The problem is that statistics are still just measurements. And what they measure is now largely unrelated to the meaning those phrases have acquired. Luis Polonia has a career .292 batting average, but he was bumped to the bench at age twenty-eight and was out of baseball four years later. Is that really the kind of guy we mean when we say ".300 hitter?" Curt Schilling and Jamie Moyer both had the same number of wins in 1997, and Moyer has thirty more wins over his career (which is just one season longer than Schilling's). But we can't seriously mean that Jamie Moyer is a better pitcher than Curt Schilling, can we?

Most statistics used to describe baseball players are misleading, worthless, or both. That is especially true of hitting stats. A hitter's value can very accurately and concisely be described using a single number called OPS, which stands for on-base percentage (OBP) plus slugging percentage (SLG). Each of those components paints approximately half the picture of a ballplayer's total offensive contributions, and when you put them together, you get a very reliable index of offensive value

That's why, throughout this book, I will refer to ballplayers' statistics with an abbreviated stat line that looks something like this: .265/.350/.450. The first number — provided only for context — is the player's batting average; the second is his on-base percentage; and the third is his slugging percentage. To get his OPS, you just add the last two numbers together, and, in this case, you'd get .800. More on that later.

I won't kid you; this book has a lot of statistics. My friends and colleagues call me a "stathead," and I take that more as a compliment than an insult. But the stathead way is more about ignoring statistics than about paying attention to them. We need to ignore most stats, because stats are constantly used by sports journalists and sportscasters in ways that confuse rather than enlighten. Moreover, a large part of the game of baseball requires one to make a snap judgment — should I pinch hit for Marquis Grissom here? Should I put on the hit-and-run? — and in those situations it is invaluable to be able to get a very good picture of a player's total ability with one or two numbers.

Unfortunately, contemporary sports journalism simply inundates us with numbers. We don't get one or two; we get thirty, fifty, a hundred. One of the few ways baseball reporting has changed in the past thirty years is the rapid proliferation of "junk statistics" making their way into columns, on talk shows, even on the scoreboard at the ballpark. Log on to the Internet; in under five minutes, you can pull up Jason Giambi's batting average during the daytime on artificial turf with less than two outs.

Some of these specialty stats are useful. If Ryan Klesko's batting average against left-handed pitchers is 100 points lower than his batting average against right-handers, that probably tells us whether Klesko should be in the lineup against a lefty.

On the other hand, how much value should we place on Ellis Burks' batting average on artificial turf? Or Jeff Bagwell's RBI per at-bat ratio? Or Carlos Delgado's strikeout-to-groundout percentage? How do we give all these specialty stats the weight they deserve?

Statistics are either *predictive* or *descriptive*. The first type is by far the more useful, because if you can interpret them, they'll give you a good idea of how a player or team is going to perform. The statistics I use in this book are almost always predictive stats. The second type tells us what has happened but doesn't offer a clue to what is going to happen in the future. They might be interesting as oddities, but they don't really help us understand the sport or the players. They're basically useless.

Unfortunately, few of the media types who report on big league baseball seem to understand the difference between the two types of stats. Play-by-play broadcasters and color analysts are some of the worst offenders. Throughout the game, batter after batter, they throw out a seemingly random barrage of numbers and factoids, few of which have any value.

With hours of air time to fill every day, I guess they can't afford to be discriminating. But this abuse of stats, mixing the trivial with the truly significant, is counterproductive to helping fans really understand the sport and how it is played. Worse, the broadcasters tend to become enthralled with certain arcane and useless stats, investing them with a significance that doesn't exist.

One of the broadcasters' favorite useless stats is a player's recent performance with the bases loaded. I'm going to spend a little time with that one here, not only because I find it particularly irksome, but because it illustrates one of the most common flaws in deceptively useless stats.

For example, every season a few hitters will put up spectacular numbers with the bases loaded. If a hitter has gone six-for-eight during the season with the bases loaded, you can be sure that the next time he comes up in that situation, the play-by-play guy is going to say that he is "hitting .750 this season with the bases loaded" — the implication being that he becomes a different hitter in this special circumstance. Never mind his mediocre bat speed and that nasty habit of chasing 0-2 sliders out of the strike zone. Because the bases are loaded, he has suddenly become as dangerous as a blowtorch in a fireworks factory.

In truth, that is almost always a fallacy. A hitter doesn't change from at-bat to at-bat. He doesn't become any more (or less) skilled when men are on base. If a hitter had a magical ability to step up the level of his game on demand in certain key situations, he would be a fool not to play at that level all the time. Spectacular success with the bases loaded is really just a good run of luck, a random occurrence that the player almost never repeats.

In 1997, Toronto outfielder/DH Joe Carter hit .600 with the bases loaded. Already legendary as a "clutch player" for his World Series heroics, in '97 it seemed Carter was collecting a hit every time he came to the plate with the sacks full. He picked up twenty RBI — nearly one-fifth of his total of 102 — from just ten bases-loaded at-bats. Carter's twenty RBI in bases-loaded situations included two grand slams and, perhaps even more surprisingly in light of his poor plate discipline, he had four bases-loaded walks.

That's some awfully impressive play. It's even more impressive when you remember that Carter hit just .234 that year. He was basically terrible in every other situation, but with the bases full, Joe Carter made Babe Ruth look like a busher. In his book written that year, announcer Jon Miller — who I think is clearly the best in the game — wrote, "If I were managing a ball club, I'd call a team meeting, bring my players together, and I'd tell them, 'Watch Joe Carter. Be like Joe Carter.'" Miller then wrote three pages of effusive praise for Carter, most of which revolved around his mentality in RBI situations.

The next year, Carter hit .111 with the bases loaded. One measly single. No grand slams. As great as Carter looked in '97, he looked completely awful in '98. The Orioles, who signed him as a free agent, were surely disappointed if they expected him to repeat his 1997 performance.

In 1997, the Brewers' Jeff Cirillo hit .625 with the bases loaded; in 1998, he hit .091. In 1997, Ken Griffey hit .857 with the bases loaded, which is awfully good, even for him. The next year, he hit .200.

These statistical flukes occur because almost anything can happen in a limited number of attempts. If I ask each of my readers to take out a coin and flip it ten times, recording the result of each toss, I know that a few of you out there are going to end up with heads eight or nine times out of ten. It's not because you have a special skill at tossing a coin: it's because true odds don't always hold over the short run.

This is sometimes known as a "small sample size," and it is a favorite phrase of statheads, who recognize that any player can look like a hero or a bum over a few dozen at-bats. This is why a player's batting average with the bases loaded over a single season is a purely descriptive stat. It tells us what he has recently done in the situation, but it doesn't give a clue to what he will continue to do. (The fact that you just threw eight heads out of ten doesn't make you any more likely to do it again.)

However, some stats *are* predictive. If a pitcher posts a 3.50 ERA for five consecutive seasons, chances are pretty good that — absent injury — he'll post an ERA around 3.50 next year, too. If a pitcher regularly strikes out 200 a year, he'll probably strike out 200 guys next year. If a batter hits thirty homers in 600 at-bats, he'll probably hit around thirty homers if you give him 600 more at-bats.

Some stats are more reliably predictive than others. A pitcher who walks 100 batters a season is very likely to continue walking a lot of hitters guys next year. A hitter's batting average is usually more consistent from year to year than the number of homers he hits, which often varies drastically.

Unfortunately, few sports reporters make any attempt to distinguish between meaningful statistics and meaningless ones. When they do manage to throw in useful numbers, they often do so in ways that marginalize the value of those stats.

Look again at Henry Schulman's candid explanation of how he integrates statistics into his reporting, at the beginning of this chapter. In essence, what he said was: *I use only the stats people have come to expect, except when I'm trying to illustrate a very narrow point.*

Yet the stats that people have come to expect are almost always misleading. Here's a typical game example from the 1998 Texas Rangers:

2B   Mark McLemore leads off the game with a solid single to right.

CF   Tom Goodwin grounds weakly to the shortstop; McLemore is forced at second base, and Goodwin is on at first on the fielder's choice.

LF   Rusty Greer strokes a single to center and Goodwin advances to third.

RF   Juan Gonzalez flies out to medium-depth left field; Goodwin tags up and scores.

1B   Will Clark strikes out.

Okay, so the inning is over and the Rangers lead 1-0. But look at who gets the glory statistics from the above scenario. Tom Goodwin gets the run, and Juan Gonzalez gets the RBI.

Is that logical? Goodwin and Gonzalez made two of the three outs! They were among the least significant players in that inning. On the other hand, McLemore and Greer both got hits and made the inning possible, and they get nothing to show for it. It's hardly fair.

I was at the ballpark once when a man in the row in front of me was getting exasperated with his girlfriend's questions about the nuances of various scoring rules. "Why," she asked, "is it an RBI when the batter grounds out and the guy on third runs home? Shouldn't you have to get a hit?" After fumbling around for an explanation a few times, the guy lamely resorted to, "Well, it's just the way the rules are."

I wanted to lean forward and tell the woman — who probably left the ballpark thinking what a stupid game baseball is — that she had a good point. It *is* silly that the batter at the plate gets an RBI for a weak grounder. If rules governing statistics are so byzantine that even diehard fans can't explain them to interested newcomers, maybe it's time to question whether the stats which those rules create have any real value. (In fact, RBI are not a good indication of a player's hitting ability. I'll have more on that in another chapter.)

Before a statistic can have any meaning for us, we have to know what is being measured, and the context in which it stands. If I were to tell you that Detroit is a very unsafe city because it had eighty-three zorbleens last year, you would probably want to know two things before deciding whether to agree with me. First, you'd want to know what a zorbleen is, and second, you'd want to know how many zorbleens other cities had over the same period of time.

That intuitive response is the heart of all statistical analysis. Any statement backing up a conclusion ("Detroit is unsafe") with data ("eighty-three zorbleens") can be broken down into two components. The first component is the *metric* — what the data is measuring. If a zorbleen is a measurement of sunspot activity, or of magnetic field strength, or of days above 90 degrees Fahrenheit, then it hardly matters how many or how few zorbleens Detroit had last year; whatever the number, it's irrelevant to the city's safety.

But suppose a zorbleen *is* a good metric; let's say it refers to death due to violent crime. Even if the measurement is relevant, however, we must have context before we can judge whether the number is high or low.

How many zorbleens do other similar-size cities experience? Is eighty-three a lot of zorbleens, or a few?

Baseball sports writing has given us a lot of zorbleens; stats that don't measure anything meaningful, which are so unfamiliar and devoid of context that we have no idea whether the number is large, small, or somewhere in between.

We need to start weeding out the zorbleens.

Let's start with batting average.

Yeah, I know, batting average is as old as the game itself. It is a part of the lore of baseball. It is synonymous with a hitter's ability.

There's only one problem: it's terribly misleading. Think about how batting average is calculated. First you take the total number of hits the player has. Then you divide by the total number of times the batter has come to the plate after subtracting out, among other things, the number of times that player has walked.

But wait a minute. If batting average is supposed to be a measure of hitting ability, why shouldn't we count walks in batting average? They certainly require skill; if they were just luck, every player would walk at about the same rate as everybody else, and we know that doesn't happen. If we're using BA as a way to judge how much a hitter helps his team at the plate, then we really ought to include walks, because any team that has trouble getting men on base is going to have trouble scoring runs. Not making an out is one of the best things a hitter can do to help his team score runs.

So why don't we count walks in batting average?

It's because BA is an historical anachronism, left over from the dawn of the game, when baseball was played with a very dead ball, under rules which required *nine* balls before the batter walked. Under those conditions, the base on balls was an accident, not a skill.

Today, however, that isn't the case. The game has changed dramatically since its inception, but we continue to use batting average as our short-cut for measuring a hitter.

So why not start off with a statistic that doesn't arbitrarily exclude as many as one-third of a hitter's plate appearances? Why not count everything the player does to help his team — both hits and walks — and measure that against how often he *hurts* the team by making an out?

To put it in numbers, take a look at the following two players. Using traditional stat lines — batting average, home runs, and RBI — they both show up as .280-25-90 hitters. But fleshing out the whole picture with walks and OBP, we can see that these two players are far from identical.

	AB	H	2B	3B	HR	RBI	BB	K	AVG	OBP	SLG
Player A	500	140	25	5	25	90	100	75	.280	.400	.500
Player B	575	161	25	5	25	90	25	75	.280	.310	.471

Both Player A and Player B have the same batting average, the same number of doubles, the same number of triples, and the same number of home runs. Both have come to the plate the exact same number of times.

Yet Player A is clearly a much better hitter than Player B. Though they've been to the plate the exact same number of times, Player B has made fifty-four more outs than Player A. When he wasn't walking, Player A was hitting for power more frequently than B. (Although they have the same total number of homers, triples, and doubles, A got his in a smaller number of at-bats, so his ratios are better.)

Player B does have twenty-one more singles, but Player A has seventy-five more walks! Sometimes a single is more valuable than a walk, but that small advantage doesn't make up for the additional fifty-four times Player A has gotten on base.

A reasonable statistic would take this into account, wouldn't it? Fortunately, we don't have to reinvent the wheel. Such a stat already exists: on-base percentage is perhaps the single most useful number you can know about a player. The best way to think about OBP is not as a measure of what a player has done, but rather, as a measure of what he *hasn't* done. OBP reflects how often a hitter comes to the plate and does not make an out.

Does a high OBP really indicate advanced hitting skill? Take a look at the 1997 American and National League leaders in OBP:

AL:		NL:	
Frank Thomas	.456	Larry Walker	.452
Edgar Martinez	.456	Barry Bonds	.446
Jim Thome	.423	Mike Piazza	.431
Mo Vaughn	.420	Jeff Bagwell	.425
David Justice	.418	Gary Sheffield	.424
Manny Ramirez	.415	Craig Biggio	.415
Bernie Williams	.408	Ray Lankford	.411
Rusty Greer	.405	Kenny Lofton	.409
Paul O'Neill	.399	Tony Gwynn	.409
Tim Salmon	.394	Mark Grace	.409

That's a pretty impressive list.

This brings us back to the Schulman quote at the start of this chapter. Beat reporters discuss a player's OBP generally only when they're talking about a leadoff hitter, and in the same sort of context in which they might also discuss that player's batting average with the bases loaded. To the reader, both statistics seem to carry about the same amount of weight.

Nothing could be further from the truth. In 1998, for example, the four teams which advanced to the American League playoffs — the New York Yankees, Texas Rangers, Boston Red Sox and Cleveland Indians — finished 1-2-3-4 in the league in OBP. The Yanks, Rangers, and Red Sox were also 1-2-3 in runs scored. (Cleveland was sixth, with 850 runs.)

The four NL playoff teams — Houston, San Diego, Atlanta and the Chicago Cubs — were 1-2-3-5 in OBP, and 1-2-3-4 in runs scored. (If you're wondering what happened to the Colorado Rockies, they're not here because I've factored out the effects of Coors Field, for reasons that will become apparent later in this book.)

In short, pick the team with the best OBP, and you're almost guaranteed to pick a winner. The Yankees, who went 114-48, led all of baseball with a .364 OBP.

On-base percentage, however, is only half the story. It fully describes the number of times a player comes to the plate and whether he makes an out or not, but it doesn't differentiate between different kinds of "non-outs." A single, a walk, a triple, a home run all count the same.

Fortunately, we can flesh out our understanding of a player statistically with just one more number. Again, there's no need to reinvent the wheel; we can use the fairly common slugging percentage (SLG). Slugging percentage is total bases divided by at-bats. A batter gets four bases to his credit for a homer, three for a triple, two for a double, one for a single.

That's it. Know a player's OBP, and you understand how often he makes an out. Know his SLG, and you know what he does at the plate when he is not making an out. Add them together and you have a pretty good number for describing the overall ability of a hitter.

Don't just take my word for it, though. Take a look at the 1997 American and National League leaders in OPS:

AL:		NL:	
Frank Thomas	1.067	Larry Walker	1.172
Ken Griffey, Jr.	1.028	Mike Piazza	1.069
David Justice	1.014	Barry Bonds	1.031
Edgar Martinez	1.010	Jeff Bagwell	1.017
Jim Thome	1.002	Ray Lankford	.996
Mo Vaughn	.980	Andres Galarraga	.974
Manny Ramirez	.953	Tony Gwynn	.956
Bernie Williams	.952	Todd Hundley	.943
Tino Martinez	.949	Craig Biggio	.916
Rusty Greer	.936	Vinny Castilla	.903

There, those guys are your top ten players from each league. Moreover, you'll notice that just about everybody on that list was pretty darn good the year before and the year after, too.

Throughout this book, I'll continue to use OPS as a baseline measure of a player's overall offensive performance, and for a couple of reasons.

OPS is a really good way to compare two players with vastly different strengths — Edgardo Alfonzo and Henry Rodriguez, for example. It correlates very strongly with runs scored, which means that it's a very reliable barometer of a player's actual overall offensive value. Any time you reduce a player to one single number, you're going to over-generalize and miss some individual nuances, but OPS is a clear cut above "quick and dirty." And you can figure it out from most newspapers, without a calculator.

I really like the feel of an OPS scale. Think of it as a test score at school — a 1.000 OPS is an A+, a .900 OPS is an A, an .800 OPS is a B, a .750 OPS is a C, and anything below .700 is pretty bad. And anyone who can't manage a .600 OPS — your Manny Alexanders and Rey Ordonezes — should be sent back a grade.

4

The Where and When of Player Evaluation

Even looking at the "right" stats, like on-base percentage (OBP) and slugging percentage (SLG), doesn't give you enough information to evaluate a ballplayer. You also have to compare a player to his peers, and that means asking two questions: *where* did this player put up his numbers, and *when* did he do so?

I'll let you in on a little secret. With the royalties I earn when this book becomes a bestseller, combined with my meager salary as a Washington, D.C. attorney, I'm planning to buy the Minnesota Twins.

But there are some drawbacks to owning the Twins, like the trash-bag-ugly Hubert H. Humphrey Metrodome and those cold winters and the fact that everybody up there sounds like Margie from the movie *Fargo*. So when I buy the Twins, I will move them to my hometown of Arbutus, Maryland (population: 3,000).

I think the good people of Arbutus are ready to support a major league team. Of course, MLB franchises are expensive. I probably won't have enough money left over to pay most of the team's salary or to build a stadium. But I have a plan. I'm going to cut everyone from the Twins except forty-year-old outfielder Otis Nixon, and sign scabs from the Catonsville High School speech and debate team to fill the other twenty-four roster spots. (Arbutus is so small, it doesn't have a high school of its own.)

38

For a stadium, I've secured the rights to the Arbutus Middle School parking lot, a flat, paved rectangle 250 feet along its longest side.

How many home runs do you think Otis Nixon — who has hit just ten home runs over fifteen major league seasons — will hit in the new Arbutus Middle School Parking Lot Field?

I'm thinking at least 150. With the deepest part of center field just 250 feet away, pretty much everything Nixon hits into the air is going to sail out of the lot and count as a four-bagger. Forget Babe Ruth, Roger Maris, Ken Griffey, Sammy Sosa and Mark McGwire — the new home run record is going to be triple digits. By June.

Sure, this team isn't likely to win (m)any games. But if three million people turned out to watch Mark McGwire hit seventy, how many people will pay their money to watch Nixon hit two to three times as many?

Okay, maybe this isn't my best idea. For one thing, according to the official rules of Major League Baseball, my park would fall anywhere from seventy-five to a hundred and fifty feet short of regulations. [Really! You can look it up – Rule 1.04(a).] There's a good reason for that rule. Hitting a home run out of a park the size of the parking lot at Arbutus Middle School would require so little skill as to be ridiculous.

Besides, fans and reporters and sportscasters would all be able to see through such a transparent ploy, right?

Well, maybe not.

Coors Field in Denver seems to be a big park. It is 350 feet down the lines, and 420 feet to center field, give or take a few feet for aesthetic asymmetricality. It doesn't *look* like Arbutus Middle School Parking Lot Stadium.

But, as everyone knows, Coors Field sits a mile above sea level. And everyone knows — at least intellectually, anyhow — that the air at that elevation does wacky things to a batted ball.

I haven't done physics equations in years, but I know someone who has: Robert K. Adair, the Official Physicist of the National League. (Really!) His book, *The Physics of Baseball*, is one of the most interesting baseball works around, presuming you've already bought several copies of this one to help pay Otis Nixon's salary.

Here's what Adair had to say about the effect of altitude on baseball, written before the era of major league baseball in Denver:

A 400-foot drive by Cecil Fielder at Yankee Stadium, which is near sea level, on a windless summer day would translate to a 407-foot drive at Atlanta on the Georgia Piedmont, at 1,050 feet the highest park in the majors before 1993. The same home run could be expected to go about 5 feet farther in Kansas City and 4 feet farther at County Stadium in Milwaukee or Wrigley Field in Chicago. These differences are not so great as to modify the game, but Fielder could expect his long drive to travel about 430 feet at mile-high Denver.

Thirty extra feet on a fly ball is a very big deal. It means that, all things being equal, a ball will travel about 7% farther in the thin Denver air. However, that doesn't mean batters hit about 7% more homers in Coors. In fact, the 7% distance boost at Coors increases homers by more than 50% over the sea-level norm.

The 350-foot foul line at Coors is the equivalent of 323 feet at sea level. The 420-foot center field in Coors is the equivalent of 386 feet to dead center in Yankee Stadium. A sea-level park equivalent to Coors would violate Rule 1.04(a).

In order to make Coors Field a park with a standard home run rate — say, the equivalent of Veterans Stadium in Philadelphia — the fences would have to be moved back to about 355 feet along the lines and almost 440 feet to straightaway center field. Playing a normal game in such a field would be virtually impossible.

Even so, the playing field at Coors is huge, extending 390 feet to the power alley in left. That's big, and it definitely affects the play of the game. It means that outfielders have more territory to cover. And when solid base hits do fall, there's plenty of room for them to find the alleys and rattle around. Furthermore, the infielders at Coors still play at normal depth, so pop flies which might be easy catches in other parks may drift out of reach and fall in for base hits. (Remember, even pop-ups travel 7% farther.)

Therefore, Coors is not merely homer heaven. It's also single, double and triple heaven as well. Over a full season, Coors Field increases the number of hits by 36%.

There's a very simple way to measure park effects. On average, a player will get half of his plate appearances at home and half on the road. Compare the two totals, and you get a sense of what sort of a difference the ballpark makes. In the 1998 Colorado Rockies, one sees some truly enormous differences between home and away numbers.

Right fielder Larry Walker hit .302/.403/.488 on the road in 1998, which is about the kind of performance he put up in Montreal in the early '90s, and quite valuable to a team. He hit .418/.483/.757 at home, numbers which would have made Babe Ruth envious. In the same number of games at home and on the road (sixty-five apiece), Walker had seventeen HRs in Coors Field, and only six at every other ballpark combined. He had 100 hits at home and sixty-five on the road.

Dante Bichette hit .279/.297/.396 on the road, which is awful for someone who also plays a poor defensive left field. He hit .381/.413/.619 at home, which is essentially MVP territory in a normal park. Of his twenty-two homers, seventeen were hit at home.

Third baseman Vinny Castilla hit .270/.311/.489 on the road, and .368/.410/.687 at home. For rookie Todd Helton, the home field advantage was the difference between .273/.340/.470 and .354/.417/.585.

Taken together, the average Rockies player got a boost of 34% in singles, 23% more doubles, 59% more triples, and 40% more home runs. So did the average *road* team's players coming in to Coors Field. Overall, a team could be expected to score 56% more runs in Coors Field than anywhere else.

Many Rockies fans (and others) seem to resist the idea of park effects. One of the reasons for that, I think, is that park effects are reported in the media in ways that seem to denigrate the players' performances, and nobody likes to hear that their favorite players aren't as good as you thought. Yet park effects cut both ways. The inflated offensive levels at Coors make Rockies pitchers appear much worse than they actually are.

Darryl Kile, for example, was widely regarded as a free-agent bust when his numbers took a nosedive after he left the Houston Astros and signed with the Rockies. Given that he left the best pitcher's park on the planet (the Houston Astrodome) for the best hitter's park (Coors Field), his drop-off wasn't surprising. Kile had a 6.22 ERA at home in 110 innings, which looks pretty bad. On the road, however, Kile put up a 4.26 ERA in 120 innings.

The rest of the '98 Rockies rotation experienced similar splits. Pedro Astacio was 7.39 at home, 4.90 on the road. John Thomson had a 6.97 ERA in Coors and a 3.45 ERA on the road. Jamey Wright had a 6.92 ERA at home and a 4.63 ERA on the road. For Bobby Jones, the difference was 6.19 vs. 4.06.

In any other organization, John Thomson would be considered a bright young pitching prospect. Because he's in Coors Field, however, he goes largely unnoticed. I am convinced that the Rockies' front office doesn't truly grasp the significance of the Coors park effects. In Steve Reed, for example, the Rockies thought they had just another run-of-the-mill relief pitcher with a 4.00 ERA. What they didn't realize is that a 4.00 ERA in Coors Field is incredibly impressive. Predictably, when Reed signed with San Francisco, he put up a 1.48 ERA in 54 $^2/_3$ relief innings.

This isn't just about Coors, either. Many other parks in MLB do have significant effects on the stats of the athletes who play there.

You cannot ignore park effects if you're going to evaluate how good a player really is. A pitcher with an 8-11 record and a 4.81 ERA, like John Thomson, may look like nothing special; similarly, a hitter who hits .331/.357/.509 is usually an All-Star. But you can't know for sure unless you know the context in which those numbers were accumulated.

Unfortunately, you can't depend on the mainstream media for much help. Most reporters and broadcasters have a vague idea that high altitude or short outfield distances pump up home totals, but they treat the subject superficially at best. Rarely does the press report that the Rockies' pitchers actually are much better than they appear to be. And I have never heard a sportscaster mention that Coors drastically boosts offense across the board — not just homer totals — or how large that boost really is, or how drastically it affects the overall play of the game.

Often park effects are not intuitive: that is, you can't always tell by looking at a park how it will affect the game. Yet, predictably, sportswriters and broadcasters usually treat park effects at a glance, without bothering to consult the stats that would tell them how the park really plays compared to the rest of the league.

In this way, some parks (like some players) acquire a reputation that is less fact than myth. For example, Baltimore's Oriole Park at Camden Yards has gotten quite a reputation as a bandbox; the marked dimensions are 333 feet to left field, and a paltry 318 to right. And there have been some suggestions that the actual distances are a few feet less than that. It looks like an easy park in which to hit home runs — and, to some extent, it is. Since it was built, the Orioles' home field has inflated home run totals by approximately 10% over the norm.

But this doesn't necessarily mean that a free-agent pitcher who signs with the Orioles is going to see his ERA go straight into the tank. Because while Camden Yards does increase the number of home runs a pitcher is likely to give up, it decreases the number of other extra-base hits. The reduced proportions allow outfielders to cover a greater proportion of fair territory, and cut balls off at the gaps. On average, batters hit 15% fewer doubles and nearly 40% fewer triples in Camden Yards. (In 1997, the Orioles hit a grand total of five triples in Camden Yards all season!) Overall, Camden Yards is actually a very slight *pitcher's* park.

Of course, a very homer-prone pitcher may very well fare quite poorly in Camden Yards. When the Orioles signed Shawn Boskie as a free agent after the 1996 season, he was coming off a year in which he'd led the American League in home runs allowed, with forty. (Amusingly enough, Boskie also led the league in hit batsmen, with thirteen.)

With Baltimore, his ERA rose by more than a full run to 6.43. He allowed fourteen homers in seventy-seven innings, and earned his release.

But the average pitcher has nothing to fear — and a tiny bit to gain — by signing with the Orioles. True, a few more would-be doubles and deep fly-outs probably will go out of the park. But many more doubles and triples will fall in for singles.

This is but one example. Rarely do the mainstream media report the other effects that distort raw stat totals. For example, team offense levels are consistently about 10% higher in the American League than the National league, due in part to the designated hitter, and also to overall park effects. You have to recognize this difference when comparing two pitchers in different leagues, for example, or when discussing variations in a pitcher's performances when he switches leagues, yet few reporters or broadcasters ever take the difference into account.

Likewise, mainstream reporters either ignore or don't grasp the fact that league offensive totals can vary widely from season to season. As I discuss below, there's no single reason for these variations. But whatever the explanation, "year effects" are real. They can be even more significant than park effects; in fact, the differences in offense levels from year to year can be so great that any comparison of raw totals, without context, is almost meaningless.

Here's an example. Playing armchair GM for a minute, would you want this guy on your team?

	GS	CG	IP	H	HR	BB	K	ERA
Pitcher	28	2	181	176	14	48	80	2.98

All things considered, this guy looks like a star, right? He gives up less than one hit an inning, rarely issues a free pass, keeps the ball in the park, and has an ERA of less than three runs per nine innings. In today's American League, he could be the ace of your staff.

But those numbers were compiled in 1968, by John Howard "Fat Jack" Fisher. Fat Jack was the fourth starter for an awful Chicago White Sox team that finished tied for ninth place, thirty-six games out of first place and just a game and a half ahead of the Washington Senators. That 2.98 ERA earned him an 8-13 won-loss record.

Is it really possible that the worst starter on one of the worst teams in baseball was a better pitcher than practically every starting pitcher in the 1999 American League? Is Jack Fisher, a career 86-139 pitcher, really a better guy to have on your team than Andy Pettitte, Pat Hentgen, Mike Mussina and David Wells?

Of course not. It just so happens that Fat Jack had the good fortune to pitch during the Year of the Pitcher, 1968, in an era before the lowered pitching mound, the shrunken strike zone, the designated hitter, and the virtual elimination of the batter's box. Fisher had an ERA below 3.00 — but so did almost every regular starting pitcher in the league. Only two teams scored more than 600 runs that year. No team scored 700 runs.

In 1998, only one AL team scored *fewer* than 700 runs — the expansion Tampa Bay Devil Rays, with 620 runs scored. Nine teams scored 800 or more runs; the New York Yankees scored 965.

In 1968 in the American League, the average team scored under three runs per game. The average AL hitter batted just .230. Oakland's Bert Campaneris led the league with 177 hits.

Today, 177 hits for the season doesn't get you anywhere near the leader board. Campaneris would have been nineteenth in total hits among 1998 AL hitters — just below Johnny Damon and Quinton McCracken.

In 1998, two dozen American Leaguers hit .300 or better. Among them were mediocre players like Gregg Jefferies, Mike Caruso and Hal Morris.

In 1968, only one player in the entire American League batted over .300 –
Boston's Carl Yastrzemski, who led the league with a .301 average. That
still stands as a record for the lowest batting average ever to win a batting
title.

(The runner up for the title that year, Oakland first baseman Danny
Cater, finished second with a .290 average and a .731 OPS. Today, a first
baseman with a .731 OPS would be sent back to the minors.)

Obviously, with such low offensive levels, pitchers' stats became superficially impressive. Jack Fisher's 2.98 ERA in 1968 would have easily led
the American League of 1996, in which no starting pitcher finished with
an ERA below 3.00. But — and this is the critical point — had a pitcher of
his ability pitched in the same conditions as the American League of 1998,
he wouldn't have come anywhere near a 3.00 ERA.

Obviously a .300 batting average, or a 3.00 ERA, doesn't necessarily have
the same significance from season to season. Yet most fans, and the media, and
baseball insiders, consider these marks as absolute standards of quality.

How can you avoid falling into this trap? Simple. You must look past
the raw numbers and see how a player compares to his contemporaries,
in any given season. If a player really is superior to the other guys playing the game, you would expect his numbers to be better than those put
up by others playing at the same time.

In this context, we begin to understand how Jack Fisher's seemingly
impressive numbers can equate to being the fourth starter on a miserable
team. In 1968, Luis Tiant led the AL with a 1.60 ERA. Five starters finished
the season with ERAs less than 1.99. In 1968, a pitcher who gave up three
earned runs a game was worse than mediocre.

We see drastic variations from the norm in other seasons, too. The next
time someone advances the silly argument that the "National League"
style of baseball is all about the bunt, the hit-and-run, stealing bases and
manufacturing runs, you might want to point him to 1930. That year in
the NL, the average batter hit .303, and the average team scored five runs
per game.

Dozens of players hit .300 or better. Bill Terry hit .401. Hack Wilson hit
56 homers — an NL record until it was obliterated in 1998 — and drove
in 190 runs, which is still the major league record for RBI. In 1930 in the
NL, the average player hit .303/.360/.448, for an .808 OPS. An .808 OPS is
about what Dodger outfielder Raul Mondesi hit in 1998. Considering that

the "average" player included catchers, middle infielders, even *pitchers*, that's mind-boggling.

Naturally, those offensive levels took a big toll on pitchers' stats.

The ace of the NL champion St. Louis Cardinals was Wild Bill Hallahan, who went 15-9 with a 4.67 ERA. He won the strikeout crown by fanning 177 in 237 innings, allowing 233 hits, giving up fifteen homers and walking 126 batters.

The rest of the Cards' staff — which included two future Hall of Famers! — put up similar numbers: Sylvester Johnson was 12-10 with a 4.64 ERA; Jesse Haines was 13-8 with a 4.30 ERA; Flint Rhem was 12-8 with a 4.44 ERA; Burleigh Grimes finished the season at 16-11 with a 4.07 ERA.

Rockies fans, remember the 1930 St. Louis Cardinals the next time some journalist writes that "the Rockies have no pitchers." When your team wins the World Series — and that will happen, sooner or later — it will probably be with a pitching staff that looks a lot like this one; maybe even worse. And just as the hitting onslaught of 1930 didn't mean that Burleigh Grimes and Jesse Haines couldn't pitch, Coors Field doesn't mean that the Rockies' starters can't pitch, either.

The more perceptive of you may have noticed that for these comparisons I picked three seasons — 1930, 1968, and 1998 — more than a generation apart. You might argue that of course the game changes over thirty years or more.

But does it really change significantly from year to year?

Often the answer is yes. I've taken 1930 and 1968 because they're the "Coors Field" of year effects. But *every* single year is its own unique circumstances, and sometimes one year makes an awful lot of difference. Offensive levels moved significantly toward normal levels in the seasons following 1930 and 1968.

For example, the composite National League batting average dropped from .303 in 1930 to .277 in 1931, while OPS went from .808 to .721, an extremely significant difference — the difference, for example, between Raul Mondesi and San Diego Padres shortstop Chris Gomez in 1998.

Chick Hafey won the '31 NL batting title with a .349 average, which wouldn't have put him anywhere near the leaders a year earlier. Chuck Klein led the league with thirty-one homers, and was the only player to hit more than thirty. Klein also led the league with 121 RBI, sixty-nine behind Hack Wilson's record total of the year before.

Similarly, hitting in the American League took a big swing back to normal after the league-wide drought in 1968, from a composite .230/.299/.339 to .246/.323/.369. That's an additional 56 points of OPS, which was more than the difference between Tino Martinez and Kevin Young in 1998.

There have been significant swings over other two-year periods as well. Most have gone largely unnoticed in the media. How many sports reporters bothered to mention that from 1987 to 1988, the American and National Leagues both lost more than fifty points of OPS?

What causes such variances? On the surface, there is no sensible reason why 1988 should have been any different from 1987 for major league hitters. Expansion and realignment, rules changes, the introduction of a new park such as Coors Field can all cause aberrations that throw off the averages.

None of those things happened between 1987 and '88. But a lot of subtle things can change from year to year. The umpires might decide — whether consciously or not — to call the strike zone differently. They might enforce rules, such as the balk or the batter's box, that have previously gone unenforced, or vice-versa. Balls may be lighter or heavier. Talent can wax and wane. New weather patterns, new philosophies, and new economics can all bring massive new inflows (or outflows) of pitching or hitting talent, disturbing the previous year's balance. And there are probably a dozen more significant factors I'm not listing.

And while it would be nice to pinpoint what changes helped to turn Jack Fisher into a 3.00-ERA pitcher in 1968, knowing the why isn't nearly as important as recognizing that these aberrations do occur, league-wide, from year to year. A 3.00 ERA isn't always a 3.00 ERA.

Remember the underlying rule: if a player really is better than his contemporaries, he'll put up better numbers than the guys he's playing with, not just better numbers than some arbitrary metric that we've come to think of as the standards.

Context is everything.

Oh, and I'm just kidding about most of those Minnesota cracks. Really.

5

Chemistry ... or Alchemy?

"Baseball is all individual. If you've got nine guys doing their jobs, you've got a team. The only thing I can do when Harold Baines is at the plate is root for him. There's no chemistry for me because I'm not at the plate. Chemistry is not the right word. I don't know what the right word is, but chemistry is not it."
— Eric Davis, quoted in the *Baltimore Sun*, April 24, 1998.

C hemistry.

It's one of baseball's staple concepts. Players and managers and GMs use the concept constantly. Almost all agree that "good chemistry" is essential to make a winning team.

But I don't believe that most baseball people really understand the concept, or how to achieve it. I'm not sure that there is any reliable, systematic way to imbue a roster with "good chemistry."

That's why I love the Eric Davis quote above. It's a rare bit of candor from someone who has played the game at its highest levels for more than a decade. You can almost picture the context. Some reporter asked Davis a perfunctory question about the Orioles' "clubhouse chemistry," and instead of a stock cliché, Davis said what was really on his mind.

Moreover, his answer is pretty insightful, too.

What is the "right word" Davis wanted? Rather than chemistry, I offer "alchemy." Chemistry is concerned with the precise combination of measurable quantities in controlled reaction. Alchemy — the ancient search for a process that would transmute base metals into gold — involves randomly mixing unknown substances in hopes that the proper combination will create a new substance with entirely different properties than its component ingredients.

Chemistry is a science — its results can be measured, tested, verified. Alchemy, on the other hand, is whimsical, random and unknown. With chemistry, the same combination will produce the exact same reaction every time; with alchemy, who knows?

The real baseball "chemist" takes the same approach. Scientifically analyze each of the ingredients (the players), document their effects (statistically), and then combine them in ways known to produce a certain outcome (maximize your talent).

Most GMs proceed like the alchemist, hoping that a player's personality will bring more to the field than his demonstrated talents; wishing that some combination can turn his lead bat into gold. There's no method to the madness; sometimes a GM tries to bring in a "fiery competitor," and other times he's looking for "good organizational soldiers." Sometimes a player is allegedly a bad clubhouse influence because he's "too immature," and other times a player is knocked for "failing to be a leader."

Of course, the same conduct can make one guy a "fiery competitor" may make another an "immature hothead." One quiet player can be described as a "solid citizen" while another quiet type is criticized for not being a rah-rah cheerleader.

Does any of it matter?

On one level, of course it matters. I know that if I'm working with people I like, I work better. I assume this is also true for ballplayers; it just makes sense to think that if the guys all like each other, they'll play a little bit harder and care a little bit more.

On the other hand, we could also imagine that a team might play better if every player hates everyone else. "I'll show him who's the winner," the third baseman thinks, as he walks up to the plate, intent on showing up the team's nine-million-dollar outfielder who just popped up to second. Or maybe on a lousy team where everyone hates everyone else, each player tries as hard as he can to do as much as possible, so as to increase his trade value or his price tag during free agency. Who knows? Can anyone really prove otherwise?

The reason why it's all alchemy, though, is that nobody really knows what the attitude in the clubhouse will be like *in the future.* Take relief pitcher Randy Myers, and his fascination with pranks, camouflage gear, and automatic weapons — will his teammates find him quirky and endearing, or annoying? Sign Bobby Bonilla — will he cast a dour mood over the clubhouse or make friends? Trade for Gary Sheffield, and will his teammates applaud the move to strengthen the club, or resent his $11 million contract?

We just don't know.

Sportswriters and broadcasters aren't much help. Almost inevitably, they project their feelings about a player into the clubhouse. Try to interview Bobby Bonilla after he's struck out in the bottom of the ninth. If he takes it out on you as the interviewer, well, it's only natural to presume that he'll take it out on his teammates, too. On the other hand, even after a loss, Andy Van Slyke was always ready to talk to reporters.

Van Slyke, usually an outfielder, once noted that he played third base "like Brooks — Mel Brooks." After an 0-for-4 afternoon in which he stranded nine men on base, Van Slyke quipped that he "couldn't have driven home Miss Daisy today." Great stuff.

Van Slyke is the kind of player a beat writer loves; if you've got another column inch to fill about a nine-run loss, you can always go get a comment from a player like that.

On the other hand, what reporter isn't frustrated in searching for a quote from Barry Bonds after the Giants have just been pounded 11-2? Interview Albert Belle ... well, just *try* to interview Albert Belle.

The reason I bring up Bonds, Van Slyke and Bonilla — but not Albert Belle, that was just a cheap shot — is that Bonilla, Van Slyke and Bonds show the consequences of roster-building by alchemy.

In 1991, the Pittsburgh Pirates were one of the best teams in baseball, champions of the NL East, with a potent lineup, a deep pitching staff and a manager quickly becoming heralded as one of the best in the game.

They also had a problem. Money. Or rather, the lack of it. Though I believe that the Pittsburgh Pirates made money during the late '80s and early '90s, their ugly, cavernous, horrific football field of a baseball stadium (Three Rivers) wasn't exactly packing in the crowds.

By 1991, it was clear that ownership was not going to pay to keep the Pirates together. Unfortunately, contracts for the Pirates' 3-4-5 hitters were all coming due around the same time.

Those three hitters, of course, were Andy Van Slyke, Bobby Bonilla and Barry Bonds. The Pirates' ownership believed that the team could afford to keep only one of those three stars. Management had to make some hard choices. I believe that the Pirates made those decisions at least partly on the basis of chemistry — or, more accurately, alchemy.

They let go Bonds and Bonilla, both of whom were known variously as moody, difficult, temperamental. The player they chose to keep was quipmeister Andy Van Slyke.

Bonilla left after the '91 season, signing a four-year, $24 million deal with the New York Mets. Through the '90s he has been one of baseball's most productive hitters; he helped the Florida Marlins win the World Series in 1997, after helping the Orioles advance to the American League Championship Series the year before.

After the '92 season, Bonds bolted Pittsburgh for San Francisco, signing a contract that made him the highest-paid player in the game, and instantly carrying the Giants from last place to more than a hundred wins. By the time he retires, Barry Bonds will have played more than a dozen years — a good career for most ballplayers — *after* having left Pittsburgh, and they're already clearing a space for his personal effects in Cooperstown.

Andy Van Slyke was re-signed by Pittsburgh and remained a Pirate until 1995, but his career as a useful everyday player was finished before his contract ran out. After leaving the Pirates, he signed as a low-budget free agent with Baltimore, was released at midseason, signed with the Phillies and helped "lead" Philadelphia to the worst record in baseball after the All-Star break. That was Van Slyke's last year in the majors.

Everybody knew as far back as '91 that the Pirates couldn't keep everybody. But given Andy Van Slyke, Bobby Bonilla and Barry Bonds to choose from, who picks Van Slyke?

The alchemist. The guy who thinks, "Sure, Van Slyke isn't quite as good a hitter as those other two, but he's a little bit cheaper and a lot better influence in the clubhouse ..."

There's another, more sinister, way in which clubhouse alchemy is used to befuddle a team's decision-making process. It works something like this: when a team plays far below or far above its expectations, club officials and sports writers look for reasons why. Usually, the answer they seize on is "chemistry."

Were I particularly ego-minded, I would call this formula "Torrez's Law of Clubhouse Alchemy." It looks something like this:

Actual Results = Preconceived Notions + "Clubhouse Chemistry"

The reasoning is lovely in its circularity. If a team is playing much better than expected, the chemistry in the clubhouse is obviously good; if a team is playing worse, the chemistry must be the problem. Bad teams always have bad chemistry; good teams always have good chemistry.

Isn't this rather silly? Isn't it possible that some truly terrible teams have had rosters full of guys who really like each other and cheer each other on and help each other out?

And isn't it possible that some great, successful teams have included a bunch of guys who loathe one another?

Attempting to draw conclusions about clubhouse chemistry from the team's record is no different from attempting to draw conclusions about workplace chemistry from a department's profitability. "Look, profits in hardware are up 200% this year — I bet those guys all really get along down there." Like many baseball clichés, once it's taken out of the sports context, the very idea is absurd.

Moreover, it leads to vastly contradictory results. In 1995, the Boston Red Sox won the American League East while using a record 53 players; the papers all talked about the positive chemistry environment in which everyone could fit in. In 1996, the Yankees won with precisely the opposite strategy, using only thirty guys all season, and media sources inevitably talked about the positive chemistry from having a stable nucleus. The 1995 World Champion Atlanta Braves illustrated how good clubhouse chemistry comes from building from within; the 1997 World Champion Florida Marlins showed how good chemistry comes from bringing in lots of free agents.

It's absurd.

Are you a chemist? Do you want to apply the scientific method? Do you want the facts, and not the rose-colored glasses? (Robert A. Heinlein once said, "If it can't be expressed in figures, it is not science; it is opinion.")

Or are you an alchemist?

Who do you want? Barry Bonds? Or Andy Van Slyke?

PART TWO

HITTING

6

Riding the `Career Curve'

"See that fella over there? He's twenty years old. In ten years, he's got a chance to be a star. Now that fella over there, he's twenty years old, too. In ten years he's got a chance to be thirty."
– Casey Stengel

Suppose that Mark McGwire and Ozzie Guillen invited you to go join them at the local batting cages and watch them take a few dozen swings against, say, an eighty-mph fastball machine.

Unless this book has fallen into the hands of a lot more professional athletes than I've anticipated, chances are really good in the above scenario that you're going to walk away with a newfound respect for Mr. Guillen. You're expecting McGwire to clobber the ball, of course, but you're going to be surprised at how well Ozzie Guillen (with twenty-four career home runs in fourteen major league seasons) looks when standing next to the Average Guy.

The simple truth is that there isn't *that* much difference between the very best player in major league baseball and the very worst. The gap is infinitesimal compared to the difference between major league ballplayers as a whole and, say, out-of-shape sportswriters.

What this means is that very minor changes in a player's overall talent mark the difference between success and failure, between heading to the minors and staying in the bigs, between fighting for an everyday job and making the All-Star team.

When I say "talent," I mean the total of a player's abilities that enable him to succeed at the game. Some of these abilities are physical attributes, such as strength and speed and reflexes and eyesight, and some are mental skills, such as judgment and discipline and experience.

(As a side note, this is part of what I love about baseball. Could Kirby Puckett, Tom Gordon, John Kruk, Cecil Fielder, Sid Fernandez and David Wells have made it anywhere near the top in any other sport? Or, as Kruk so eloquently put it, "I ain't an athlete... I'm a baseball player." These guys had tremendous baseball *talent*, which is more than just physical conditioning.)

But athletic ability changes over time. Let's examine some of the attributes above.

Eyesight: Visual acuity is a steadily declining curve, starting around age two to three, and dropping along a straight line. It's impossible to improve one's eyesight naturally, but there are many things one can do to make it worse.

Strength and Speed: The male body continues to grow through puberty and into early adulthood, stopping around age eighteen to twenty. From that point forward, physical conditioning is largely a function of exercise. It is possible for a very healthy twenty-five-year-old to be stronger and faster than he was at age twenty. It is extremely unlikely that a healthy athlete who was always in good physical shape will be stronger and faster at age thirty than he was at age twenty-five.

Reflexes: A steadily declining curve, starting at mid-puberty.

In short, the ballplayer's physical abilities are likely to improve from year to year — assuming he works hard — until the early or middle twenties. After that, it's going to be "one step forward, two steps back" for most ballplayers; a guy might be able to bench press ten more pounds at age twenty-eight than he could at age twenty-five, but his eyesight and reflexes and overall health are three years worse.

A graph of physical abilities over time would look something like this:

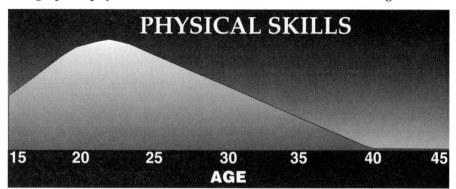

What about the second set of skills, the mental ones? For most players, the function will increase over time, at least for a while; that is, every year of baseball experience helps a ballplayer of any age learn more about what it takes to play the game. However, this learning process isn't going to be a straight line. You would expect a player to learn a lot during his first few professional seasons, even after he has reached the majors. A rookie might swing at that tailing slider out of the strike zone fifty times his first year in the bigs. You would hope, after a year's worth of seeing the wicked slider and working out in the batting cage and on videotape, he swings at those pitches less often the year after that. But after a while, that kind of learning will level out.

Graphically, a player's mental skill development might look like this:

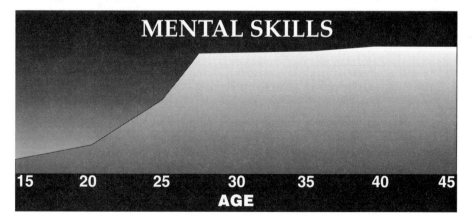

58

Both of these sets of skills, in combination, determine a ballplayer's overall talent.

Ted Williams is a good example of the interplay between physical and mental skills. He was obviously a great player, with terrific natural talent, a solid work ethic, and a tremendous head for the game.

In 1939, when Ted Williams was twenty, he walked 107 times during a full season (672 plate appearances). He also hit .327, smacked thirty-one homers, drove in 145 runs — well, you get the picture. Having the talent to put up a season like this before he turned twenty-one is one reason Williams is the second-best player in baseball history.

Ten years later, when Williams was thirty, he walked 162 times in a full season (728 PA). He raised his batting average to .343, and, for good measure, won the Triple Crown with 43 HR and 159 RBI.

Why should Ted Williams draw about half again as many walks as a thirty-year-old than he did when he was twenty? Clearly his eyesight was ten years worse. Was Williams in better shape at thirty than he was at twenty?

The answer, of course, is that Williams had more than made up for any drop in his physical attributes by improving his mental skills

At the far opposite side of the talent spectrum from Ted Williams is former utility infielder Kim Batiste. A lifetime .234 hitter in the majors with marginal power, Batiste spent parts of five seasons with Philadelphia and San Francisco. In 1996, the Giants sent Batiste down to AAA. He was twenty-eight years old and had been hitting .208 in the National League.

With the AAA Phoenix Firebirds, Batiste hit .297. Although he had just ten career home runs in his five major league seasons, Batiste hit fourteen dingers for Phoenix in just forty-two games. His .636 slugging percentage would have looked pretty good from Frank Thomas, let alone a backup shortstop.

Five years earlier, that same Kim Batiste had hit just one home run in 122 games in Triple-A. Clearly, Batiste had learned quite a bit about the mental aspect of baseball during his five years in the majors, and those skills outweighed whatever physical advantages he would have enjoyed at age twenty-three. But his mental improvement wasn't enough to keep him in the game. Despite his spectacular two months at AAA, not a single team was interested in his services the next year. Batiste was out of professional baseball at age twenty-eight.

By putting together the two graphs of a player's physical and mental skills, you get a picture that looks something like this:

THE "CAREER CURVE"

| 15 | 20 | 25 | 30 | 35 | 40 | 45 |

AGE

The "Career Curve" is a graphical representation of a very simple concept: all things considered, you should expect a player to get better each year if he's twenty-five or younger, and you should expect a player to get worse if he's thirty or older. Around ages twenty-six to twenty-eight, a typical player should be at the "peak" of his career.

The Career Curve has gotten some publicity, mostly in publications discussing Rotisserie baseball, as advice to would-be Roto players in predicting how their players will perform during the coming year. Roto magazines have heavily over-hyped the Career Curve, generally by making statements such as, "A player will have his best year at age twenty-seven."

That's silly. If looking at a birth certificate was the sole requirement for projecting a player's performance, teams could save millions on scouting reports.

When I use the Career Curve, I use it in the same sense that one might say "on balance, men are taller than women." The statement is true, but it doesn't mean that you can't find WNBA players who look down on the top of my head.

Similarly, the Career Curve is not a promise that a player's absolute best year will come at age twenty-seven. It does say, though, that if a team signs a thirty-year-old free agent to a six-year contract, that team should expect some severe decline in that player's effectiveness before the contract runs out.

Let's look at some actual career curves.

First, we'll go back to Ruth. On the Y-axis, I've plotted his OPS, and on the X-axis, his age. Ruth spent the first three years of his career exclusively as a pitcher, so the values are skewed somewhat, but you can still see an obvious pattern:

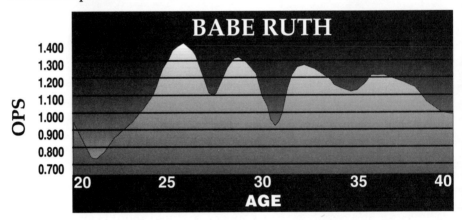

R uth's best year came at age twenty-five (1920, a 1.378 OPS), his second-best year at age twenty-six (1921, a 1.358 OPS), and his third-best year at age twenty-eight (1923, a 1.309 OPS). After 1923, the Babe never again managed an OPS above 1.300, although he was still an incredible ballplayer.

I've deliberately started off with discussing the Career Curve for the greatest player in the history of the game, because I think it's important to set out what the curve does and does not show. The curve concept is not an argument that all players are washed up after age thirty, just that they're on the decline. Babe Ruth on the decline was still better than most major leaguers in their prime.

Moreover, the curve doesn't predict individual seasons with pinpoint accuracy; Ruth had relative down years in 1922 (age twenty-seven) and 1925 (age thirty). He rebounded from both quite nicely the next year. Indeed, from 1918 to 1931, there were only two years during which Babe Ruth did not lead the league in homers — 1922 and 1925.

But the career curve does uphold the general rule expressed above. In years before 1920, it was reasonable to expect Ruth to improve the following year; in the years after 1925, it was reasonable to expect Ruth to decline.

Now let's look at another career curve, this one for a player who is not quite Babe Ruth.

Dale Murphy came up through the Atlanta Braves organization as a catcher. After two seasons, he was moved to first base, and then to center field, where he excelled for nearly ten years. Murphy was a pretty fair hitter: a lifetime .274 batting average, more than 350 career homers, and seven seasons during which he hit thirty or more homers. In the graph above, I've only listed Murphy's years as a regular; he debuted in 1976 as a twenty-year-old but got only 72 plate appearances, and he was scrapping for playing time as late as 1992, with the Colorado Rockies. But his regular career began at age twenty-two in 1978, and was over at age thirty-five, in 1991.

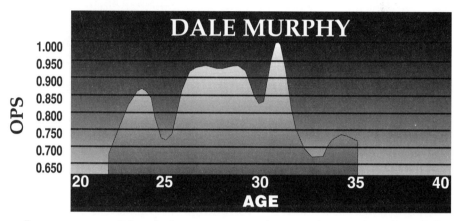

In some ways, Murphy's career curve is more instructive than Babe Ruth's. For one, when Ruth's skills began declining, the drop was more gradual and difficult to notice. When you're Dale Murphy, however, four years can make the difference between the best season of your life and fighting for a fifth outfielder spot.

That Murphy's single best year came at age thirty-one is not unusual. Many players will show an isolated spike later in their careers. Overall, though, if your team signed Murphy to a six-year contract in 1986, they would have been disappointed five years out of six. And that's the point of the Career Curve.

Let's look at another one:

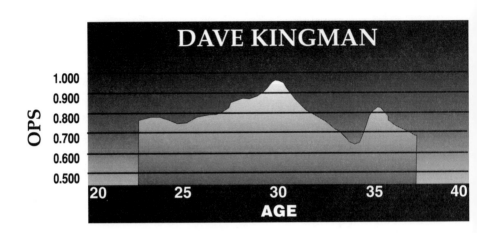

I picked Dave "King Kong" Kingman to demonstrate that the career curve applies even to very extreme players.

Some future edition of Webster's New Standard Dictionary will have Kingman's picture next to the definition of "one-dimensional." Sportswriters like to throw that term around a lot whenever a big slugger has a low average and strikes out a lot — in particular, it was often inappropriately applied to Mickey Tettleton — but Kingman really was one-dimensional.

In 1973 — a typical year for him — Kingman batted .203, with sixty-two hits in 305 at-bats. Of those hits, twenty-seven were singles, ten were doubles, one was a triple, and twenty-four were home runs. He drew forty-one walks and struck out 122 times.

In other words, when King Kong strode to the plate, his chances of striking out were better than one in three. He was much more likely to strike out than to get a hit. On the off-chance that he got a hit — only once out of every five at-bats — he was as likely to hit a homer as a single.

Kingman finished his career with 442 homers. His best year was at age thirty; his second-best, at age twenty-nine; and his third-best, age twenty-eight. Like Murphy, Kingman delivered a late-career spike at age thirty-five; also like Murphy, Kingman dropped off rather rapidly from his peak.

What about someone whose skills were very much different from Kingman's?

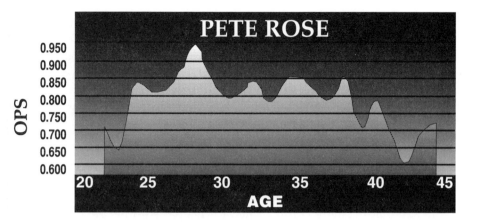

Although they have virtually identical career OPS (.786 for Rose versus .783 for Kingman), Rose derived nearly all of his value from high batting averages, good walk rates and doubles power. Kingman drew most of his value from the occasional moon shot. Kingman hit forty-eight homers in 1979; Rose never hit more than sixteen, and had sixteen seasons in single digits. Rose finished with a lifetime average of .303; Kingman, .236.

And yet their career curves look very familiar.

Finally, since we've mostly been dealing with very good hitters, let's look at a guy who was unequivocally lousy with the stick:

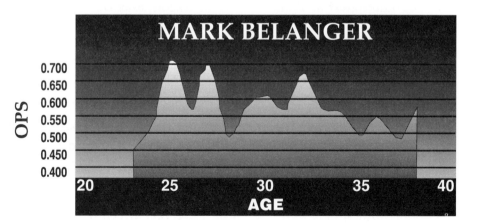

Mark "The Blade" Belanger was Earl Weaver's dependably outstanding defensive shortstop from 1968 to 1980, a span during which the Orioles won six pennants, one World Series and an impressive 1,244 games. For thirteen years, the Orioles averaged ninety-six wins per season, a truly amazing record.

Throughout this astonishing run, Belanger slapped out an occasional base hit, drew a walk now and again, and, every once in a while, managed to knock one for extra bases. His career high in average was .287, set in 1969, one of only three seasons he managed to get his average above .228. His career high in homers for any season was five; for doubles, twenty-two; for RBI, fifty; for hits, 152.

To say that Belanger compensated for his bat with his glove would be an understatement.

Yet the career curve works for him, too. Belanger's best season was 1969, in which he hit .287, managed twenty-three extra-base hits, drove in a career-high fifty runs, and put up a .699 OPS. Belanger was twenty-five in 1969.

Belanger's second-best season came two years later at age twenty-seven; after that, he would have just two more seasons in his career in which he cracked the .600 OPS barrier. (Today, most players with a .600 OPS — even spectacular defensive shortstops — don't last long in the major leagues.)

Players do follow a "Career Curve" determined by their experience and declining physical abilities. In major league baseball, even a small variance in skill can produce a huge difference in performance. So even small drop-offs in a player's ability are obvious on the field. Those nagging injuries that are just a bit more severe once you're past thirty; the slight drop in bat speed, can make the difference between a productive player and one who is a drag on his team.

And this holds true across the spectrum of talent. It's true for big sluggers, for balanced players, for all-or-nothing home run hitters, and for guys who stroke lots of singles and doubles. How many other generalizations hold true for both Babe Ruth and Mark Belanger?

Scouting Tools and Stats

The essence of baseball savvy is being able to forecast a hitter's performance over his next season or two.

For good players in their peak years, that's not so tough. If your star center-fielder puts up a .310/.414/.607 season at the age of twenty-six, you can be pretty sure that if he stays healthy, he'll be putting up All-Star numbers for the next few seasons to come, and you probably ought to dig down deep and sign him to that multi-year contract.

A bigger challenge is to differentiate among the players at either "tail" of the career curve. Among young players, we want to be able to cull gems with true potential from the pseudo-prospects. We want to find playing time for youngsters who have a good chance to blossom next year, but we don't want to waste a roster spot on someone who isn't likely ever to make an impact in the big leagues.

Among older players, we want to know who can continue to be useful for the next couple of seasons, and who is due for that big tailspin that will end his career.

I'll treat declining veterans later. But this chapter will be devoted to evaluating young players: picking prospects.

Let's take a look at two players, and what each did one season in the American League:

	AB	R	H	2B	3B	HR	RBI	BB	SO	SB	CS	AVG	OBP	SLG
Player A	455	61	120	23	0	16	61	44	83	16	7	.264	.329	.420
Player B	465	59	121	29	1	13	51	39	65	6	7	.260	.328	.411

These look to be two fairly evenly matched. Player A has a bit more speed and a few extra RBI, but the two players have roughly the same average, number of hits, plate appearances, walks and extra-base hits.

Moreover, suppose I told you that Player A was an outfielder, while Player B was a good defensive shortstop. Who would you pick as more valuable to your team?

Before you answer, take a look at two more guys:

	AB	R	H	2B	3B	HR	RBI	BB	SO	SB	CS	AVG	OBP	SLG
Player C	413	72	92	26	3	16	48	65	102	36	7	.223	.330	.416
Player D	416	49	97	17	1	17	68	53	111	0	1	.233	.324	.401

Between these two, there's a big difference in speed, but not much else. Player D has twenty additional RBI; Player C has twenty-three more runs scored. Player D has one extra homer and a batting average ten points higher than Player C, although C has nine more doubles and two extra triples. Player C is a left-fielder; Player D is a first baseman.

If you were running a major league team, would you have a strong reason to prefer Player A to Player B, or Player C to Player D? And, more important, would you really want *any* of these guys on your team? A .223-hitting outfielder? Absent additional context, chances are good that the only guy you'd really want is Player B, the shortstop.

Player A is Ken Griffey, Jr., at age 19. Player C is Barry Bonds, at age twenty-one. They're headed for the Hall of Fame. Player B is one year in the career of Mike Bordick, a nondescript shortstop who has played for the Oakland Athletics and Baltimore Orioles, and who will have to stand in line to buy tickets to Cooperstown with the rest of us. And Player D is Cecil Fielder, in probably his last season, who was released by the Anaheim Angels during a pennant race, signed by the Cleveland Indians, and promptly relegated to the back of the bench.

So how does a GM tell the difference between a prospective Ken Griffey and the next Mike Bordick?

It starts with scouting. And it starts when the would-be phenom is a pimply teenager.

Scouting young players is a very hard job. It's harder than you think, and then it's harder again than that. When a team sends its scouts around the country and overseas to look at fifteen-year-olds, it is trying to make the most educated guess possible in a multitude of very wild guesses. The only winning strategy at that level, it seems, is to draft fifty or sixty players per year, sign another dozen internationally, throw them all into the hopper, and see if the cream rises to the top.

But how does a team select which of those sixty-odd players to sign? When John Smith hits .735 for the year for the Catonsville High School Comets, what does that mean?

(Answers: Probably nothing. Maybe something. Who knows? And yes, that's a real team. Yankees' pitcher Jeff Nelson played for the Comets in the early '80s.)

I love baseball statistics, but when it comes to amateur teenagers, stats aren't worth a damn. They're useless, because there is no equalization of competition. The .735-hitting Smith may never have faced a single competitor good enough to play college ball at a Division I school; Smith may be the biggest fish in a small pond, but how will he perform in the ocean of professional baseball? On the other hand, it would be silly to presume that Smith *can't* hit, simply because his competition may or may not be any good.

Scouts, then, learn the importance of judging a kid's physical tools and athletic talent. Moreover, they see their methodology validated when a scrawny teenager bulks up, adds fifty pounds of muscle, and turns into the power hitter that the scout envisioned. The Texas Rangers signed Juan Gonzalez out of Puerto Rico when he was sixteen.

For every Juan Gonzalez, though, there are dozens, perhaps hundreds, of "tools" projects who just don't pan out. That's to be expected; scouting is a very imprecise process, and that's why there are multiple levels of minor leagues in which the wheat can be sorted from the chaff.

And scouting has risks in the other direction, too. Mike Piazza went in the sixty-second round of the 1988 draft, after more than fifteen hundred other kids had been taken. Oops. And every year, a couple of major league teams find players in the Mexican and Independent leagues who went previously undrafted (and unnoticed) by their scouts, and who have the talent to help a big league team. Sometimes, quite a bit of talent. Francisco Cordova of the Pittsburgh Pirates is a recent example.

The old saw in baseball is that even the best players fail six times out of ten; in scouting, even the best guesses fail about ninety-nine times out of a hundred. It's hard: scouting by physical tools is risky and fraught with failure.

Teams don't have a choice when they are scouting teenage amateurs. Yet, as risky as that method is, teams continue to use it even when they are scouting older players in the minors, players with several years of professional experience. They judge minor league talent by the same unreliable scouting methods *even though a much better system is available.*

Imagine that you were given the job of assembling the finest baseball team in creation, and that you had an infinite amount of money and access to every player in the world. How would you go about it? Would you hire scouts to watch videotapes and tell you which players are the most fundamentally sound, which players look best on the field, which have the most raw talent? Of course not. You'd go out and sign the best players in major league baseball, based on the way they've played so far. Alex Rodriguez wouldn't be your starting shortstop because he looks good in a uniform or because scouts say he's got a great swing; he'd be your starting shortstop because he's the best player on the planet.

In fact, some major league stars look pretty ugly when they're playing. I'm astonished that Gary Sheffield can manage even one hit a week — let alone earn $11 million a year — with his crazy wave-the-bat-until-the-last-possible-second stance. Geronimo Berroa was the same way, and so are a number of others. Better yet, watch any disciple of the Charlie Lau school of hitting — the approach that involves taking one hand off the bat during the follow-through. Jose Canseco hit forty homers that way; I'm not sure I could hit a wiffle ball forty feet one-handed. Cal Ripken changes his batting stance every couple of weeks, and has been doing it for fifteen years.

None would impress a scout as fundamentally sound at the plate.

When John Olerud was flirting with .400 in 1993, you couldn't open a newspaper without reading a story about what a "sweet swing" Olerud had. With the same swing, Olerud slipped below .300 for the next four seasons, and suddenly those stories disappeared.

Olerud, of course, *does* have a sweet swing. And he *is* a good hitter. But

Sheffield and Canseco and Ripken are (or were) great hitters as well. We know that, not because of artistic impression, but because they have demonstrated over the seasons that they can pound the ball. This is such a simple proposition that I'm almost embarrassed to be stating it.

Then why don't teams use a player's demonstrated hitting ability when judging minor league talent? Why do scouts examining a twenty-three-year-old young man in the minor leagues employ the same methodology they use when evaluating a fifteen-year-old kid in Puerto Rico?

Here's the way most teams scout minor league players. A minor league scout will receive his assignment to prepare a report. He then goes to the minor league game, and takes notes on his particular assigned player(s).

Typically, those notes will be recorded on scouting forms, which are then passed along to the general manager or his subordinates. The GM creates a file on the player, possibly comes out and watches the prospect once or twice, and prepares his recommendation. These recommendations are greatly influenced by a young player's performance in spring training, when the GM and others have a chance to look at the prospects work ethic, attitude and skills on a day-to-day basis.

In short, minor league scouts function as gatekeepers. There are thousands of players in the minor leagues; GMs feel that they can't waste time looking for signs of life in every outfielder scrapping along at a .250 average in single-A (although some .250 hitters *are* prospects). So they rely on scouting reports. Fail to impress the scouts and you'll rarely, if ever, have the opportunity to impress the GM.

Scouting reports traditionally have five categories in which ballplayers are graded (usually along a scale of 1 to 5, although this can vary) — hitting for average, hitting for power, speed, defense, and throwing arm. From these scouting reports, the term "five-tool talent" has crept into the baseball lexicon; a "five-tool talent" means a player who, in the eyes of a scout, excels in all five areas on the report.

The standard "five tools" approach has already started to come under a great deal of criticism from professionals both within and outside of the baseball business. John Sickels, for example, has noted that "defense" and "throwing arm" overlap an awful lot, and that neither ought to be judged with the same weight as "hitting for power." In his published works, he identifies seven "skills" that he uses to judge players, and it's a much-improved system.

I contend that scouting minor league players can, and, in some cases, *must* be done from the armchair, rather than the stands.

This is not to suggest that observation plays no role in evaluating a young player's talent. However, observation is primarily an indicator of *negative* factors. Good scouts will spot the pitcher who can muscle the ninety-five-mph fastball past A-ball hitters, but likely lacks the control or movement to pull off the same trick in the majors; a slugger with a long swing who connects fairly frequently off of other eighteen-year-olds, but isn't likely to get so lucky at higher levels; the shortstop whose arm just isn't strong enough to sling the ball over to first on a regular basis. All of these observations (and many others like them) are absolutely critical to an organization's success in developing talent.

But these subjective, personal observations of physical "tools" are only one measure of a player's potential as a big leaguer. To understand really how a player might perform in the majors, teams also should consider objectively that player's past performances. Unlike high school-age players, minor leaguers *do* have an established record of one or more seasons against relatively equal competition.

Players at AA are already well-sorted. If Steve Slugger hits .300 with thirty-five home runs off AA pitching, that tells us a lot about his talent. It's not like he's teeing off against the Catonsville Comets any more; in AA, Steve faced many pitchers who will go on to AAA and the majors, and he still managed to beat them up pretty good. That's a fairly good indicator of potential major league success, isn't it?

You would think so. Many teams' general managers, however, would disagree with you. When they are judging minor league talent, most continue to rely on subjective scouting reports rather than closely evaluating a player's professional record.

This isn't a problem with most top-notch prospects. Both the "tools" and the "stats" approaches will agree on the very best players. Among players who will likely be proving themselves as you read this, both tools-based scouts and statistical analysts have tapped Adrian Beltre, Ben Grieve and Travis Lee as top prospects. These players look the part, they have great physical tools, and they also have the minor league numbers to back up the hype.

The problem comes at the next level of prospects, young players who aren't on the fast track to superstardom, but who nevertheless project as regulars players in the major leagues. Here, a team will often have to choose between players who show up well in the scouting reports but fare relatively poorly in actual game performances, or players who fail to impress the scouts but somehow manage to get the job done. Who gets that twenty-fifth roster spot out of spring training — Dante Powell, a fantastically athletic first-round draft pick who has struggled at every level of the minor leagues, or Roberto Petagine, a twenty-six-year-old first baseman who has never impressed the scouts but has torn the cover off the ball at every level of minors? Does your team sign Preston Wilson, a scout's dream, or Arquimedez Pozo, a scout's nightmare?

I believe that, when picking hitters, in every instance a team should take the player with the minor league record of performance over the player with the glowing scouting reports.

This doesn't mean simply scanning the agate type in a few of the back pages of *Baseball Weekly*. This is the superficial approach teams use when giving lip service to a player's minor league stats: "Oh, yeah, and he also tore up AAA pitching." A .300 average one season at Colorado Springs isn't much of an indicator. You must understand the context in which certain numbers were accumulated, and it is absolutely critical to use the right measures of performance.

When I'm evaluating minor league statistics, I use seven indicators: age, context, plate discipline, secondary skills, experience, sample size and position.

Age

Having studied the professional careers of thousands of players, I believe that the single most important factor, one which is all but ignored by most sportswriters and vastly underappreciated by GMs, is a player's age.

Most high school draft picks are sent to rookie ball; they're often nineteen or twenty years old before they move on to the lowest A-ball leagues. Similarly, most college picks start off directly in A- or even AA-ball.

But sometimes, players break that mold. A college player might decide to play another sport, like football or basketball, and he may be twenty-three by the time he's drafted and signed by a major league team. A college player who is well-regarded by scouts but doesn't hit well in his first year at A-ball may repeat a level. Or one team's organizational philosophy may move young players through the system more slowly than another. All of these factors can result in one player being older — sometimes significantly older — than his peers.

When a twenty-three-year-old is in low-A ball, he is literally a man among boys, an athlete in probably the best physical shape of his career, playing against nineteen- and twenty-year-olds. He has the advantage of several years of physical and mental growth. That gives him a temporary edge, but it doesn't make him a prospect.

Here's an example from the franchise that is dear to my heart.

In 1997, the Orioles convinced a highly regarded prospect named Ryan Minor to give up on his basketball career and play baseball in their minor leagues. He was twenty-three years old when he signed his first pro contract. He had played four years of college baseball and basketball. In that first season of pro baseball, he hit .307/.387/.545 for the single-A Delmarva Shorebirds of the South Atlantic League, in the Orioles' organization. He hit forty-two doubles, twenty-four home runs, and drove in 97 runs in 134 games, and when he got a few hits during spring training in '98, some people started to regard him as the Orioles' best hitting prospect.

But that was way premature.

In 1998, Minor ran into all kinds of problems at the plate when he moved up to AA, where the competition tends to be somewhat older and more experienced. His numbers slipped all the way down to .250/.296/.397, which is bad, even for a third baseman with a good glove.

The extreme advantage Minor had over the kids at single-A was already starting to disappear when he faced competition closer to his own age. Minor may yet contribute in the major leagues , but that 1997 season at Delmarva is far less impressive when put in its proper context.

One of Minor's teammates at Delmarva in 1997 was a big first baseman by the name of Calvin Pickering. He had a year at the plate that was virtually identical to Ryan Minor's:

	AB	R	H	2B	3B	HR	RBI	BB	SO	SB	CS	AVG	OBP	SLG
Minor	488	83	150	42	1	24	97	51	102	7	3	.307	387	.545
Pickering	444	88	138	31	1	25	79	53	139	6	3	.311	.395	.554

In 1998, Pickering was promoted to the AA Bowie Baysox along with

Ryan Minor. While Minor struggled, Pickering got even better, hitting .309/.425/.566, launching thirty-one homers, drawing many more walks, and striking out less frequently.

From looking at the statistical lines above, how could one have reasonably guessed that Minor would get worse at AA while Pickering would get better? Easy. Pickering and Minor were virtually identical in every meaningful statistic except one: birth date. Calvin Pickering was twenty years old during Delmarva's 1997. Those three years make all the difference. Had Minor been nineteen or twenty when he hit .307 in the Sally League, he would have been an outstanding prospect.

Even after their respective 1998 seasons, most scouts and general managers consider Minor to be the superior prospect — as does practically everyone in the Orioles organization.

I believe that most of these individuals are making this judgment call based on exactly one comparison: Ryan Minor is 6 feet 7 inches, 225 pounds, and extremely athletic; Calvin Pickering is 6 feet 5 inches and weighs between 285 and 300 pounds. Minor looks like he was sculpted out of marble in ancient Athens; Pickering was sent by the Orioles to a special weight-training camp.

(Mind you, I've met Pickering, and he's not what I'd call fat. And the statistics back that up, too; after all, he stole ten bases between '97 and '98.)

Oh, sure, there are a few other differences between the two players that favor Minor: Minor plays a more difficult defensive position (third base as opposed to first base) and plays it well; Minor hit well in spring training in 1998 while Pickering did not; and Minor got six hits in fourteen at-bats during a September call-up.

But, mostly, these are factors that GMs use to justify their built-in prejudices. Teams prefer Minor because he *looks* more like a prospect than does Pickering. And that's silly.

The other end of the spectrum from guys like Ryan Minor are the exceptionally talented high school players who sometimes shoot through the ranks of the minor leagues, holding their own (and more) against players four or more years older than themselves. When an eighteen- or nineteen-year-old doesn't embarrass himself in the upper minors or the major leagues, that's a terrific accomplishment.

One of those high school phenoms was Ken Griffey. His first year in the major leagues saw him hit .264/.329/.420 and play an erratic center field; that's hardly unique. But when you consider that Griffey was a mere nineteen years old at the time, it seems awfully impressive. And, of course, it was a great indicator of what he would do when he got a little older.

Ivan Rodriguez hit .264/.276/.354 when he was nineteen, and .260/.300/.360 when he was twenty. Juan Gonzalez hit .264/.321/.479 as a twenty-year-old. Sammy Sosa hit .233/.282/.404 when he was twenty-one. Barry Bonds, Jeff Bagwell, Bernie Williams, all had some early success in the majors at an age when most players are struggling in the minors. If you can hit big league pitching as a teenager — even just a little bit — odds are overwhelmingly in your favor that you're going to be a great one.

Age isn't everything. No team should trade a twenty-four-year-old AAA shortstop hitting .320/.400/.525 for a nineteen-year-old outfielder hitting .205/.235/.280 in A ball; the AAA shortstop is probably going to be an All-Star, while the nineteen-year old may never be more than minor league roster filler. But age does provide context; without it, you can't accurately judge a player's minor league stats. If that shortstop is thirty years old when he hits .320 at AAA, he might never make the big leagues.

If he were nineteen instead of twenty-four, he'd be Alex Rodriguez.

League context

In evaluating minor league stats, you must always compare his raw numbers to the numbers put up by other players in his league. This seems obvious, but it isn't, because we keep thinking of certain benchmarks — like a .300 average or thirty home runs — as absolutes. But they're not.

In the AAA Pacific Coast League (PCL), for example, many teams play in high-altitude stadiums with shallow dimensions that are known for inflating offensive statistics. (This effect was even more pronounced before the American Association was folded into the PCL in 1997.) In 1998, nine PCL teams hit .280 or better. The league's batting leaders hit .372, .355, .353, .343, .330, .329, and .328. Jeremy Giambi (who won the batting title at .372) is a very good prospect, but almost everybody else on that list isn't a prospect at all. Darryl Brinkley, who finished second in the batting race at .355, is a twenty-nine-year-old outfielder signed out of the independent Northern League; Derrick White (.343) is a twenty-eight-year-old journeyman outfielder with a career average more than sixty points below his '98 totals; Dave Hajek (.328) is a thirty-year-old slap-hitting infielder recording his fifth consecutive season at AAA. And so on.

It's simple: if a player is better than his peers, you would expect him to hit better than his peers. If his peers are all hitting .300, and he's hitting .295, then .295 is a poor performance. Never mind that .295 *looks* like a nice batting average; in that context, it isn't. A .300 hitter in Peoria would be a .400 hitter in Colorado Springs.

We see the opposite effect in the low-A South Atlantic League, sometimes known as the "Sally League." In 1998, nine starting pitchers in the league finished the season with ERAs below 2.75. The stats of the best pitcher in the PCL (Brady Raggio of Memphis, 8-9 with a 3.07 ERA and 100 strikeouts in 154 innings) wouldn't have shown up anywhere near the top in the South Atlantic League.

Two pitchers in the Sally League — Josh Kalinowski of Asheville and John Sneed of Hagerstown — each struck out more than 210 batters during a 140-game season. All but two pitching staffs in the league struck out at least 1,000; that's about eight strikeouts per game over the season. The average South Atlantic League team puts up pitching numbers that would lead the major leagues in virtually every pitching category.

Obviously, though, the Hagerstown Suns' pitching staff isn't superior to that of Toronto Blue Jays. Nor is the offense of the Albuquerque Dukes more powerful than that of the New York Mets. To understand minor league stats, you have to put the numbers into a league context.

Plate discipline

A good hitter, at any level, must be able to lay off the bad pitches in order to be successful. This is particularly true in the minors, and one of the best indicators of future major league success is a minor leaguer's plate discipline. This involves looking at how often the player walks, how often he strikes out, and the ratio between the two.

It's important to note that strikeouts are not significant in rating a hitter's offensive ability. They don't affect team offense. Basically, an out is an out, and over the course of a season, strikeouts aren't worse than any other kind of out. True, sometimes a ground ball or deep fly out will advance a runner, but that advantage is almost entirely counteracted by the fact that putting a ball into play can also lead to double plays. Some of the greatest offensive players in the game strike out a lot: Mo Vaughn is always among the league leaders in strikeouts, averaging about 150 a season over his career, and Sammy Sosa has had back-to-back seasons of more than 170 strikeouts. Although nothing may be more agonizing than watching a player swing through strike three to end a game — particularly if the tying and go-ahead runs are on base — the truth is that strikeouts aren't a serious detriment to a player's run-producing abilities.

However, strikeouts *are* important in evaluating the future of minor league prospects. A high strikeout rate is a red flag because players who strike out a lot tend to have trouble advancing to the big leagues.

I don't know the exact cause and effect. Perhaps a struggling hitter tends to become overly aggressive and swings at pitches out of the strike zone; maybe it's because hitters with expanded strike zones are more easily exploited at the higher levels. Most likely, it's a little of both.

Whatever the reason, high strikeouts — particularly when matched up against low walks — indicate a problem.

Here are the composite minor league walk and strikeout totals, as well as the ratio of the two, for some randomly-selected players who made it to the majors. Ranked in descending order of plate selectivity, the list looks like this:

	Total Walks	Total Strikeouts	Ratio
Brady Anderson	286	167	0.58
Tino Martinez	215	135	0.63
Rafael Palmeiro	107	88	0.82
Jeff Bagwell	99	82	0.83
Gary Sheffield	159	135	0.85
Craig Biggio	79	72	0.91
Barry Bonds	70	83	1.19
Mark McGwire	192	241	1.26
Mo Vaughn	147	213	1.45
Greg Vaughn	257	398	1.55
Jay Buhner	247	388	1.57
Walt Weiss	149	243	1.63
Jose Canseco	149	259	1.74
Bobby Bonilla	65	118	1.82
Brian McRae	203	383	1.89
Joe Girardi	88	181	2.06

Cecil Fielder	127	266	2.09
Royce Clayton	195	409	2.10
Eric Anthony	157	405	2.58
Mariano Duncan	53	155	2.92
Glenallen Hill	308	960	3.12
Archi Cianfrocco	134	489	3.65

That list is not perfectly sorted in descending order of talent, but the relationship between talent and plate discipline in the minors is pretty clear. The worst players, in terms of minor league strikeout-to-walk ratios, are not the big, free-swinging sluggers, but just the worst overall players. Mo Vaughn, for example, shows up much better than Walt Weiss, Brian McRae and Joe Girardi — even though Vaughn in the majors strikes out more than any of them.

There are exceptions.

Sammy Sosa, in the first five years of his professional career, seemed to have absolutely no clue about the strike zone. Here is his career leading up to the major leagues:

Age	Year	Level	Walks	Strikeouts	Plate Appearances	K/BB	PA/BB
18	1987	A	21	123	548	5.86	26.3
19	1988	A+	35	106	549	3.03	15.6
20	1989	AA	15	52	295	3.47	19.6
		AAA	9	14	97	1.56	10.8
21	1990	ML	33	150	579	4.55	17.5
22	1991	AAA	17	32	137	1.88	8.1
		ML	14	98	338	7.00	24.4
23	1992	ML	19	63	291	3.32	15.4

Sosa's plate discipline ranged from bad to worse during his time in the minors. The last two columns represent the ratio of strikeouts to walks and the ratio of plate appearances to walks. In 1987, Sosa struck out approximately six times as often as he walked, and he averaged one base on balls in twenty-six trips to the plate. That is about one walk per week. Yuck.

Still, Sosa moved very rapidly up the ladder to the major leagues. He went from A-ball in 1988 to splitting time between AA, AAA, and the majors the next season, when he was only twenty years old. By the time he was twenty-three, he had spent most of three years in the majors. That's outstanding. And, by and large, his plate discipline improved at each level.

So a player can have poor plate discipline and ultimately still be a very good major league ballplayer, as Sosa is. Of course, if Sammy Sosa had had all of those things *and* had good plate discipline, then he would have been Ken Griffey.

At age seventeen, Griffey drew 44 walks and struck out forty-two times in 228 plate appearances for Bellingham of the Northwest (A) League. The next year, the eighteen-year-old Griffey drew thirty-four walks against 39 strike-outs in 256 plate appearances in the California League. The year after that, he was in the majors for good.

Sosa is a good ballplayer with a fantastic season and an ill-deserved MVP trophy on his shelf; Griffey is a Hall of Famer. That's the difference plate discipline makes.

Secondary skills and "perks"

By "secondary skills," I mean those aspects of a player's hitting that don't show up in batting average but which do add significant value.

Let's look again at Barry Bonds' first season in the majors:

	AB	R	H	2B	3B	HR	RBI	BB	SO	SB	CS	AVG	OBP	SLG
Bonds	413	72	92	26	3	16	48	65	102	36	7	.223	.330	.416

A .223 average isn't impressive, but drawing sixty-five walks in 478 plate appearances is very good, as is knocking forty-five extra-base hits. As a bonus, Bonds was an excellent defensive left-fielder (and capable centerfielder) with outstanding speed.

The walks and the power are secondary skills; they show up in the OBP and SLG calculations. The speed and the defense are "perks" — they're certainly nice to have, and they add value, but they're meaningful only insofar as the player also shows potential of being able to hit. The minor leagues are full of speedy outfielders who play fantastic defense but hit for poor average, can't get on base and have no power.

Here's why secondary skills are important. When a player is young for his league, or still adjusting and learning, he may have difficulty making consistent contact with the ball and, consequently, have a low batting average. This is all part of the learning process. Secondary skills tell us what the player is doing *when he is successful.*

In effect, secondary skills at the minor league level represent a player's potential. When a guy produces a .746 OPS despite being overmatched by major league pitching, it's a fairly good indicator that if he ever does catch up, he's going to hit the ball awfully well.

For Bonds, it took four years. After struggling along to a .223 average in his rookie season, Bonds hit .261 the next year, .283 the third, and slumped to .248 in his fourth full season in the majors.

The next year, 1990, Bonds won the National League Most Valuable Player Award, hitting .301/.406/.565 with 52 steals in sixty-five games and a Gold Glove. The next year, he finished runner-up in the MVP balloting to Terry Pendleton. In 1992 and 1993, Bonds won the MVP back-to-back.

Could one have predicted, back in 1986, in looking at Barry Bonds' minor league and rookie numbers, that they were looking at a Hall of Famer in the making? Probably not. But you certainly could have seen that Bonds' secondary skills were a good indicator of potential stardom if his average came around.

On the other hand, here's Hal Morris in his rookie year with Cincinnati, when he was twenty-three, and Garret Anderson in his first full season in the majors, when he was twenty-two:

	AB	R	H	2B	3B	HR	RBI	BB	SO	SB	CS	AVG	OBP	SLG
Morris	309	50	105	22	3	7	36	21	32	9	3	.340	.381	.498
Anderson	374	50	120	19	1	16	69	19	65	6	2	.321	.352	.505

Those are obviously fine years for young ballplayers, and both Morris and Anderson went on to have solid major league careers. Yet neither turned into anything like Barry Bonds.

The difference is in the secondary skill numbers. Garret Anderson had a batting average 100 points higher than Bonds', but his on-base percentage was a mere twenty points higher. For one year, Anderson was much more productive than Bonds; but a smart scout would have expected Bonds to bridge that gap rapidly. (And he did.)

This item is really strongly related to the previous one; hitters with a good eye for the strike zone — like Bonds, of course — are naturally going to have good OBPs, and are more likely to have higher SLGs as well.

Experience

Ordinarily, experience is a good thing. For evaluating prospects, however, it can be deceiving. When a player repeats a year of the minor leagues, he often comes back much stronger the second time around. Unfortunately, this performance almost never translates well into success at the next rung of the ladder.

This makes sense when you consider that most minor leagues have a high turnover every season, with a high proportion of players moving up from the lower levels. New players often have a period of adjustment that may be as long as half a season or more (particularly when they move up to AA). A player who stays at the same level for two or more seasons will be skipping that period of adjustment; essentially, he'll have a head start that can help him pad his stats. But his true talent level hasn't changed.

An extreme — but by no means isolated — example is Webster Garrison, a journeyman second baseman in the Oakland organization. In nine minor league seasons, his best "season" was 168 plate appearances for AAA Syracuse in 1989, where he hit .285/.368/.344 with zero home runs.

In 1993, Garrison hit .303/.369/.414, with a career-best thirteen home runs. The next year was even better, .302/.356/.459. He would hit 44 more homers over the next three years, after hitting twenty-two in his first nine.

Did Garrison turn in to a bona fide slugging second baseman? I doubt it. He just mastered AAA and stayed there.

This is not to say that a player's improvement is never for real, or that guys who take a year or two to master a level of the minors have no place in the big leagues. But a healthy dose of skepticism is usually in order when a struggling player suddenly seems to turn his career around in his second or third season at a given level of the minors.

Sample size

At any level of baseball, in the majors or minors, a player can have a "fluke" season far out of line with his actual potential.

This often occurs when a player is repeating a season at a certain level, but it can happen even when he is advancing.

P.J. Forbes, once an infield prospect in the Angels' system, is one example. In 1990, his first season as a professional, he hit .247/.335/.312 at A-ball; the next year he hit .266/.342/.335, a slight improvement, in a slightly tougher A-league. The following season, he hit .282/.356/.367, again at the A level. That performance earned him a promotion to AA Midland, where he hit .319/.357/.464, with twenty-three doubles, fifteen homers and 90 runs scored. Forbes had had four career home runs before 1994; with that one season, he quintupled his total.

A breakthrough? Not quite. The following season, he was back down to .286/.331/.374, with one home run. He hit one more in '95, and another one in '96, before leaving Anaheim as a six-year minor league free agent.

Take a look at a player's entire career when deciding whether he is a true prospect; if his previous three seasons were mediocre, be wary of two or three hundred at-bats at AA or AAA which make him look like a potential star.

Position

Finally, the position a prospect plays is relevant in two ways: first, it gives an indication of the player's long-term relative value to his team; second, it can explain poor performances if a player is shifted around to multiple defensive positions.

When Ron Gant was first promoted to the majors, he hit .259/.317/.439 with Atlanta; he was an erratic, scrawny second baseman who made twenty-six errors in 122 games at second base. Sent back to AAA Richmond in 1989 to learn how to play the outfield, Gant hit .262/.345/.484 — hardly impressive numbers — before being recalled to the majors.

The next year, Gant hit .303/.357/.539 as a center-fielder.

On the other hand, Donnie Sadler was a middle infielder posting respectable numbers for three seasons in the Red Sox organization; in 1997, the Sox decided to jerk him around from shortstop to second base to center field, and he slipped to .212/.295/.326. In 1998, Sadler spent some time in the majors, and hit .226/.276/.395 in 130 plate appearances. That's not terribly impressive, but it does suggest that Sadler's '97 was artificially deflated due to his changing defensive positions.

None of these rules is absolute, nor are they necessarily easy to apply. But, as you'll see from the following chapters, knowing which stats to apply, and how to evaluate them in context, can help an armchair analyst outperform professional journalists and general managers.

Seven Rules for Picking Prospects

• The younger a player is, relative to the league in which he plays, the more highly his performance ought to be valued.

• Always compare a minor leaguer's statistics to the league and park in which he played.

• All things being equal, the hitter with more command of the strike zone is the better prospect.

• Look for a player who can put up solid OBP and SLG numbers even when his average is low.

• Always look to make sure this year's stats aren't the result of a year or more head start on the competition. A player who hits .300/.400/.500 in his first stop at AAA is a much better prospect than the one who hits .300/.400/.500 on his third go-round at that level.

• Look for a trend of consistent development when a player advances through the minors. Don't discount a bump upwards in production as necessarily a fluke, but don't get excited by a small number of plate appearances that makes a hitter look better than he actually is.

• All things being equal, a second baseman is more valuable than a right-fielder, but a second baseman struggling in the field may take his defensive woes up to the plate with him.

8

Undervalued Talent

P rofessional baseball isn't fair.

Maybe I'm naïve to believe that it should be. But you'd think that in such a highly competitive sport (and business), a highly promising young player would always be given a legitimate chance to prove himself, and genuine value would always rise to the top.

But it doesn't work that way. Truth is, dozens and maybe hundreds of players with true major league ability find themselves stuck in the minors while less able players build time toward their pensions. And more often than not it is because those "failed" players didn't impress their team's manager and front office within their first few dozen big league games.

This chapter is about undervalued and unappreciated talents, players with demonstrable big league ability who find themselves languishing for years in minor league uniforms, victims either of bad luck or (more often) the myopia of managers and GMs and personnel directors.

Mainly, it is the story of one of the truly undervalued players in pro baseball, Roberto Petagine. I could have chosen plenty of equally talented minor leaguers who have been just as badly shafted. But I have a soft spot for Petagine, as I have been promoting him as a potential standout since 1993.

I have never met Roberto Petagine. I've seen him play a few times, and once watched him during the televised broadcast of the AAA All-Star

Game. I know absolutely nothing about his personality, work habits or extracurricular activities.

I do know that he can hit the snot out of the ball. I also know that he's been twice voted the best defensive first baseman in his league. And I would be tempted to label him the Unluckiest Man in America, except that his story is far too common among minor leaguers.

Roberto Petagine was a blue-chip prospect in the Houston Astros' organization, a left-handed first baseman who hit for average and power, knew how to draw a walk and was also well-regarded defensively. In 1993, he hit .334/.442/.529 at AA, and earned a spot on the Astros bench the next year when Sid Bream started the year on the disabled list.

You might suspect that the backup first baseman behind Jeff Bagwell probably isn't going to play much, and you'd be right; after all, Bagwell is better than Petagine in nearly every conceivable way. That's no crime – Bagwell is an All-Star first baseman, and he is better than many players with seven-figure annual incomes.

Petagine never had a shot to crack the Houston Astros. He had Bagwell in front of him at first base, there was no DH, and the team didn't even consider placing a slow first baseman out in the cavernous outfield of the Astrodome. Petagine managed only seven at-bats in two call-ups with Houston in 1994, going 0-for-7.

Clearly, Petagine needed to get out of Houston. If he had been given his choice of teams to which he'd like to be traded that year, he might very well have picked the San Diego Padres. The Padres were an awful team that had recently shipped off its stars during a 1993 "fire sale." Outfielder Gary Sheffield was sent to Florida, and starting first baseman Fred McGriff went to Atlanta and almost single-handedly carried the Braves to the playoffs. Unsurprisingly, 1994 was a dismal season for the Pads; their 47-70 record was the worst in baseball when the strike shut down major league ball for the rest of the year.

In 1994, while Bagwell was hitting .368 in Houston (with Petagine stuck behind him on the organizational depth chart), the Padres were auditioning a cast of makeweights at first base, including Rule V draftee Tim Hyers (.254/.307/.280), Phil Clark (.215/.255/.356) and Dave Staton (.182/.289/.394). The Padres even managed to sneak out a fantastic hundred-odd at-bats out of softball refugee Eddie Williams, but no one seriously expected him to hit .331 again.

December brought new hopes — and new ownership — to the Padres. An ownership group led by Larry Lucchino and John Moores acquired the club and quickly made efforts to reassure the fans in San Diego that they were serious about bringing a winner to the city. A few days after Christmas, on December 28, 1994, Padres fans were treated to an historic thirteen-player deal that brought them Steve Finley and Ken Caminiti, among others.

One of those "others" was a young first base prospect named Roberto Petagine.

With his new team, Petagine quickly made the most of his opportunity. He broke camp with the big league club, having won the starting first base job out of spring training. In the first two weeks of the regular season, he reached base via a hit or walk in fourteen of his first fifteen games. Soon afterward, he was injured.

When he came back, Petagine couldn't get started, couldn't hit, and couldn't win back his starting job. For the year, he made just twenty-two starts at first base and hit .234. Yet even at this low-water mark, Petagine managed to draw twenty-six walks in just 150 plate appearances, for a .367 OBP. Solid peripheral numbers like that almost always indicate a solid foundation of talent.

However, few teams are going to make room for a .234-hitting first baseman with three career major league home runs, even if he does have a decent batting eye. And the new Padres ownership, encouraged by a nearly respectable season, felt that the best way to signal their continuing commitment to building a winner was to trade for a veteran first baseman in the offseason. The Padres sent second baseman Bip Roberts to Kansas City for Wally Joyner.

Petagine could only wait during the off-season. The Padres clearly weren't going to give him another shot at first base, and few National League teams have the luxury of carrying a rookie first baseman as a bench player.

His relief didn't come until March 17, 1996, during the middle of spring training, when he was shipped off to the Mets for two players you've never heard of. The Mets already had a first baseman, Rico Brogna, who had hit .282 with twenty-two homers in his first season the year before. But Brogna had torn his medial collateral ligament two weeks previously, and the Mets were in the market. Once again, Petagine was seemingly headed to the right place at the right time.

By now you can probably guess where this is going.

Major league ballplayers have bad weeks, bad months, even bad years; it's all part of the game. When Frank Thomas hits .265, everyone knows that's not his true level of ability. Ken Griffey can go 0-for-the-month-of-April, and Lou Piniella isn't going to bench him.

A prospect with 150 miserable plate appearances on his major league resumé, however, cannot afford to get off to a slow start. And Petagine did just that, hitting .232 in 108 plate appearances with the '96 Mets, losing the first base job to Butch Huskey.

Even when the Mets traded Rico Brogna to the Phillies in late November of 1996, Petagine was still behind Butch Huskey on the depth chart.

Then the Mets traded for John Olerud less than one month later. Olerud is almost exactly the same sort of hitter Petagine is: a left-handed line-drive hitter with decent power and a superb batting eye. But Olerud had seven full seasons in the majors and a career average near .300 under his belt at the time; Petagine had two hundred and some at-bats and a career average of .233.

Previous teams during previous seasons had been able to trade Roberto Petagine once he no longer fit into their plans. That is what comes with being regarded as a "blue chip prospect" — which Petagine was in 1994 — rather than a shopworn "minor league hitter," the reputation he had acquired by the end of 1996. Other teams come calling for a prospect who's blocked by a veteran, but there's no demand for a career minor leaguer.

By the end of 1996, there were no takers for Roberto Petagine, and he spent most of 1997 at AAA.

This drastic transformation from prospect to suspect took just over two years. From 1994 to 1996, Petagine was given 265 plate appearances — less than half of one full season in the majors. Any player can have a lousy stretch of 265 plate appearances. Given his injury, and the fact that most of his appearances were as a part-timer (a role that most players find difficult) Petagine's problems at the plate weren't surprising.

Even some tremendous players have struggled to start their careers. When Barry Bonds broke in, he hit .223 in almost twice as many plate appearances as Petagine got in three seasons. Top prospect Andruw Jones hit .217 when called up to Atlanta in August of 1996, hit .231 for all of

1997, and then hit .218 in April of 1998, and the Braves *still* stuck with him.

Nobody called Andruw Jones a "failed prospect" or "minor league hitter" despite 662 plate appearances during which he couldn't hit at all. (And rightly so; Jones hit .282 for the rest of 1998 to finish at .271/.321/.515, with thirty-one homers and twenty-seven stolen bases.)

Why had three teams given up on Petagine after one-third the playing time that Andruw Jones was given to prove himself?

I suspect it has to do with two things.

First, both Jones and Bonds played outstanding defense in the outfield; and second, both Jones and Bonds were very fast and stole a lot of bases. A team often will show some patience with a prospect if he plays a key defensive position well, or if he steals a lot of bases. But when a player's main skills are as a hitter, his trial is apt to be a *lot* shorter.

In the short term, this makes sense: a Gold Glove center-fielder who can't hit will still help his team more than a first baseman who can't hit. But it is an absurd way to predict a young player's long-term development. What does Jones' ability to steal bases or play the field have to do with his ability to learn how to hit major league pitching? Absolutely nothing!

And yet the slow-footed, lead-gloved hitter who needs more than a handful of at-bats to adjust to life in the majors is inevitably tagged as a "minor league hitter." The implication is that his numbers in the minors no longer count; that the AAA leagues are somehow stocked with rejects from your local forty-and-over slow-pitch softball league, slopballers who serve up hanging breaking balls and seventy-five-mph heaters right down the pipe, near-amateurs putting in six months a year as batting practice pitchers before heading back to their "real" jobs running the Slushee machine in the Huntington, Iowa Wal-Mart cafeteria.

This is nonsense, of course. Were it true, then Ken Griffey and Barry Bonds and Frank Thomas would have hit .500 and smacked seventy-five homers a season during their time in the minors. There isn't *that* much difference between the International League and the American League. (I'm not the first to say that: Earl Weaver used to say it, too.)

If Andruw Jones can adjust to the majors after more than a year's worth of futility, why can't Roberto Petagine?

Alas, that question was not answered in 1997. Petagine spent nearly all of 1997 at AAA Norfolk, winning the International League's MVP award, hitting .317/.430/.605, going 1-for-15 in a brief major league call-up. (No, this was not some fluke; Petagine had hit .318/.421/.529 the year before at Norfolk.)

Petagine declared free agency after the 1997 season and signed a minor league contract with the Cincinnati Reds, another rebuilding team with a lot of holes to fill. But the Reds traded Dave Burba for a highly regarded first base prospect, Sean Casey, with just a few days remaining in spring training. Later in the season, they acquired another first base prospect, Paul Konerko, from the Dodgers.

Still, Roberto managed to get in a brief audition late in the season with the Reds; tried in right field, he didn't embarrass himself defensively, and managed to hit .258/.405/.468. Against right-handers, he hit an excellent .291/.426/.527.

As this was being written, Petagine was preparing for 1999 spring training with the Reds. Will he finally get the legitimate shot that he deserves? Probably not. He isn't really a long-term solution in the outfield, and he isn't likely to displace Sean Casey at first base.

Roberto, if you're reading this, take heart from the tale of Pittsburgh's Kevin Young. He started off just as you did, a sure-fire, can't-miss prospect. In 1992, when he hit .314/.406/.447 at AAA, he was the American Association's Rookie of the Year.

The Pirates gave Young the starting third base job in 1993. He hit .236/.300/.343 in 485 plate appearances and played his way off the team.

In 1994 and 1995, Young got two more chances to prove himself and didn't, hitting .205 and .232 in 319 trips to the plate over those two years. He was released, and signed with Kansas City.

In 1996, he got just 143 plate appearances with the Royals. Despite a respectable .771 OPS — including a .470 slugging percentage and eight home runs in 55 games for the power-starved Royals — Young was released again.

In 1997, Kevin Young went back to Pittsburgh, the organization that had drafted him. He broke camp with the big club in a reserve role, but slowly won the starting first base job. He finished the year with .300/.332/.535, leading the team in homers (18) and RBI (74), despite only 349 plate appearances. In 1998, he played all year and hit a respectable .270/.328/.481.

There are many similar stories: Troy O'Leary, Matt Stairs and Geronimo Berroa all spent way too much time in the minors before being given a legitimate chance in the majors (and finally succeeding). But for every one who finally gets the chance, there are many others who still wait, like Petagine, Pat Lennon, Mark Leonard and Arquimedez Pozo.

Give them a chance and, like Kevin Young and Matt Stairs and Geronimo Berroa, they *will* hit.

The Cruelties of Age

P rofessional baseball is a young man's game.

The cruel law of the career curve is that by the time a player is established as a star, the best part of his career is already finished. This holds true for nearly everyone. As fans, we all want to believe that the Hometown Heroes can play forever, that they are always capable of improving, but never subject to decline. They play at their peak level until it's time to pack up the spikes and retire gracefully.

In the real world, it doesn't work that way. Athletes get old. Abilities deteriorate. The difference between a successful major leaguer and an struggling one is incredibly small. One-tenth of a second in triggering the swing of the bat. One-tenth of a second in breaking to the left off a batted ball up the middle. One tiny notch downward in the quality of your vision. These changes are inexorable and they're reflected in a player's day-to-day performance. They mark the difference between being a star and merely being a contributor, between being an everyday player and scrapping for a role on the bench.

When do these declines begin? That depends somewhat on the individual. Tony Phillips played his best baseball after age thirty. So did Paul Molitor. But thousands of major leaguers never played past thirty at all. Mostly, "old man" territory for baseball players starts after age thirty-two.

H I T T I N G

If you think that's being overly pessimistic, maybe it's because we tend to remember the ones who did manage to sustain their careers into their late thirties: Dave Winfield, Wade Boggs, Eddie Murray, Andre Dawson, Cal Ripken. We forget about Bob Geren and Candy Maldonado and Mitch Webster and Bill Pecota, not because they were abysmal ballplayers, but because they were just average. And the life expectancy of an average ballplayer is very low.

Winfield, Murray, Dawson and Ripken were good players into their mid-thirties in part because they were *great* players in their mid-twenties. Hard work and conditioning probably helped to preserve their skills to some extent, and they may have been gifted with exceptional talent as well.

All these factors may delay the disastrous, career-ending decline, but even the great ones and exceptional cases will have slumped drastically by the time they reach forty. At that age, even the greatest Hall of Fame hitters can't keep up with major league pitching. Look at Babe Ruth's numbers when he was forty. Or Murray's. Or Dawson's. There's an exception here and there, but not many.

For most players, the nosedive comes much earlier. Ballplayers who begin with marginal skills have nowhere to go but down, and often very quickly.

Consider this list of all major league players who were thirty-three or thirty-four years old when they entered the 1994 season:

Wally Backman, Kevin Bass, George Bell, Rob Deer, Tom Foley, Dave Gallagher, Bob Geren, Rene Gonzalez, Tony Gwynn, Brian Harper, Billy Hatcher, Kent Hrbek, Tim Hulett, John Kruk, Mike LaValliere, Steve Lyons, Candy Maldonado, Don Mattingly, Kevin McReynolds, Randy Milligan, Charlie O'Brien, Greg Olson, Junior Ortiz, Spike Owen, Mike Pagliarulo, Dan Pasqua, Bill Pecota, Terry Pendleton, Gerald Perry, Geno Petralli, Kirby Puckett, Randy Ready, Harold Reynolds, Ernie Riles, Cal Ripken, John Russell, Nelson Santovenia, Steve Sax, Mike Sharperson, Larry Sheets, Mickey Tettleton, Ron Tingley, Dave Valle, Gary Varsho, Jim Walewander, Mitch Webster and Curtis Wilkerson.

This list was compiled impartially — by selecting all position players with a birthday from late 1959 to early 1961. It yielded forty-eight names in all.

Two years later, going into the 1996 season, all but nine of those forty-eight players were out of major league baseball.

The nine were Deer, Gonzales, Gwynn, Mattingly, O'Brien, Pendleton, Tettleton, Ripken and Valle. Three of those — Deer, Gonzales and Valle — got only a handful of at-bats in '96, and played terribly.

A year later, in the 1997 season, only four of the original group of forty-eight got as much as a single at-bat in the majors.

That is to say, only one in twelve of the players who were thirty-three or thirty-four years old to start the 1994 season was still playing three years later. The ratio isn't unusual: it holds up pretty well for almost any year's group of thirty-three- and thirty-four-year-old players.

Those odds ought to be burned into the forehead of every general manager who considers signing a thirty-three or thirty-four-year-old free agent to a three-year contract. The chances of that player completing his contract are terrible. And even if he does manage to hang around on the roster through the full term, he will probably end up playing so badly that he hurts his team.

Some players beat those odds. I would love to have Ken Griffey on my team when he is thirty-four. But Griffey at that age won't be nearly as good as he was seven years earlier.

Since turning thirty, Barry Bonds has slugged .597 — awfully good. But between ages twenty-seven to twenty-nine, Bonds slugged .651, which is considerably better. His batting average and on-base percentage, too, were significantly higher during those earlier seasons. Like almost everyone else, Bonds wasn't quite the player after thirty that he had been before.

Of course, the difference between Barry Bonds and, say, Gary Varsho is stark. Nobody offers Gary Varsho a long-term contract at age thirty-four, but Barry Bonds is probably worth the risk if the price isn't too high. The hard questions lie in between the extremes, the great majority of players who are better than Varsho and worse than Bonds.

Here are some considerations that would help teams to minimize the possibility of paying big money to a player whose age will soon make him completely useless as a major leaguer.

Pooling the risk
One of Branch Rickey's maxims is that "it is better to trade a player a year too early than a year too late." In light of the odds against a player remaining useful into his mid-thirties, this seems like true wisdom.

Unfortunately, most teams take precisely the opposite approach, in part because people in the game tend to over-value experience, but also because of great pressure from media and (hence) fans to retain veteran players. Trading a popular veteran or allowing him to leave via free agency is viewed as a defeat, the sort of concession that fans in Milwaukee or Montreal have to go through, but that fans of "real" franchises shouldn't have to endure.

Fan loyalty is important to team owners, and fans can be terribly demanding. Boston fans still haven't forgiven the Red Sox for allowing Wade Boggs and Roger Clemens to leave as free agents when they still had productive seasons left in their bodies. And fans want to believe that their teams are at least trying to contend for a championship; "rebuilding" is a dirty word and is seen as a surrender.

The decision is reduced to a stark dichotomy. If you're a big league GM, you either prove that you want to compete by signing older players to long-term contracts, or else you throw up your hands and admit that you're in a rebuilding phase in which you allow your veterans to leave indiscriminately for greener pastures, while you plug the holes with younger and cheaper alternatives.

But there's a third choice, which is to avoid rebuilding by constantly working in young players. Every team pays lip service to this idea, but few seem to recognize that if a team is to work a young player into the lineup, it has to be willing to let go of an older one, even if he still has some value.

The Atlanta Braves have been able to pull this off better than most, as demonstrated by a series of moves that began before the 1996 season, when the Braves let go Kent Mercker to free up a rotation spot for Jason Schmidt. Then, during the season, they traded Schmidt for Denny Neagle (seemingly a step backward in age, but with a purpose). In the next offseason, the Braves allowed Steve Avery to leave via free agency, traded David Justice and Marquis Grissom for Kenny Lofton, and swapped Jermaine Dye for Michael Tucker. The Braves declined to sign Lofton for '98 and gave Avery's rotation spot to rookie Kevin Millwood. Then, after 1998, the Braves traded Neagle and Tucker to Cincinnati for Bret Boone.

If you were playing Rotisserie ball, these were horrible moves. The Braves got nothing for Mercker and Avery; got one year of Lofton for Justice and Grissom; and, after trading four outstanding prospects, have wildly inconsistent second baseman Bret Boone to show for it.

But look beyond the obvious.

Mercker's departure opened up an opportunity for Schmidt. Avery's departure allowed them to take a look at several young pitchers, and ultimately to work Kevin Millwood into the rotation. The departure of Grissom and Justice freed up a spot for Andruw Jones, who, in turn, made Kenny Lofton expendable. The trade of Neagle will leave an open path for top pitching prospect Bruce Chen, and by timing Chen's arrival until Millwood had a successful major league season under his belt, the Braves avoided having two rookies in the rotation at once.

Remember, the Braves were already the best team in the National League when they began these moves. For most teams, dominance is an excuse to stand pat. Instead, the Braves continually cycled in prospects and divested themselves of aging veterans, including Fred McGriff, Jeff Blauser and Mark Lemke among the others mentioned above.

Yet they continued to win, and nobody accused them of "rebuilding."

McGriff, Blauser and Grissom all declined in 1998 (badly, in some cases). And by the end of the season, Lemke, Avery and Mercker were struggling to even keep a job in pro baseball.

Most important, the Braves didn't just help themselves by getting rid of veterans who were ready to take a nosedive. Freeing up those spots allowed them to develop excellent young players who were ready for full-time jobs. (Obviously, none of this would have been possible without the Braves' fine farm system.)

In 1998, Andruw Jones (.271/.321/.515 while playing a great center field) was easily more valuable than any of the veterans Atlanta traded away or allowed to leave. Kevin Millwood (17-8, 4.08 ERA) was a better pitcher than Avery or Mercker. Even though they ended up without Schmidt, giving him a spot in the rotation enhanced his value so much that they were able to trade him for Neagle, whose 16-11 record and 3.55 ERA in '98 was the long term payoff for allowing Mercker to leave in '96.

The Braves would not have won the National League East in 1998 if they had stood pat on their team in '96.

These moves involved some risk. What if Kevin Millwood hadn't panned out? Or if Andruw Jones had had more trouble adjusting to the major league strike zone? Or what happens in '99, if Bruce Chen blows out his rotator cuff? Baseball, like everything else in life, is sometimes unpredictable. Young players do entail some risk (although Andruw Jones' emergence as a big-league hitter was as close to a certainty as you could get).

But remember: *major league veterans are risks, too.* Older players, especially those not quite in the elite, can take career-ending declines at any time. Steve Avery and Marquis Grissom were nearly worthless within a year after the Braves declined to re-sign them (to the consternation of many fans and media critics).

The Braves did what teams must do if they're to remain successful over several seasons: they pooled their risk. In any given year, a "proven veteran" may indeed be less of a risk than an "untried rookie." But over several seasons, that risk accumulates to the point of near-certain disaster.

The Braves, clearly, have begun to figure this out. Most other teams don't yet get it. When they look at a prospect they see only the risk, not the potential reward. When they look at a veteran they're dazzled by the success of his peak years (which are usually far behind him). They don't see the risk involved in keeping him around until his career-ending decline arrives like a fast freight.

Teams — particularly so-called "large market" teams — also face pressures from within and without not to become the Montreal Expos. Indeed, "Expos" has become synonymous with refusing to field a competitive team or play major league baseball.

Because of budget restraints, the Expos are forced to rely on young players throughout the lineup, and they're unable to hold on to their better players once they become eligible for free agency. This would be a nightmare scenario for most teams.

But how horrible, really, is that nightmare?

In 1993, the Expos won 94 games and missed out on the NL East division title by three games. For most teams, that's a signal to consolidate, maybe make a few moves to bolster the team in an attempt to win the division. Instead, during the off-season, Montreal traded away one of the key players on their roster, gifted (and arbitration-eligible) second baseman Delino DeShields, who went to the Los Angeles Dodgers for two pitching prospepcts.

It was the beginning of a long series of moves that would come to define the Expos, to convert them from a mere baseball franchise into a media buzzword. Penny-wise and pound-foolish. Short-sighted. More concerned with saving a buck than with winning a title.

And yet the 1994 Expos — depsite dumping salary instead of adding it — had the best record in baseball when the strike hit. Nearly every year, the Expos manage to confound their critics by playing better than the experts predict.

From 1994 to 1998, following the DeShields Dump, the Expos had the following won-loss records: 74-40 (.649), 66-78 (.458), 88-74 (.543), 78-84 (.481), and 65-97 (.401). That's a five-year record of 371-373. Had the 1994 season not been cut short by the strike, the Expos would have been a winning franchise over those five seasons.

In other words, despite trading or releasing every single player from that '93 team, the Expos finished essentially in the middle of the pack, coming in ahead of some teams with much larger payrolls.

This was possible in part because the 1994 trade of DeShields brought in Pedro Martinez. The 1997 trade of Martinez brought in Carl Pavano. And, in a few years, Carl Pavano will bring a couple prospects in when he is traded (and he will be).

Don't get me wrong: this is no way to run a franchise. Trading a twenty-six-year-old Pedro Martinez for salary reasons, even for one of the best pitching prospects in baseball, really *is* pound-foolish.

The Montreal Expos represent the absolute worst, most foolish, most idiotic implementation of a commitment to use young (and cheap) players. Despite the egregious nonsense of this approach, the Expos from '94 to '98 were only *one-half game worse* than the New York Mets, a quintessential big-market, big-payroll franchise.

The Expos are a powerful object lesson about getting younger and growing old in baseball.

Plotting career curves

Okay, we know in general that players after thirty are a bad risk, and that players over thirty-three are a terrible risk. That's fine as far as it goes, but a good GM would want to know the particulars. Who can we expect to get old in a hurry, and who will beat the odds? Who might fizzle out at age thirty-two, and who is a decent bet to continue on through age 39?

Often the answer can be found in career curve plotting.

Here's the career curve of Chris Sabo, the 1988 NL Rookie of the Year, a scrappy third baseman with the Cincinnati Reds who earned the nickname "Spuds Mackenzie" for his all-out enthusiasm and hustling style of play:

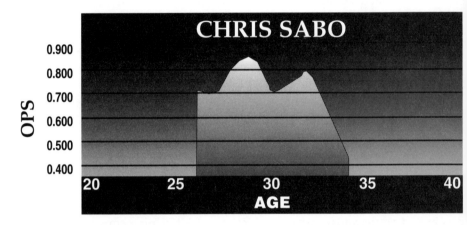

In that 1988 Rookie of the Year balloting, the next three position-players spots after Sabo were Mark Grace, Ron Gant and Roberto Alomar. Ten years later, those three were still playing and Sabo was long finished.

What happened?

A big part of the answer is that Chris Sabo was twenty-six years old when he broke in, while Grace and Gant were twenty-three and Alomar was just twenty. Even in his rookie seasons, it should have been obvious that Sabo probably had fewer productive years head of him than did younger but talented players who were also breaking into the majors at the same time.

Furthermore, his minor league career didn't show much potential for enduring stardom. Sabo was drafted out of college and sent straight to Double-A Vermont of the Eastern League, where he hit .213/.288/.295. Given another shot at AA in 1985, Sabo hit .278/.360/.400. (Remember, a player repeating a level in the minors may sometimes experience a big upward bump in his numbers that doesn't really reflect his talent level.) Even so, this wasn't a particularly impressive year for a corner infielder — Sabo hit just 11 home runs in a full season — but it was enough to earn him a promotion to AAA the next season. Perhaps the Reds understood the pointlessness of keeping a player at the same level for three consecutive seasons.

Sabo spent two years at AAA, hitting .273/.346/.412 as a twenty-four-year-old, and .292/.362/.438 at age twenty-five. In 1988, at age twenty-six, he opened the season on the Cincinnati Reds' bench as a utility infielder. But when veteran starting third baseman Buddy Bell got off to a miserable start, hitting .185 with no extra base hits and three RBI during all of April, Sabo got a chance to start at third.

He played well, if not spectacularly: 271/.314/.414, no more or less than his minor league numbers had suggested. Sabo also stole 46 bases in '88, which he never again came anywhere close to repeating.

In sum, it was enough to nail down the third base job in Cincinnati and win Sabo the best-rookie trophy.

When a rookie hits .271 with forty doubles, as Chris Sabo did in 1988, fans and baseball insiders get excited about his future. Sometimes that enthusiasm is justified. When a young player pops a lot of doubles, those long hits into the gaps sometimes turn into homers as he matures, adds strength and becomes more familiar with big league pitching. Vladimir Guerrero had twenty-two doubles in just over half a season with Montreal in 1997; the next year, he hit 38 home runs.

But Guerrero was twenty-two when he broke in. Chris Sabo at age twenty-six didn't have nearly that much untapped potential. Eventually he did add a bit of power, peaking at twenty-six homers in 1991. Still, within three years after his debut, Sabo was already on the down side of his career. He played on until 1996, when he was thirty-four, but his productive days as a regular ended after just six years in the majors.

This period in his career had an ugly side. When Sabo lost the Baltimore Orioles' starting third-base job in 1994 to the injury-prone, defensively challenged Leo Gomez, he snarled to the local press that Gomez "was no Mike Schmidt." Sabo, himself no Mike Schmidt, was moved to the outfield, where his defensive play earned him the nickname "Galatea," after the famous mythological statue. Over the next two years, Sabo bounced from the Orioles to the White Sox to the Cardinals and back to the Reds, totalling just over 200 more at-bats in those two seasons before hanging up his spikes for good.

Compare Sabo to the following player, who first appeared in the majors a year ahead of Sabo, at the age of twenty-one (his Career Curve is on page 100).

I'm including Jay Bell's 1987 and 1988 years, even though he spent more than half of each season in the minors.

But that is the key difference between Jay Bell and Chris Sabo. When Sabo was twenty-two, he was struggling badly at AA; when Jay Bell was

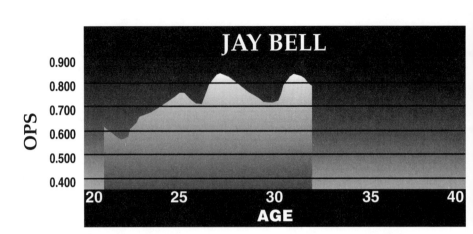

twenty-two, he had already spent a season putting up an .844 OPS at AAA and a .621 OPS in 145 plate appearances in the majors.

You must have a player's full career laid out in front of you as a curve before being able to make any sort of rational prediction about that player's future. Taking a selected slice just won't do it.

During the prime of their respective careers, Chris Sabo and Jay Bell were virtually indistinguishable as hitters. Sabo's career best was .305/.354/.505 as a twenty-nine-year-old in 1991; Bell hit .310/.392/.437 as a twenty-seven-year-old in 1993. Sabo's career high in homers is twenty-six; Bell's, twenty-one. Their career averages are .268 and .267. Sabo's career OPS is .771, Bell's is .763. So why was Sabo washed up at age thirty-two while Jay Bell at the same age was putting up a near-.800 OPS?

The answer is in the career curves. Bell's shows a player who made adjustments, settled in at the big league level, and delivered consistent, if unspectacular, seasons at the plate while playing a key defensive position. Sabo's curve shows a player who was capable of starting in the big leagues, but only for a limited window during his peak years.

Knowing how to separate Chris Sabo from Jay Bell is the key to predicting when a player's production will fall off the table.

Sabo offers another, deeper lesson.

He was a fan favorite, a hard-nose competitor, a grinder who wasn't afraid to sprawl out, dive far to his left, get his uniform dirty, take the extra base when the pitcher was napping.

He played the game all-out, every day, and the people in the seats loved him.

And he was washed up by age thirty-two. Not because he played hard, but because his skills were never much more than average.

It's a painful reminder of the principle I've tried to lay out throughout the book. Wishing doesn't make an average player good, or a good player great. No amount of adulation from the fans can extend a baseball career when a player's skills hit the wall.

Extreme peak years in perspective

Here, through the '98 season, is the career curve of outfielder Kenny Lofton. Note the big spike at age twenty-seven:

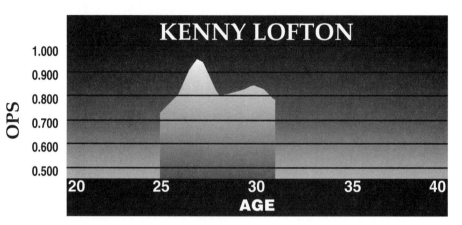

Lofton gets on base, he is an effective base stealer, and he is terrific in center field. Kenny Lofton is a good player. Many fans and media types seem to think that he's a great player, one of the elite, yet he's not nearly at that level.

Take a look at Lofton's OPS breakdowns since becoming a regular at age twenty-five in 1992: .727, .816, .948, .815, .818, .834, .784. Lofton did have a single great season, at age twenty-seven. He hit .349, with thirty-two doubles, nine triples, and twelve homers. In a shortened season in which he played just 112 games, Lofton scored 105 runs and drove in fifty-seven from the leadoff spot.

I think the memory of that single year is the reason his reputation exceeds the reality.

Unfortunately for Lofton and his fans, he isn't likely ever to duplicate that season again. (Especially not as he approaches his mid-thirties.) Take out Lofton's .948 OPS from that year, and you find him around a solid .815 OPS, season after season.

So if you're a major league GM, what do you predict Lofton will hit in 1999? Do you expect that at best he'll stay around .815 OPS, or would you be looking for him to get back over .900 again? This book is being written before the start of the '99 season; I'll risk making myself look silly for posterity when I say that I expect him to be around an .815 OPS, at best, in '99.

And what does his career curve portend for Lofton's longevity? If you disregard his extreme peak season, he is not one of those rare great players whose superior skills, even though eroded, will keep him useful past the age of thirty-five or thirty-six. He's better than average, but not that much better.

Enduring skills
Take a look at one more chart:

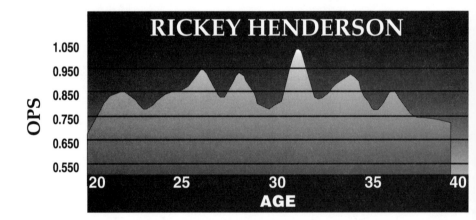

Rickey Henderson is one of those no-doubt-about-it Hall of Famers. That he remained a valuable player into his late thirties is no great surprise, since his talents were so far superior to almost anyone who has played the game over the last two decades. But Henderson also has a special skill that has been the secret of his longevity.

He knows how to lay off bad pitches.

Over his career, Henderson has done this better than any of his contemporaries, averaging 117 walks per season. That's phenomenal. And that's why Rickey has continued to be a valuable ballplayer well into dreaded Old Man territory, despite a dip in his batting average from a high of .325 to its current neighborhood south of the .250 border.

I suspect that the ability to recognize bad pitches, while somewhat dependent on eyesight, probably degrades slower than bat speed. And knowing how to work the count doesn't depend on physical skills; it's a mental exercise which can actually improve with age and experience, up to a point.

If a player is to remain effective through his mid-thirties, he must make adjustments. Rickey Henderson would have been out of the game several seasons ago if he had constantly been stuck trying to fight off 0-2 fastballs. But because of his strike-zone judgment and discipline, he has been able to work the count to his advantage and occasionally still drive the pitches he *can* hit.

If you insist on placing any bets on twelve-to-one long shots, I suggest picking the horse who knows a ball from a strike.

PART THREE

PITCHING

Making the Most of a Brief Career

Conventional wisdom holds that pitching is nearly impossible to predict for all but the very best of pitchers; moreover, conventional wisdom holds that teams cannot be contenders or win championships without excellent pitching. Sometimes, this latter pearl of "wisdom" is expressed by a slick-haired sportscaster with the cliché, "Pitching is 75% of the game." (Or some other arbitrarily high percentage.)

Conventional wisdom is wrong on both counts.

Pitching can be predicted. The same things that are true about hitting are also true about pitching. By and large, a pitcher's performance in the major leagues can be accurately predicted from his performance in the minors, if those minor league numbers are properly understood. By and large, most teams evaluate pitchers poorly, from scouting to promoting to signing free agents. By and large, teams fail to understand the way pitching has changed with the game of the '90s. And by and large, most teams spend money on pitching in foolish ways.

And pitching is not "75%" of a winning ball club. It is important to distinguish between the argument that pitching controls the game (which is false) and the argument that good pitching is harder to find than good hitting (which is true). Essentially, this is the difference between total utility and marginal utility.

Think about it this way. Suppose you really like salmon. Now imagine that you're stranded in a mountain cabin with nothing to subsist on but canned salmon. Mountains of canned salmon. Enough canned salmon to last a year. After two weeks of salmon for breakfast, lunch and dinner, you are delighted to discover a small piece of chocolate hidden in the back of a cabinet. At that moment, the chocolate is going to taste awfully good.

Nothing about the total utilities of the situation is any different: canned salmon still has a lot more value to you than chocolate. Salmon is what's keeping you alive, while chocolate is a happy bit of variety. But chocolate has a higher *marginal* utility because you have canned salmon anytime, but this is the only chocolate to be found.

The same concept holds true in baseball. A first baseman, like Eric Karros, may hit .270/.325/.475, with 25 homers and 95 RBI. Now Karros' *total* worth as a player is certainly positive; after all, he drove in 95 runs. It would be strange to argue that he didn't help the Dodgers.

But Karros is the baseball equivalent of the canned salmon in the cabin; he, or someone like him, can be found almost anywhere. If you cannot sign Karros, you can sign his virtual clone in Lee Stevens or Reggie Jefferson or Brad Fullmer or Rico Brogna or Butch Huskey or ... well, you get the picture. In other words, a slugging first baseman often has a high total utility, but negligible marginal worth to his team, simply because there are an awful lot of these guys out there who could do just as well.

The exact opposite is true of starting pitching. Pitching isn't the most important thing to winning ball games — indeed, it's less than half of it. On one side of the ledger is the total number of runs a team scores — the offense. That's exactly half the game. On the other side is the number of runs a team allows — the defense. This half is then further split into two components — pitching and fielding. If you assume that the pitcher is four times as valuable as every other defensive player, that would amount to 40% overall — a far cry from our sportscaster's "75%" figure.

But pitching does have a higher *marginal* utility, because it's more difficult to find. While .270-hitting first basemen abound, on every major-league team and in the minors, 4.50 ERA starting pitchers are harder to find. Pitching, because of its scarcity, is the far more valuable commodity.

The Atlanta Braves do simply too many things right for there to be just *one* lesson of what "The Braves Way" is, but certainly stockpiling of dependable starting pitching has to be considered one of the hallmarks of "The Braves Way."

However, one of the things few people realize is how good the Braves' *offense* has been during their run of greatness called the 1990s. Since 1991, Atlanta consistently has ranked among the National League's leaders in OPS. Replace the Braves' good offense during that time with a mediocre or poor one, and nobody would be using the Braves as a model for anything.

In other words, pitching is no requirement for success, much less a guarantee of success. The Cleveland Indians made it to the World Series in 1997 with a world-class offense and a relatively sad pitching staff. The 1989 Oakland A's made a nineteen-game winner out of Storm Davis, who threw just 169 innings and allowed four and a half runs per game. One year later, those Mark McGwire-Jose Canseco-led A's turned Bob Welch into a twenty-seven-game winner, tops in all of baseball in the '90s.

Bob Welch?

Of course, it's rare to see a championship club with lousy pitching, but that's because it's rare to see a championship club with lousy *anything*. If you assemble a great offense and back it up with poor pitching, you're probably going to play about .500 ball; similarly, if you assemble a great pitching staff but have poor hitting, nobody is going to be spraying champagne anywhere near your clubhouse in October.

For much of the '90s, the AL team with the best pitching staff, year in and year out, has been the Kansas City Royals. And during the late '90s, the AL team with the best offense has been the Seattle Mariners. And between these two franchises you find fewer World Championships in the past decade than the Florida Marlins. World Championship teams almost always need both; you can't sacrifice pitching for hitting, but you can't make it work the other way, either.

So how *do* you assemble a great pitching staff?

Know the risks

The chart below examines the fortunes of the fifteen best starting pitchers headed into the 1994 season. The names were drawn from starting pitchers who topped both the ERA and the Wins leaderboards; that's a good rough measure of any of the top starters in baseball. In other words, if you could assemble a Super Team for 1994 from the available starting pitchers in baseball, you probably would have taken these 15 guys to be your pitchers.

Take a look at those fifteen names. Other than a thirty-eight-year-old Danny Darwin, and the talented but fragile Jose Rijo, you won't find any obvious indications of an imminent dropoff. Steve Avery was twenty-four. Jack McDowell was the talk of the American League. Billy Swift was pilfered from the Seattle Mariners in the Kevin Mitchell felony.

The average age of that group was just over twenty-nine years. Twenty-nine-year-olds aren't washed up, are they?

Age	Player	Going into 1994	1996	1998
26	Kevin Appier	18-8, 2.56	14-11, 3.62	1-2, 7.80
24	Steve Avery	18-6, 2.94	7-10, 4.47	10-7, 5.02
38	Danny Darwin	15-11, 3.26	10-11, 3.77	8-10, 5.51
24	Alex Fernandez	18-9, 3.13	16-10, 3.45	—
31	Chuck Finley	16-14, 3.15	15-16, 4.16	11-9, 3.39
28	Tom Glavine	22-6, 3.20	15-10, 2.98	20-6, 2.47
27	Pete Harnisch	16-9, 2.98	8-12, 4.21	14-7, 3.14
30	Randy Johnson	19-8, 3.24	5-0, 3.67	19-11, 3.28
33	Jimmy Key	18-6, 3.00	12-11, 4.68	6-3, 4.20
33	Mark Langston	16-11, 3.20	6-5, 4.82	4-6, 5.86
28	Greg Maddux	20-10, 2.36	15-11, 2.72	18-9, 2.22
28	Jack McDowell	22-10, 3.37	13-9, 5.11	5-3, 5.09
31	Mark Portugal	18-4, 2.77	8-9, 3.98	10-5, 4.44
29	Jose Rijo	14-9, 2.48	—	—
32	Billy Swift	21-8, 2.82	1-1, 5.40	11-9, 5.85

Yet look at the fortunes of that group both two and four years later. By 1996, five had losing records, a sixth was out of baseball, and three more had their seasons cut drastically short due to injury. None of the original fifteen won more than 16 games, and all but two who managed to pitch a full season recorded double-digit losses.

All of our original elite starters posted an ERA of 3.37 or less. Two years later, all but two of those pitchers had an ERA *above* 3.37.

And two years after that, only seven pitchers managed to give up as few as five runs per game. In other words, of the fifteen best starting pitchers at the start of the 1994 season, fewer than half were even slightly useful to their teams by 1998.

And four years earlier, these had been the *very best pitchers in baseball*. Major league veterans are thought to be predictable; this is one of the rationales for their higher value. With hitters, there's some truth in this. Sign Luis Gonzalez, for example, and you can pretty much count on a .270 average, thirty doubles, fifteen homers, fifty-five walks, seventy-five runs and seventy-five RBI. There will be a little variation from year to year, of course, and maybe you'll luck into his 1998 season. Overall, though, if you sign a hitter who isn't at the beginning or the end of his career, a look at what he has done in the past couple of years will give you a good idea of what you're going to get over the next couple of years.

But what about the pitching equivalent of Luis Gonzalez, the guy who pitches to about a 4.00 ERA, a .500 record and can log 180 to 200 innings? What predictability do those guys show, if star pitchers have a success rate of less than 50%?

Returning to 1994, the Gonzalez-style pitchers meeting those criteria were: Rene Arocha, Tim Belcher, Tom Candiotti, Doug Drabek, Cal Eldred, Kevin Gross, Jose Guzman, Chris Hammond, Erik Hanson, Greg Harris, Charlie Hough (!), Danny Jackson, Mike Morgan, Armando Reynoso, Scott Sanderson, Greg Swindell, Kevin Tapani and Bobby Witt.

Ugh.

Even two years later, you'd be hard-pressed to find more than a couple of those guys with any value whatsoever. Most of them became downright awful immediately thereafter.

If pitchers are almost certain bets for mediocrity at best, then what's the value of signing a veteran?

I don't know either. Would teams clamor to sign Luis Gonzalez if he alternated between seasons hitting .270/.350/.450, and ones in which he hit, say, .235/.290/.335? I should hope not. But when it comes to pitching, teams do exactly that. They give multi-year contracts to Tim Belcher and Erik Hanson.

Would teams really be any worse off giving a shot to a Dave Eiland, Kirt Ojala or Mickey Weston?

If you haven't heard of any of those guys, you're not alone. Most major-league GMs haven't, either. In the next chapter, I'll discuss how to analyze minor-league pitchers and spot the guys who could step in and be at least as good as Erik Hanson.

Know the context

By now, you probably know that a 4.00 ERA today is quite a bit different than a 4.00 ERA before 1990. Today, the average American League starting pitcher gives up ten hits and five runs per nine innings — not that the average pitcher can even go nine innings these days.

This has implications far beyond just comparing ERAs. As offense increases, innings become longer. More patient hitters foul off more pitches, forcing deeper counts. A pitcher in the American League can't coast once every two to three innings, facing a .100 hitter who can rarely hurt you. With smaller ballparks, pitchers can't rely on the time-honored strategy of putting the ball in play; increasingly, those balls put in play wind up landing beyond the outfield fence.

All told, you need more pitches to complete an inning in 1999 than it did in 1989.

This is part of why throwing 230 innings a year for a starter today is much more grueling than throwing 230 innings in 1968. (It's also why you don't see nearly as many 230-inning starters these days.)

Additionally, several other factors combine to make an inning in the 1990s much more difficult to complete as compared to an inning in the game of baseball of years gone by.

Strikeouts

In 1998, the average National League pitcher struck out 6.8 batters per nine innings.

In 1988, the average was 5.7 strikeouts per nine innings.

In 1978, the average was 5.1 strikeouts per nine innings.

Pitching strikeouts are at an all-time high. Throw out the 1990s, and the highest seasons in baseball featured pitchers who struck out an average of six men per game. Today, it's nearly seven — and possibly still increasing.

As strikeouts increase, innings become longer and more grueling. You must throw at least three to notch a strikeout (six or seven is more like it).

Now consider that the *average* pitcher is striking out an extra two guys a game, and working deeper into the counts on everyone else in order to set up those two strikeouts. It's just another reason why an inning today is a lot more grueling than an inning just a few decades ago.

Conditioning

It isn't fair. Not only have most changes in the game over the past twenty years tended to favor the hitter, but breakthroughs in training and conditioning over the past couple of decades also have much more long-term benefit for hitters than for pitchers.

Hitters work out more often, bulk up, and generally keep themselves in better shape than they did twenty years ago. Although a batter can become over-muscled, proper weight training and conditioning generally improves a batter's strength and power and overall physical conditioning. Shape. They don't just hit the ball harder; they can play longer and sustain their performance for more years.

A pitcher may gain an edge through weight training and conditioning, but that improvement is often at the expense of his long-term career. Greater power means greater stress on the arm, heightened risk of injury. Pitchers from the dead-ball era routinely note in their accounts that they rarely threw with full effort on every pitch. That's no longer possible: today's pitchers rarely can get away with throwing at anything but maximum effort. And the advanced weapons today's starters add to their arsenals — particularly sliders and split-finger fastballs — add to the risk of injury, particularly if thrown with poor mechanics.

No wonder pitchers often flame out after a year or two of solid work, or suddenly add a run and a half to their ERA, or go down with rotator cuff surgery. The pitcher nowadays faces an uphill struggle against the league, the rules, the players, the ballparks and his own physique just to try to keep pace with offense run wild.

So how can a team use that knowledge to assemble a great pitching staff?

First, be cautious when bringing along a rookie pitcher: establish moderate pitch count limits and stick to them.

Second, pool the risks. Avoid giving multi-year contracts to all but the very elite arms; remember that even the best starters from one year may wind up on the discard pile just a year or two later.

Third, recognize true value. Two hundred innings and a 5.00 ERA in Coors Field is a very good performance, even though that runs counter to every standard we have ever seen in big league baseball.

Above all, teams need to expand their horizons and give the guys who have proven they can pitch in the minors a chance to show their stuff in the majors. Since long, successful careers are the exception among starting pitchers, teams should constantly be working in young pitchers. To rely on a staff of veterans is to invite disaster.

11

Predicting Performance: Ignore the Radar Gun

Q uick, which of these minor league players is the better prospect?

	GS	CG	IP	H	R	ER	HR	BB	K	WHIP	K/9	W–L	ERA
A	25	5	173.2	154	67	56	16	46	177	1.152	9.17	13-8	2.90
B	24	1	132.1	118	69	51	2	90	115	1.572	7.82	6-13	3.47
C	29	0	151.2	93	84	77	4	131	186	1.477	11.04	10-9	4.57

(WHIP is the average number of walks and hits per inning; K/9 is strikeouts per nine innings.)

Since you're undoubtedly familiar with some of my tactics by now, I'll also flesh out the context by informing you that all three players were roughly the same age at the time these numbers were compiled. Pitcher A was twenty-one, Pitcher B, nineteen, and Pitcher C, twenty. Moreover, both Pitchers A and B compiled their numbers in AA ball. Pitcher C's numbers come from about a hundred innings at AA and fifty more at AAA.

So who's the better prospect? Pitcher A had the best record, the lowest ERA, the most complete games, put the fewest number of men on base, and struck out more than a batter an inning. Pitcher B was the youngest, allowed the fewest number of home runs, and had an ERA in between A and C. And finally, pitcher C allowed the fewest hits and struck out the most batters.

Depending on how much you've managed to get inside my head throughout the course of this book, you may or may not be surprised to learn that Pitcher A is Oakland A's right-hander Jimmy Haynes, who has a career 5.53 ERA in parts of four major league seasons; that Pitcher B is phenom-gone-bust Todd Van Poppel; and that Pitcher C is Kerry Wood.

So how can you tell the difference between the next Kerry Wood and the next Jimmy Haynes? Here are some guidelines.

It's not a crapshoot

There's a popular belief that you can't project a young pitcher's career in the majors. Proponents of this argument — a popular one in pro baseball — tend ignore minor league performance, preferring to rely on scouting reports and subjective impressions.

Brien Taylor generally is trotted out as Exhibit #1 for the proposition that "predicting pitching is a crapshoot." Taylor was a high school pitcher whom scouts liked so much that he became the top pick in the 1991 draft.

Taylor signed with the Yankees, and got off to a nondescript start in rookie ball. Then, in 1993, he suffered an off-season injury. He returned to professional baseball in 1996, with less-than-stunning results. That year he pitched sixteen innings for single-A Greensboro, going 0-5 with an 18.73 ERA. The next year, he lowered his ERA to 14.33, and the year after that he pitched twenty-five innings, reducing his ERA all the way down to 9.59!

At this pace, Taylor should be ready for the majors by 2068 or so.

When you draft a high school stud, like Taylor or Todd Van Poppel or Matt White, you're essentially playing the roulette wheel. Too many injuries have taken down too many "can't miss" high school pitchers. Brien Taylor is yet proof of the fact that there's just too much distance between Martin High School and the American League.

But that's not the same as looking at a pitcher who's had four solid years of success moving up the rungs of the minor leagues and stands poised to advance to the bigs. A pitcher with such a background *is* predictable, though not as reliably predictable as a hitter. Sometimes a very good minor leaguer pitcher struggles in the majors. But, by and large, the same principles hold for pitchers as for batters. If a pitcher has demonstrated ability in the minors, chances are very good he'll demonstrate ability in the majors.

The second argument-by-analogy from the "it's all a crapshoot" school of thought is to point to the 1995 Mets' trio of "Young Guns" — Paul Wilson, Bill Pulsipher and Jason Isringhausen. All were top-notch pitching prospects. All were being counted upon as rotation anchors, and not a one of them made it.

This argument, too, misses the point. Wilson, Pulsipher and Isringhausen were all worked to death in the minors by an organization that couldn't keep its minor league pitchers on appropriate training regimens, pitch counts and innings limits. (The lawyer in me knows there's a tort in there somewhere.) All three suffered — not from ineffectiveness, but from arm injuries.

So, a pitcher's previous work load should be a factor when evaluating a pitcher's prospects for future success. But that's an argument that pitching *is* predictable, not the reverse. If a player has thrown 750 innings in four minor league seasons, then he's probably not a good bet for success.

As a side note, work load is often very difficult to ascertain from raw minor league innings pitched totals. A pitcher who throws 175 innings in a five-month minor league season is almost certainly being worked harder than one who throws 200 in a full six-month season. A pitcher with higher walk and strikeout rates probably is throwing more pitches per start in the same number of innings as a pitcher who puts the ball in play.

Frankly, I'm surprised at the popularity of the "It's all a crapshoot" mentality. Not only does that approach come at an opportunity cost — the forsaken chance of identifying a young star before his time — but it has a tangible cost to the team that is stuck playing a mislabeled "prospect" because some scout likes his arm.

As an illustration, I give you Todd Van Poppel.

Todd Van Poppel is a scout's dream pitcher. He's a big, 6'5", 210-pound right-hander. He can throw nine innings' worth of ninety-five-mph fastballs in two hours. He was drafted in the first round way back in 1990; the only reason he fell to the fourteenth pick overall was because most teams believed that he could not be signed, that he was headed for college. The Oakland A's used a compensation pick, took a

118

chance on Van Poppel, and wooed him with a then-record signing bonus in seven figures. Van Poppel spent two years in the minors and made 32 starts before earning a trip from double-A to the Show during a September call-up.

During that first cup of coffee, Van Poppel allowed five runs in the fifth inning of his only start of the year. He finished 1991 with a 9.64 ERA.

In the seven years since that disastrous first start, Van Poppel has thrown more than 500 innings.

His career ERA is 6.24.

I'm not sure that anyone tracks the record for most career earned runs allowed, but I've got to think that Van Poppel must be closing in on it; not only does he give up a ton of runs, but he continues to tantalize teams with his fastball and imposing physique. Usually, when a guy allows six or seven runs per game, he is soon pursuing alternative lines of work. But not Van Poppel. He continues to tease teams with his "tools" and then bring them back to reality with his "talent."

Van Poppel's best season, if you can call it that, was in 1995. That year, he went 4-8 with a 4.88 ERA. He was able to nudge his ERA just under five by pitching in long relief, notching a few somewhat effective mop-up outings during blowouts. It's the only season Van Poppel has *ever* allowed fewer than five runs per game.

In 1998, Van Poppel had an 8.84 ERA with the Texas Rangers and was acquired by the Pittsburgh Pirates and thrown into the starting rotation!

I shouldn't have to tell you that something is drastically wrong if your team is acquiring and starting Todd Van Poppel.

Here is the consequence of believing that it's all a crapshoot:

G	GS	CG	W	L	ERA	IP	H	R	ER	HR	BB	K
135	80	2	22	37	6.24	509.1	534	371	353	80	299	353

That's Todd Van Poppel's major league career line through 1998. Why would rebuilding, small-revenue Pittsburgh give this guy eighteen appearances and seven starts? You know the answer. After all, if it's all just a crapshoot, then what can it hurt to take another look at that guy who throws Real Hard?

Or maybe — if you're not a Pirates fan — you're tempted to think "who cares, it's only Pittsburgh, and it's not like they could do better." But you always want to win as many games as possible, even if it's sixty-five instead of sixty-two. And a team is willing to put up with a six-plus ERA, why not take a look at a guy who might actually *help* your team in the future? Give that above-average AAA starter a start or six to see what he can do against major leaguers.

It's *not* a crapshoot. Teams who think that it is inevitably get stuck with a ton of extra runs allowed, and a few more games in the loss column.

Ignore the radar gun

Scouts and coaches and managers love to pick pitching prospects by the numbers on a radar gun.

This, in spite of the fact that anyone who knows pitching knows that pure velocity is only one of the tools of a successful pitcher. Movement, location, pitch selection are all more important than the reading a radar gun. Pure velocity alone won't keep a pitcher in the majors.

At one hundred miles per hour, a fastball reaches home plate in just over four-tenths of one second. At eighty-five miles per hour, that same fastball reaches home plate in just under half a second. About seven one-hundredths of a second separates the best fastball in baseball from the very mediocre.

Not only is a difference of seven one-hundredths of a second insufficient to humble Mark McGwire, it won't even humble Ron Coomer. Put the average major leaguer into a batting cage against a machine firing straight, 100-mph fastballs over the heart of the plate, and he'll hit moon shot after moon shot. With very rare exceptions, a hitter simply won't make it to the majors if he can't hit a fastball.

Pure velocity is at best secondary to a pitcher's success. Movement is more important. So is location. So is pitch selection. In fact, a good pitcher with good stuff will keep hitters off balance all day by mixing pitches, putting pitches where they can be hit, varying velocity — sometimes all with the same pitch.

Okay, throwing ninety-five mph is better than throwing eighty-five, if a pitcher has all the other tools. But that rarely happens. Usually, teams will have to weigh tradeoffs and choose between a pitcher with better velocity and one with better control. Yet teams almost always choose the player who throws harder.

My method is to pick the player who has the least to learn. And the best way to do that is to look at the numbers. A guy who's walking ten men per game doesn't just have "one thing" to learn — he's about as far from being an effective major league pitcher as I am, and I haven't thrown a fastball in ten years.

Here are the minor league numbers of a guy who's made seventy-nine major league appearances during a five-year career in the major leagues:

	LVL	G	IP	H	R	ER	HR	BB	K	WHIP	BB/9	W–L	ERA
1989	R	15	64.1	50	58	47	2	74	81	1.93	10.35	2-7	6.58
1990	A	32	106	81	89	61	12	121	142	1.98	10.27	4-9	5.18
1991	A	59	66.2	48	40	34	5	69	101	1.77	9.32	1-6	5.40
1992	A/AA/AAA	56	76.1	37	22	19	2	54	105	1.19	6.37	3-5	2.59
1993	AAA	17	15.2	12	11	6	0	13	19	1.60	7.47	1-2	3.45

Except for 1992, this pitcher was uniformly awful in the minors. And even during his best season, he still walked a lot of batters, though he was virtually unhittable. The next season, he was back to his bad old self, walking a batter an inning.

So how has this player done in the majors?

	G	IP	H	R	ER	HR	BB	K	WHIP	BB/9	W–L	ERA
Totals	79	75.2	67	64	59	12	89	83	2.06	10.59	4-9	7.02

Pretty much what you'd expect, right? Two base runners per inning — one via walk and one by base hit, and a ton of runs allowed. The only question, of course, is why this guy got five years to prove that he can't get major leaguers out.

And you know the answer: he throws hard. Really hard. *And* he's left-handed, so it's a double whammy. His name is Brad Pennington.

I'd love to set up the scouting equivalent of a "blind taste test," and put Brad Pennington and Todd Van Poppel into blank uniforms and let them pitch off against soft-tossers Rick Reed (career 38-35, 3.75 ERA in 104 starts) and Jamie Moyer (career 104-93, 4.25 ERA in 262 starts).

I'd wager a year's salary that there isn't a scout alive who would tell you to take Reed or Moyer over Pennington and Van Poppel. And that, in a nut-shell, is why you need to put aside the radar gun when evaluating a pitcher.

This isn't to say that scouts play no role in selecting successful pitchers.

It's just that the order needs to be reversed. The smart GM should identify prospects based on their established levels of performance, and then use scouting reports to differentiate carefully between otherwise similar pitchers. Between two minor leaguers with roughly identical statistics, the better bet is the guy who throws harder. But the radar gun reading shouldn't take priority over the live trial-by-fire that pitcher has faced against real hitters.

If you're still unconvinced, I have one irrefutable argument why pure velocity is irrelevant.

His name is Greg Maddux.

I know that Maddux is often rated at eighty-nine to ninety mph on radar guns. I also know that those same radar guns routinely clock forty-one-year-old Jesse Orosco at ninety, too.

Maddux is probably throwing closer to eighty-six. But that doesn't matter: in fact, the precise number really is beside the point. What is important is that Maddux clearly does not throw any harder than an average major league pitcher.

Yet he is the best starting pitcher of our generation, and we might some day make a plausible claim that he has been the best starting pitcher of all time.

That's a powerful argument that pitchers can succeed without blazing heat.

Look for the stats that matter

You may pat yourself on the back if you're willing to accept the proposition that the readings on a radar gun are only moderately important in predicting the career of a young pitcher. Now take another deep breath, because I'm going to ask you to accept another tough one.

Throw out a pitcher's ERA.

I don't just mean adjust a pitcher's ERA to reflect the ballpark and league in which he plays — although you must do that, too. I mean toss out the stat itself.

Let's go back to the comparison between Todd Van Poppel and Kerry Wood. In AA, Van Poppel put up a 3.47 ERA; that's more than a full run lower than Wood's 4.57. But Van Poppel also allowed 11 more unearned runs than Wood.

If we calculate "RA" for Wood and Van Poppel — that's ERA, without the "E", reflecting total runs scored per nine innings — then we get a 4.69 RA for Van Poppel and a 4.98 RA for Wood.

Disregarding runs scored through errors can be misleading, especially when dealing with minor league pitchers, since errors are distributed strangely in the minors. There's no reason to specifically reward pitchers who play for error-prone teams.

In the comparison with which I opened the chapter, Kerry Wood starts to look much better than Von Poppel when we look at RA, instead of ERA; they both allowed roughly the same number of runs, but Wood allowed fewer hits, fewer base runners and struck out more batters.

If we compare the full careers of each of the pitchers — which you must do when evaluating minor leaguers, whether hitters or pitchers — the differences between Wood and Van Poppel are even more stark.

The statistics that are most meaningful in evaluating a young pitcher are his ratio of base runners per inning (WHIP), his strikeout ratio (K/9), his walk ratio (BB/9), and the ratio between the two (BB/K).

An overpowering pitcher records lots of strikeouts; a pitcher with good control will avoid putting men on base and will strike out many more hitters than he walks.

If the pitcher *can't* do that, he resembles Brad Pennington. Remember that Pennington generally struck out around a batter an inning, but he allowed more than two base runners per inning — the quintessential "one step forward, two steps back."

Here's how Van Poppel and Wood match up in those four categories:

	WHIP	K/9	BB/9	BB/K
Van Poppel	1.572	7.82	6.12	0.78
Wood	1.477	11.04	7.77	0.70

The choice seems a lot easier now. Both pitchers have a problem with control, but Wood is a lot more overpowering, and much less easy to hit.

Jimmy Haynes? Let's look at his numbers:

	WHIP	K/9	BB/9	BB/K
Haynes	1.152	9.17	2.38	0.26
Wood	1.477	11.04	7.77	0.70

Wow, Haynes looks a lot better than Wood, doesn't he?

But Wood was more than a year younger than Haynes, and pitched for part of the year at a level higher than Haynes. At this point in their careers, Jimmy Haynes was clearly more polished than Kerry Wood. This is what we would expect from an older player at a lower level of the minors. Again, a reasonable comparison looks at the full careers and progression of each pitcher.

And I was deliberately misleading in describing Haynes as a "career 5.53 ERA pitcher" — after all, he is just twenty-six years old, and still may turn into a dominant starter.

In Greg Maddux's first full season in the majors, he threw 155 $^2/_3$ innings, went 6-14, and compiled a 5.61 ERA. The year before, he'd gone 2-4 with a 5.52 ERA in five starts. John Smoltz had a 5.48 ERA in *his* first season. David Cone debuted as a reliever with a 5.56 ERA.

This puts Jimmy Haynes in some pretty good company. Haynes may never compare to Kerry Wood, Greg Maddux, John Smoltz or David Cone. But he's no Todd Van Poppel, either.

Finding Relief

"Here's the choice: You can have a proven, dominant closer to preserve your late-inning leads, or you can have a closer-by-committee arrangement, with capable pitchers but blurred responsibilities. Which do you want? The dominant closer, of course, particularly if you have designs on winning a World Series, as the Orioles do in 1998."
— John Eisenberg, *The Baltimore Sun*, February 20, 1998.

H ere's another choice, using actual stat lines from a recent major league season. Among the following three players, which one would you rather have pitching in relief for your team?

	IP	H	RA	HR	BB	K	W-L	ERA
Reliever A	68.2	61	24	2	25	57	5-1	3.01
Reliever B	62.0	56	23	9	10	48	0-9	3.34
Reliever C	63.2	54	23	9	21	69	2-3	2.83

All three pitchers are right-handed short relievers. Relievers A and C were thirty years old at the time. Reliever B was twenty-eight.

You can make a pretty good argument for any one of them. Reliever C had the most strikeouts and the lowest ERA; Reliever B was two years younger, and put the fewest number of men on base; while Reliever A had the best record and the fewest number of home runs allowed.

Moreover, none was flawless, either. Reliever A put the most runners on base, Reliever B lost nine games and struck out only forty-eight batters, and Reliever C allowed nine home runs. And each gave up around three runs per game.

These three pitchers were quite similar.

So is there any reason why one of these pitchers should make $6.5 million a year, another $3.5 million, and the third the league minimum?

The main distinction among these three pitchers is a stat that I didn't include: the number of saves. Among relief pitchers, salaries vary as a straight function of saves, which is to say that the more saves a pitcher records, the more money he earns.

I can understand why ballplayers like to count certain statistics. Stolen bases, home runs, RBI are the batter's equivalent of a gold star on his resumé.

For starting pitchers, those gold stars are wins. For closers, the gold stars are saves.

Do gold stars reflect a player's ability? Some do — home runs, for example. But saves are determined entirely by a pitcher's usage patterns. Mariano Rivera was the best reliever in baseball in 1996, yet he got only five saves, because the Yankees didn't use him in the ninth inning (John Wetteland was their closer). The next year, the Yankees traded Wetteland, made Rivera the closer, used him in the ninth inning, and his total jumped to 43 saves. He didn't pitch any better — if anything, he was a little less outstanding than he had been the year before — but his save total jumped substantially.

It happens all the time. Jeff Shaw went from four saves in 1996 to forty-two in 1997 and forty-eight in 1998. Tom Gordon went from zero saves to forty-six. Bob Wickman, from one to twenty-five. Mike Jackson went from six to fifteen to forty. Duane Ward, Mel Rojas, Randy Myers all started as non-closers and promptly began racking up saves when their teams decided to use them differently.

Closers also depend on their teams to get them into save situations. After all, a closer needs a lead in the ninth: his save total almost always suffer when he is pitching on a bad team.

So the argument that a closer is more valuable than other relievers because of his saves is like saying that the acrobat at the top of a human pyramid is the tallest.

A great mystique has grown up around the role of closer. We're told that closers must have a special mentality, an intimidating personality and preferably a blazing fastball. Yet practically every successful middle-reliever who has been given save opportunities — no matter what his pitching style or mental attitude — has become a successful closer.

There's really no mystery to it.

It involves being a decent pitcher and having your manager hand you the ball in the ninth inning with a lead of three runs or less.

That's all.

Supposedly a closer faces more "pressure" than does a middle reliever or a set-up man. The staggering number of non-closers who have readily adapted to the "pressure" of closing seems to belie this argument, but fans and general managers and media continue to say it all the time, so I guess it deserves at least some comment.

Consider a situation so commonplace as to be completely taken for granted, one that is a "no-brainer" for every manager and fan of today's game. The Anaheim Angels lead 7-4 on the road against the Kansas City Royals. Due up in the ninth are the Royals' 7-8-9 hitters: right fielder Jermaine Dye (.606 OPS), catcher Sal Fasano (.691 OPS) and shortstop Mendy Lopez (.611 OPS).

What happens in this situation? Ninety-nine times out of a hundred, Terry Collins brings in Troy Percival to shut down that bottom third of the lineup and pick up a save so easy that it ought to be considered a gift.

How much pressure does that involve? Not a whole lot, wouldn't you say?

If I were managing the Angels, chances are very good that I'd want to use my second- or third-best reliever in that situation (unless Percival hadn't pitched in a while and needed the work). Even a mediocre pitcher is unlikely to give up three or four runs in one inning of work, regardless of who he is facing, and that isn't exactly Murderer's Row due up in the Royals' ninth. More important, I might need Percival to face Frank Thomas, Albert Belle and Robin Ventura in a 4-3 game tomorrow.

That scenario is an extreme example, but over the course of any team's season, there will be others times, less obvious, when someone other than the closer ought to be used in a "save situation." Yet nearly all managers, nearly all the time, will reflexively go to his closer when there's a save on the line, thereby padding that closer's save total, as well as his reputation and future salary.

The last effect is the most pernicious. When the manager helps pad the save totals of his closer to the maximum, that's more money that the team will have to pay for him in arbitration, and a greater chance that the team won't be able to afford him for another year. The manager's largesse is often repaid by having that player pitch against him next season.

A team with only one good reliever — like Johnny Oates and the 1997 Texas Rangers — has an even more serious problem. What does he do when his opponent has the bases loaded in a 5-2 game with nobody out in the seventh inning? No conventional manager brings in his closer, but I sure would. Put your best guy on the mound, minimize the damage, and give your mediocre pitchers a decent shot at holding a 5-2 or 5-3 lead.

If you do it in reverse, and trust the dregs to save a 5-2 lead with the basis loaded and no one out in the seventh inning, your expensive closer probably won't have a chance to earn his money with a save in the ninth.

Why should a team plan on giving the game away in the seventh and eighth innings for the privilege of holding on to whatever leads they manage to take into the ninth? Conversely, when a set-up reliever is pitching well with the game on the line in the seventh and eighth innings, why should his manager be afraid to use him with the game on the line in the ninth?

The way that you get to that lead, of course, is by having competent *middle* relievers who can withstand the "pressure" of situations like the one discussed above. After all, most middle relievers and setup men come in with men on base, while most closers come in at the top of the inning, with the bases clear.

Which situation involves more "pressure?"

Not only do I believe that teams don't use their closers properly, I would even say that in many instances a club is wasting its resources in pursuing a closer with a reputation and big save totals.

The problem is economic. Every major league franchise has a limited budget for player contracts, even though in many cases that limit seems astronomical. No matter how deep the owner's pockets, every GM must put together the most competitive team possible for a given amount of money, getting the best bang for the buck.

When teams face a tradeoff between paying $6.5 million a year to one "established closer," or paying $6.5 million to, say, *three* quality middle relievers, it doesn't seem to make any sense to take the former option. Why pay for sixty good innings when you could get 200?

To return to my question at the top of this chapter, Reliever A is Mike Trombley of the Minnesota Twins. Chances aren't good that you've heard of him. Reliever B is Rod Beck, now with the Chicago Cubs. And Reliever C is the Rangers' John Wetteland.

That season, 1996, Trombley saved six of nine games; Beck, thirty-five of forty-two; and Wetteland, forty-three of forty-seven.

Trombley earned minimum wage the next season; Wetteland bolted the Yankees and signed a contract with Texas that paid him around six and a half million dollars.

Trombley allowed exactly one more run than Wetteland over the course of the season, while pitching five more innings. He walked four more hitters, and allowed seven extra hits. In effect, Trombley was Wetteland plus this decent stat line: 5 IP, 7 H, 1 R, 4 BB.

Wetteland did strike out twelve more batters than Trombley; but Trombley allowed seven fewer home runs. Think about it this way — Trombley was effective despite putting more pitches in play; Wetteland was effective despite giving up a fairly frequent number of homers.

Perhaps, after this comparison, you might still believe that John Wetteland is a better pitcher than Mike Trombley. Fair enough; he probably is.

But is he *fifty times* better than Trombley?

Is he *six million dollars a year* better than Trombley?

Even on a team with the highest payroll in baseball, economics still matter. Six million dollars spent on a closer is six million less the team can spend upgrading its second baseman, or luring a free agent starting pitcher, or on international scouting, or to sign its top three draft picks, and so on.

The Rangers would probably justify that money to Wetteland this way: "Sure, every once in a while, someone like Mike Trombley will turn in a good season, but how can we predict that? By acquiring Wetteland, we get a guy who will predictably shut down the opposition in the ninth. And that's worth six million bucks."

This is really two arguments. First, that proven closers, unlike random middle relievers, are more predictable from year-to-year; and, second, that the best closers will consistently shut down the opposition in the ninth inning.

As to the first claim, there is certainly some truth that teams ought to pay a bit more for predictability. But not significantly more. Mostly, that's because pitchers as a whole aren't very predictable from year to year. This is even more the case with relief pitchers. You will pay a lot more and to sign Jose Mesa or Mark Leiter after a killer year, but you're not really increasing your predictability by much, and the cost of doing so is huge.

Take a look at the following ERA progression, put up from 1990 to 1997: 3.55, 4.29, 3.11, 3.79, 3.88, 3.53, 1.51

I'm guessing that even without the bold face type, that 1.51 ERA would stand out as completely out of line with this reliever's established history. He has a bunch of ERAs ranging from 3 to 4, and then one fantastic, aberrant season at the end.

Moreover, if I told you that this particular reliever was thirty-five when he put up that last number, would *you* have gone out and signed him to a three-year deal for nearly twenty million dollars?

Me neither. But that's exactly what the Toronto Blue Jays did. That 1.51 ERA belonged to Randy Myers in 1997, his second and last season with the Baltimore Orioles. At the end of the season, the Jays — convinced that they needed a "proven closer" in order to contend for the post-season in 1998 — hurried out to sign Myers, who promptly compiled a 4.92 in 1998. Myers didn't last a season with Toronto. Before the season was over, he had been traded for a nondescript minor leaguer, and demoted to mop-up duty behind Trevor Hoffman with the San Diego Padres.

Another sad example of the unpredictability of relief pitchers is that of former Atlanta closer Mark Wohlers; he was among the league's save leaders in 1997, and suddenly forgot how to throw a strike, skyrocketing to a incredible 10.18 ERA in '98.

Although what happened to Wohlers was an extreme fluke, it underscores the proposition that paying top dollar for a big-name closer doesn't really net a team all that much in terms of predictability.

The second part of the Wetteland argument is that a proven closer can completely shut down the opposition. I believe this attitude, as well as the current practice in using closers exclusively in ninth-inning save situations, derives almost entirely from Tony LaRussa and Dennis Eckersley.

Tony LaRussa's decision in 1987 to convert Dennis Eckersley from a starter to a reliever is probably the second-most momentous shift in the history of baseball, right after the Yankees' decision to move a quality southpaw named Babe Ruth from the mound to right field.

Eckersley was a very successful pitcher when he came to Oakland in 1987. He had 151 career victories at the time, and was thirty-one years old; that's a very impressive number. (When David Cone was thirty-one, he had just 111 wins. John Smoltz had 146. Orel Hershiser had a mere 99.)

Eckersley had been a two-time All-Star, and he was the starting pitcher for the American League in 1982. He had thrown a no-hitter, struck out 200 batters in a season, and notched more than 100 complete games. But in 1986, his third year with the Chicago Cubs, he slipped to a 6-11 record and compiled an ugly 4.57 ERA. Eckersley still managed to lead the Cubs in both strikeouts (137) and innings pitched (201), but that wasn't enough to save his job in Chicago. He was traded (along with Dan Rohn) to Oakland A's for Dave Wilder, Brian Guinn and Mark Leonette.

No, you're not the only person who's never heard of the rest of those guys.

Eckersley had two disappointing starts with Oakland in 1987; he lost both and was moved to the bullpen, where he immediately was successful. When closer Jay Howell suffered an injury, Eckersley got a chance as a closer, and he immediately began to prove that he was something special.

Beginning in 1988, many around baseball began to suspect that the word "Eckersley" was actually Sanskrit for "scoreless ninth inning." Not only was he exceptionally effective, but LaRussa began to use him in what was then atypical fashion, almost exclusively in the ninth innings when the A's had a lead of three or fewer runs. Previously, closers had racked up more than a hundred innings per season, coming into games in the seventh and eighth innings and pitching until it was over.

The Eck changed all that. Starting in 1988, LaRussa used Eckersley almost exclusively in ninth-inning save situations. He made sixty appearances that year, of which all but six were save situations. Eckersley pitched a total of 72 2/3 innings, picking up forty-five saves, four wins, and two losses. He finished the year with a 2.35 ERA, 70 strikeouts, 52 hits allowed, and just 11 walks. He finished second in the Cy Young balloting, losing out to Frank Viola of the Twins.

The Eck really was absolutely dominant. From 1988 to 1992, his ERA ranged from a high of 2.96 to a low of 0.61. In 1990, he allowed *five runs* all season. In sixty-three appearances! That year, and for several seasons that followed, Tony LaRussa knew that he could virtually guarantee ringing up a "0" on the scoreboard in whenever he brought in the Eck with the game on the line. Here are Eckersley's save totals from 1988 to 1992: 45, 33, 48, 43, 51.

Eckersley became the paradigm of baseball relief. Other clubs rushed to copy LaRussa's innovation, using their best relievers exclusively in ninth-inning save situations. Save totals began to skyrocket.

But those other guys weren't Dennis Eckersley. Yet teams and managers and GMs seemed to think so. That's because they based their judgments primarily on raw save totals.

Here are Randy Myers' save totals since 1992: 38, 53, 30, 43, 31, 45.

(That is fudged slightly, since Myers played in two short seasons as a result of the '94 strike, so I projected out his actual saves — twenty-one in 1994 and 38 in 1995 — to a full, 162-game schedule.)

Now, it doesn't take much imagination — if one works solely from the premise that a closer is evaluated by his save totals — to argue that Myers is *almost* as good as Eckersley.

I believe this is what happened in the general perceptions of relief pitching over the past decade. In the rush to "Be Like Eck," teams looked to guys who had put up forty, fifty saves over the course of a season, not realizing that a great many of those saves came as gifts, with the team leading by two or three runs. You have to be a pretty bad reliever to *not* convert most of those 2- and 3-run leads when you only have to pitch the ninth. And so, somewhere along the line, people got fooled into thinking that Bobby Thigpen and Heathcliff Slocumb and Jose Mesa were almost as good as Dennis Eckersley.

The crucial difference is that Eckersley was virtually a guaranteed zero during his prime. On the other hand, Randy Myers' career ERA is 3.19. Rick Aguilera's is 3.55. Rod Beck's is 2.98. These guys are going to give up runs. Used in one inning stints, that averages out to a run every third outing. They're not guaranteed to shut down the opposition; they're just like every other reliever with a 3.00 ERA.

Jim Corsi's career ERA is 3.16. Steve Reed's is 3.54. Jesse Orosco's is 2.96. As in the comparison of Relievers A, B and C, I don't think anyone can make a convincing case for Myers over Corsi, Aguilera over Reed or Beck over Orosco.

And that's really the point of this chapter. I don't have anything against the "proven closers" of the world. What team couldn't use a Rick Aguilera or a Rod Beck in the bullpen? The problem isn't absolute performance, it's opportunity cost. When you pay Aguilera fifty times as much money as you could have paid Corsi, it means that your team gets shorted in some other way. Maybe you can't hold on to your ace starting pitcher, or your team doesn't sign its first-round draft pick, or can't afford to make that crucial stretch run acquisition to put them over the top. Even for the New York Yankees, money matters, and money spent on an "established closer" is almost always poorly spent.

PART FOUR

DEFENSE

Range, Positioning and the Defensive At-Bat

What makes a good defensive player?

With the exception of catchers, who have their own unique role, the purpose of a defensive player is to convert batted balls into outs. The better a player is in the field, the greater the percentage of potential base hits he will turn into outs.

But how can we tell whether one player is better than another?

Both fans and professionals turn to four sources of information about a player's defensive abilities in order to draw conclusions about his value on the field: personal observation, media sources, expert opinion and statistics. Each method suffers from numerous flaws.

Personal observation

The most common way to judge a player's defensive ability is through first-hand observation. And since baseball is more than a century old, we have a pretty good idea of what we're looking for. Even a casual fan knows that being a good fielder is not the same as simply being athletically gifted. Good fielding — like every other attribute in baseball — is a package of skills, some physical, some mental. Good fielding includes seeing the ball off the bat, predicting where it will go, breaking the right way, keeping your eye on the ball, being fast enough to catch up with it, taking the right path to the ball, making the right decision whether to dive or to play it on a hop, being coordinated enough not to slip or to drop the ball, having a strong arm, throwing to the right base, and more.

But some aspects of fielding can be deceptive to even a skilled observer. One of the most important skills a fielder can have is knowing where to position himself before the pitch is delivered and the ball is put into play. Good positioning can make up for a lack of speed, while poor positioning can negate the advantage of the fastest center-fielder.

Similarly, how do you evaluate a shortstop who seems to dive to his left more often than other shortstops? Is he a brilliant fielder extending his range? Or is he a gifted athlete playing out of position and/or getting a late jump on base hits?

By and large, though, I believe that a dedicated fan or a skilled professional, watching one team night after night can form a fairly good picture of the defensive abilities of that team's players. I think the scout still has an important role to play in evaluating defense.

The problem comes in comparing one player to another. Unless you're a Milwaukee Brewers fan, how many opportunities do you get to watch, say, Jeromy Burnitz play the outfield? Fifteen games? Obviously, no one can fully appreciate a player's talents based on a small handful of appearances. Maybe Burnitz plays a bad couple of games in the field when the Brewers come to town against the Braves; if you're a Braves fan, you might be tempted to conclude that Burnitz can't field.

So for context, we have to turn to other sources.

Media

The greatly expanded televised coverage of baseball has been a mixed bag. Most days in the season, a fan with cable service or a satellite subscription can choose among the broadcasts of several big league games. We get a lot more opportunities to view a lot more players, and that's good.

But the coverage on sports shows, which is usually based on quick clips of a few seconds each — the "highlight reel" approach — is biased and misleading.

What makes a highlight reel play?

I have done extensive research on this question. (One of the great things about writing a book about baseball is that you can sit in front of the TV, watching SportsCenter, and call it "research" with a straight face.) After copious research, I have concluded that the following defensive plays form the bulk of ESPN's highlight reel plays:

- diving catches
- outfield assists, and
- errors.

That's it. The highlight clips on other national and local sports shows usually follow the same pattern. Oh, sure, every once in a while you'll see a fluke double play, or a lighting-quick stab at third base, or some such. But those three plays are the bread-and-butter of the highlight reel.

The problem is that the highlight reels don't tell us anything about a player's range, positioning, or any of the other subtle attributes that separate a good fielder from a mediocre one. Watching those selected samples day after day leads us to conclude that the better fielders are the ones who make the most diving catches and outfield kills, and that the poor fielders are the ones who make the most errors.

But that is silly. The outfielders with the best arms record, at most, a dozen or so assists over a season, but they may have 500 balls hit to them. What's more important: 500 outs or ten outs?

Similarly, the worst middle infielders generally make no more than thirty errors in a season — that's thirty plays, out of a thousand balls hit up the middle over 162 games.

Of course, some flashy players who show up on SportsCenter day in and day out also are legitimately good fielders. Jim Edmonds is an obvious example. There's nothing wrong with a guy who can make the routine play and also sparkle now and again. The problem is that highlight reels cover only the extraordinary; we don't see the other hundreds of chances that the player has had.

A flashy catch by one fielder is often a ball that another outfielder could have reached routinely. And even if the catch is extraordinary, it's still just one more out. Diving is not inherently bad. But it is misleading. Most fans and analysts tend to view the diving fielder as being defensively superb, but often that isn't accurate. Rey Ordonez has built his defensive reputation on highlight catches, but his defense really isn't great. Or watch Roberto Alomar carefully sometime — you'll see that he makes a lot of flashy diving stops on infield hits. A dive tells us very little about a player's position, natural range or any of the other talents that make a good fielder.

Experts

When we talk about "expert opinion" in terms of fielding, we're usually talking about Gold Glove awards. After all, Gold Gloves are selected by major league professionals, and they must know the difference between the good, the bad, and the truly great, right?

Certainly, most players who win Gold Gloves are at least good fielders.

But Gold Gloves — and, more generally, good defensive reputations — are awarded in very curious ways which make me question whether those players are the *best* fielders at their positions.

For example, players who shift from demanding defensive positions to easier positions almost never win the Gold Glove.

Consider Jose Offerman and Jeff King.

Offerman came up as a shortstop with the Los Angeles Dodgers, but had problems making the long throw from short. He was traded to the Kansas City Royals, who moved him to first base for most of 1996.

You would expect that any fielder with the range to play shortstop would be an excellent first baseman, almost overqualified for the position. Yet Offerman's defensive play at first caused barely a ripple. After that season, the Royals shifted him to second base, where he played very well in '97 and '98.

If Jose Offerman was an excellent defensive second baseman in 1997 and '98, isn't it almost certain that he was otherworldly with the leather at first base in 1996?

So why does J.T. Snow have the 1996 AL Gold Glove for first base on his mantle?

Offerman's replacement at first was Jeff King, who had played both second and third base earlier in his career. Like Offerman, King was by all accounts ludicrously overqualified to play first — after all, he was used to handling a far more difficult defensive position. By most accounts, King was superb at first base. And yet in 1997 the little statue went to Baltimore's Rafael Palmeiro.

All of the available statistics — more on those in a minute — indicate that Offerman and King were far and away the best first basemen in the AL in '96 and '97, respectively.

The only reasonable explanation for the Gold Glove voting is a subtle bias against players who move from a difficult defensive position to one not so demanding. The theory seems to be that if they're not good enough to play their "real" position, we shouldn't think of them as good enough to play the one they've been moved to, either.

(Interestingly enough, I believe this holds in reverse, too. When catcher Craig Biggio was moved to second base, he began to merit immediate and serious Gold Glove consideration. He's currently at four Gold Gloves and counting — even though his defense seems to be nothing more than adequate at second. I believe that the professionals are rewarding a guy who made a more *difficult* defensive shift at the major league level, and successfully pulled it off.)

This is not to say that Gold Gloves are worthless. But they're not a very reliable indicator of whether one player is necessarily better than another.

Statistics

Ideally, statistics ought to be able to give us as complete a picture about a player's fielding as they do about a player's hitting.

We're quite far from that ideal. But at least we're learning.

In the beginning, there was fielding percentage. Fielding percentage is a very simple statistic; it is the number of chances a player successfully handles divided by the number of chances the player handles overall. The more errors a player makes, the lower his fielding percentage.

In theory, fielding percentage is designed to help us differentiate among the players who are capable of reliably making the routine play, and those who cannot. At the close of the nineteenth century, this may have been a reliable indicator of defensive value. At the close of the twentieth, it certainly is not.

Official scorers award errors when a fielder attempts to make a play that could have been turned into an out "with ordinary effort," and fails to turn it into an out. Notice, of course, that if the fielder doesn't bother to try and make the play, he gets no error. Or that if the fielder attempts an extraordinary play and botches it, he doesn't get the error.

So in theory, fielding percentage is designed to reward the player who makes the routine play. But why should routine plays earn a fielder extra credit? After all, it's not as if his team gets an extra out when a routine play is executed, or is penalized a run when a routine play is botched. If a fielder com-

mits an error and allows a runner to reach base when he should have recorded the out, it has the *exact same cost* to his team as if he had simply watched it
skip by him for a base hit.

Think about how three different left-fielders might go after the same fly
ball. Left-fielder A has the athletic ability to catch up with the fly, but is poorly positioned, so he can't make it in time, and the ball drops in for a base hit.
Left-fielder B is positioned properly, but is slow, and so he can't make the
catch, either, and it falls in for a hit. And Left-fielder C is both positioned properly and is fast enough to catch up with the ball. He dives, sprawls out, catches the fly — and then drops it.

Of those three players, only C gets charged with an error, despite the fact
that he's probably the best fielder of the three. Isn't that silly?

Do you know which team has the all-time record for best fielding percentage and fewest errors committed per game?

Unless you're a Baltimore fan — and perhaps even if you are — you probably wouldn't guess the 1998 Baltimore Orioles. After all, that team fielded the
oldest average starting lineup of all time, and finished a disappointing 79-83.
It's hardly the sort of team you'd classify as a great defensive outfit. Yet the '98
Orioles finished with only 69 errors by their position players, and a team fielding percentage of .987. The team allowed just thirty-one unearned runs all
year.

What kind of a team managed to set this all-time fielding record? Take a
look at the Orioles, position-by-position, for their regular defensive alignment
for most of the year:

C: a sore-armed, 33-year-old Chris Hoiles and career backup Lenny
     Webster;
1B: 33-year-old Rafael Palmeiro;
2B: Roberto Alomar, recuperating from a serious shoulder injury;
SS: pedestrian 32-year-old Mike Bordick;
3B: a 38-year-old Cal Ripken, learning a new position;
LF: catcher-turned-third-baseman-turned-first-baseman-turned-
     left-fielder B.J. Surhoff, who may have been the Orioles' best
     overall fielder;
CF: thirty-four-year-old converted left-fielder Brady Anderson; and
RF: thirty-seven-year-old Joe Carter, who retired at the end of the
     season.

Palmeiro is a legitimately good fielder, and Alomar certainly was a good fielder at one time and may have been above average in 1998. And Cal Ripken, even at 38 and out of position, is still Cal Ripken. But the rest of those old, broken-down guys? Does anyone out there want to argue that this was the greatest defensive team of all time? Or even close?

Sometimes when I criticize standard statistics, like batting average, I do so to point out that the correlation between what the statistic is supposed to represent and what it actually does isn't as tight as conventional wisdom leads us to believe. This is the case for RBI, for example. Although RBI aren't as good an indication of hitting skill as most people believe, the correlation still holds up to a certain extent. It's difficult to be an absolutely terrible hitter and still rack up a lot of RBI.

But errors are not just misleading; they're *completely unrelated* to a fielder's actual defensive ability. Therefore, since fielding percentage is basically an error rate turned inside out, fielding percentage is also completely unrelated to a player's defensive ability.

Some years ago, analysts outside the baseball establishment began calculating more advanced statistics designed to differentiate between plays made and plays not made. One effort which survives to this day is the STATS Range Factor (RF), which is simply the sum of a player's putouts, assists and errors, divided per nine innings.

The theory behind RF is fairly simple: by determining how often a fielder makes plays, he can be compared to other fielders around the league. Over time, the better fielder will make more plays.

But there's a huge flaw in this approach. A fielder's opportunity to make plays is heavily dependent on his team's pitching staff, whether those pitchers tend to give up fly balls or ground balls, the influence of his home park, the number of strikeouts the pitching staff records, and other factors.

In the 1990s, Atlanta infielders have consistently shown up around the bottom of the league in RF. Why? Because Atlanta has the best pitching staff in baseball. Braves' pitchers put fewer balls in play, and that means that Braves' fielders have fewer opportunities to make defensive plays.

Or consider three starting pitchers. In 1997, Scott Erickson allowed 440 ground balls and 153 fly balls — a ratio of nearly 3:1, the most extreme of any starter in the majors. Picking another name at random, John Smoltz allowed 325 ground balls and 247 flies. And at the other end, Bobby Witt allowed 275 ground balls and 254 flies.

Move the same shortstop from Baltimore to Atlanta to Texas, and his overall chances will drop significantly, even if all three pitchers are otherwise evenly matched.

RF and related stats which are calculated by looking at total chances are really the best that we have for retrospectively grading fielders who played before the 1980s. And that's part of what makes it so hard to compare today's fielders to their counterparts of yesteryear. It's really easy to see that Ray Oyler was a miserable hitter; it's right there in indisputable black and white. It's much more difficult to determine whether, say, Bobby Sturgeon (1940-1947 White Sox) was a good fielder. *Total Baseball* gives him FR ratings ranging from -3 to 4 over his career, and his chance totals are unremarkable. So how do we know?

The short and sad answer is that we really don't.

Fortunately, we are now beginning to accumulate statistics that will help us to make meaningful judgments about a player's defensive ability.

The approach is similar to the way we track hitting data. Every time a player steps to the plate, an official scorer makes a notation that a plate appearance has occurred, and also records exactly what the hitter did during that at-bat. In this way, we can get large, unbiased sample sizes that tell us everything we need to know about a batter's hitting.

Essentially, that's what STATS Inc.'s Zone Rating (ZR) does for fielders. An official scorer tracks every ball put into play and notes where it is hit. To do this, the scorer divides the field into "zones of responsibility." Every ball hit into that zone is charged as a kind of "defensive at-bat" against the fielder who occupied it. ZR then reflects the percentage of outs made in each defensive at-bat. Errors — say from dropped fly balls — count exactly the same as fly balls that fall in for singles without the fielder's assistance.

How are zones selected? According to the STATS guide, Zone Rating "measures all the balls hit into the area where a fielder can reasonably be expected to record an out, then counts the percentage of outs actually made."

This is not a judgment call. The STATS scorer has a sheet dividing the playing field into twenty-six wedge-shaped slices. After each ball is hit, the scorer indicates distance from home plate and into which pie slice the ball was hit. Most zones are assigned to a fielder, although some are unassigned, reflecting STATS's judgment that some balls are "uncatchable."

Intuitively, this approach seems right. Of course, as with any new tool, there are some empirical questions surrounding the way it is carried out. Should there be "uncatchable" zones? Should zones be large or small? What about a fielder who catches a ball in someone else's territory?

Because of these questions about the methodology of zone-based fielding statistics are still unresolved, the best way to get a true picture of a player's defensive ability is to rely on statistics from multiple sources. Both STATS and the *Baseball Prospectus* offer fielding methodologies based on the "defensive at-bat" approach. *Total Baseball's* Fielding Runs (FR) and the STATS Range Factor (RF) are both essentially counting statistics based on total chances.

Using a "defensive at-bat" approach we can come up with some idea of the opportunity cost or marginal advantage of playing one particular fielder over another. By judging how many base runners each fielder would allow, we can estimate the number of runs a team would save by playing the superior defender. And then we can match this number up against the number of runs playing the superior hitter would create for the team.

In some cases, we don't have any real work to do. If the best hitter is also the best fielder, then the call is easy. Usually, however, a team is faced with a choice between a much better hitter and a much better fielder. How should a team decide in that situation?

Historically, teams have taken the better fielder, at least at key defensive positions. Consider that Ray Oyler (a lifetime .175/.259/.251 hitter) and Rafael Belliard (.221/.270/.259) have each had regular or semi-regular jobs in the major leagues, and have played six and seventeen seasons, respectively. They are among the very worst hitters to ever play the game.

Has a team ever given one of the very worst fielders a regular job at shortstop? In the 1980s, Davey Johnson played Howard Johnson at shortstop for parts of several seasons. I can't think of many others.

But this probably ought to happen more often. If you were managing the Tampa Bay Devil Rays, and could trade Kevin Stocker for Jeff Bagwell, under the condition that Bagwell would have the play short, would you do it? I would. I just can't imagine that the defensive dropoff — huge though it may be — would be as large as the offensive gain.

Before leaving this discussion of defense, a few words need to be said

146

regarding New York Mets shortstop Rey Ordonez, a player who epito-
mizes the "defense vs. offense" debate.

Considering that he plays in the offense-rich 1990s, Ordonez is possibly the worst hitter in the history of the game. Here are his statistics from
his debut through 1998:

G	AB	R	H	2B	3B	HR	RBI	BB	K	AVG	OBP	SLG	OPS
151	502	51	129	12	4	1	30	22	53	.257/	.289/	.303	592
120	356	35	77	5	3	1	33	18	36	.216/	.255/	.256	511
153	505	46	124	20	2	1	42	23	60	.246/	.278/	.299	577

TOTALS

G	AB	R	H	2B	3B	HR	RBI	BB	K	AVG	OBP	SLG	OPS
424	1363	132	330	37	9	3	105	63	149	.242/	.276/	.289	565

That's three years of utter and complete offensive futility. Ordonez has
demonstrated, in more than 1,400 plate appearances, that he cannot
hit for average, cannot draw walks, and cannot hit for power. Moreover,
Ordonez hasn't been a good base stealer, either, with just fifteen steals in
twenty-nine attempts.

In 1997, Ordonez earned the distinction of putting up one of the worst
offensive seasons by a major league regular in the history of the sport,
barely breaking the .500 barrier of OPS at .511. Remember my rough rule
of thumb, that you should consider a player's OPS as if it were a score on
an exam? What would you say to a student who continually scored
around 50% on his exams?

Okay, so Ordonez can't hit. "But," some might argue, "Rey plays shortstop! He's in there for his defense, and anything he provides on offense is
a bonus!"

Unfortunately, in this era of professional baseball, all fielders must contribute offensively if they're to be of value to their teams. Ordonez's outs
still count, and he makes far too many of them.

How good would Ordonez have to be with the glove in order to make up for
his bat?

The flippant — and true — answer, is "ungodly, otherworldly good." And he
isn't nearly there. Let's take a look at the numbers.

Baseball Prospectus rates Ordonez a 94, on a scale where 100 is average.

STATS computes his range factor (RF) as 4.63, which is slightly above average. However, they compute his Zone Rating (ZR) as .896, well below the 1998 major-league average of .934.

Rey Ordonez simply doesn't measure up. He's acrobatic. He has soft hands and an accurate arm. I find him entertaining and exciting. But I'm forced to conclude that he shouldn't be an everyday major leaguer.

I realize that many people, including the management of the New York Mets, aren't ready to accept this. And because statistical analysis of fielding is still relatively undeveloped, his supporters may never be convinced that Rey Ordonez costs the Mets far more with the bat than his glove can ever make up. (Of course, they probably don't accept what a really awful hitter he is, either.)

Nevertheless, we're making progress in quantifying this basically ephemeral quality. I believe that before long we'll be able to gauge accurately a player's fielding ability with statistics, and that we'll then be able to match that against his offensive numbers and reliably deduce how many runs he is worth to his team on balance.

Actually, that's the easy part. Much tougher — as always — will be getting The Powers in professional baseball to accept the conclusions.

14

The Catcher's Quandary

"[Mike Piazza's] greatest improvement this spring has come in blocking the plate, but when it comes to throwing out runners, he's still a long way from being among the average defensively in the National League. Weaknesses behind the plate could prevent Piazza from becoming an all-time great ...

Piazza will never be listed among the game's greatest catchers ... because Piazza is never going to win a Gold Glove for fielding."
— Mel Antonen, *USA Today*, April 12, 1998.

Years ago, when I first logged on to the rec.sport.baseball USENET newsgroup, I encountered a pithy little saying called Nichols' Law of Catcher Defense, after its creator, Sherri Nichols.

> **Nichols' Law of Catcher Defense: A catcher's rumored defensive abilities are in inverse proportion to his batting skills.**

While there are exceptions, this insightful little principle basically holds true: catchers who hit poorly are almost always believed to be excellent behind the plate (probably because people assume that anybody who has

150

trouble hitting .200 with little power must be good at something) while catchers who hit well are often, inexplicably, assumed to be a liability behind the plate.

Consider this tale of two catchers. One was a young kid with a sterling defensive reputation, a catch-and-throw guy who was nevertheless sent to the waiver wire at age twenty-seven by a .500 ball club after back-to-back seasons around the Mendoza line (.204 and .194).

The second catcher was a big, slow, strong slugger. He was a switch-hitter who mashed 245 home runs and finished with a career OPS comparable to Don Mattingly. This second catcher wasn't well-regarded defensively, however, and was tried at first base and in the outfield — with poor defensive results — and ultimately DH-ed.

Both catchers are Mickey Tettleton.

In 1984, Mickey Tettleton was a starting catcher in the AA Eastern League All-Star Game despite his .255 average and five home runs. Tettleton, a fifth-round draft choice by the Oakland Athletics in the 1981 amateur draft, fell into a deep homerless slump after that minor league all-star game and watched his average plummet all the way to .231.

Oakland called him up to the majors before the year was out.

In 1985, Tettleton spent the entire season as the A's backup catcher, getting into seventy-eight games. That offseason, the A's traded starting catcher Mike Heath to the St. Louis Cardinals for pitcher Joaquin Andujar, and Tettleton took over behind the plate.

After the trade, Tettleton watched his average fall from .251 in 1985 to .204 in 1986. When he slumped even further, to .194 in 1987, Oakland gave him his unconditional release. Even a good defensive catcher can only be carried so far, and .194 is awfully far.

At this point Tettleton signed with one of the worst teams ever to play baseball, the 1988 Baltimore Orioles. Yes, those Orioles. The team which set a major league record for futility by losing its first twenty-one games in a row. A team which would finish 54-107.

Tettleton responded by smacking eleven homers in 283 at-bats — his new career-high in HR at any professional level. The next season, while the Orioles were undergoing a renaissance of Italian proportions, Tettleton hit .258/.369/.509 and obliterated his previous personal career best by clubbing twenty-six home runs. It was also the year when he revealed his breakfast cereal preference, sparking a strange shortage of Froot Loops in the greater Baltimore metropolitan area.

Right about this time, the Orioles started grumbling about Tettleton's weak throwing arm from behind the plate.

Tettleton enjoyed one more season in Charm City before being shipped off to Detroit for Jeff M. Robinson, a nondescript right-hander who allowed, on average, six earned runs per game.

How could Tettleton, a player who very nearly carried the Baltimore Orioles from worst to first in one season, a switch-hitting catcher who smacked fifty-two homers in three seasons, be traded for the worst starting pitcher in baseball? What happened?

Nichols' Law happened. Tettleton suddenly had a rep of being shaky behind the plate. And he never overcame that rep. Within one year after Tettleton arrived in Detroit, the Tigers added supposed defensive whiz Chad Kreuter at catcher and moved Tettleton all around the field, to first, to right field, to left field and, ultimately, to DH.

You don't have to be a rocket scientist to figure out that a thirty-homer-a-year DH is an awful lot less valuable than a thirty-homer-a-year catcher.

Was it necessary? I can't believe that Tettleton, the superb game-caller of 1985, had suddenly become such a bad catcher that the Tigers couldn't keep him behind the plate. Tettleton's abilities didn't change that much. Perception of them did — public perception, which was shaped by media perception, which in turn was probably influenced by perception within the game itself.

Which brings us to Mike Piazza.

Let me make my case known up front: Mike Piazza is the best catcher of all time. He's as much a standout at his position as Babe Ruth, Mike Schmidt and Honus Wagner are at theirs.

The total value of a player can be thought of as follows: runs driven in with the bat plus runs saved with the glove. When it comes to catchers, though, how do we value that glove? How do we avoid doing to Piazza what the Orioles and Tigers did to Mickey Tettleton?

Defensively, a catcher has five responsibilities:

1. Calling pitches.
2. Catching pitches — including framing pitches at the plate for strikes, avoiding passed balls, holding on to tipped third strikes, and stopping potential wild pitches.
3. Blocking the plate on throws to home and tagging the runner.

4. Fielding his position, including ranging after pop fouls, fielding bunts, and throwing to first on bunt attempts.
5. Throwing out would-be base stealers.

That fifth job is the most visible aspect of a catcher's defensive game. It is also the least important. Yet grumblings about Mike Piazza's defensive shortcomings, based mainly on his throwing, have dogged him throughout his career and probably played no small part in the Dodgers' decision to trade him in 1998. Indeed, when in return for Piazza the Dodgers got Charles Johnson — widely regarded as the best defensive catcher in the National League — many suggested that overall the Dodgers improved their catching position.

Is this so? Is the defensive improvement of Charles Johnson's arm worth the offensive loss of Mike Piazza's bat? Overall, how does Piazza's bat plus Piazza's glove compare against Johnson's bat and Johnson's glove?

Let's start with the easy part. Here's what those two players did at the plate in 1997:

Piazza

G	AB	R	H	2B	3B	HR	RBI	BB	K	SB	CS	AVG	OBP	SLG
152	556	104	201	32	1	40	124	69	77	5	1	.362/	.431/	.638

Johnson

G	AB	R	H	2B	3B	HR	RBI	BB	K	SB	CS	AVG	OBP	SLG
124	416	43	104	26	1	19	63	60	109	0	2	.250/	.347/	.454

Both players had career years with the bat in '97; Piazza's career totals through 1997 were .332/.395/.571; while Johnson's were .241/.331/.412. Projecting their career averages out to a full season of equal usage, you get the following lines:

G	AB	R	H	2B	3B	HR	RBI	BB	K	SB	CS	AVG	OBP	SLG
135	512	84	170	22	1	33	106	53	82	2	2	.332/	.395/	.572
135	502	55	121	24	1	20	64	68	126	0	2	.241/	.332/	.412

All things being equal, replacing Piazza's bat with Johnson's costs a team thirty-four outs and eighty-six extra bases. And all things aren't equal. Piazza's career numbers are hurt more by Chavez Ravine than Johnson's are by Pro Player Stadium, so the real difference between these two is even larger. In fact, Johnson's hitting suffered when he started playing half his games in Chavez Ravine. But I'm trying to be as charitable to Johnson as I can in this analysis. That's also why Charles Johnson is getting credited for more games than he actually played, and Piazza, fewer. In real baseball, Piazza's durability is yet another point in his favor.

Now, let's factor in the defense.

1. Calling pitches

This is an incredibly difficult aspect of a catcher's game to measure, and it's probably also the most important part of a catcher's job in the field. If Mike Piazza is so bad at game-calling, if he makes such poor decisions as to cost his pitchers an additional run per game every time he plays, that will seriously cut into the value of his bat.

How can we tell whether Piazza is any good at calling a game or not? STATS, Inc. tracks a statistic called "Catcher's ERA" (or CERA), which is the ERA of pitchers with that particular catcher behind the plate.

Unfortunately, CERA isn't particularly useful in comparing one player to another, because the number is skewed by how good the catcher's pitching staff is. Eddie Perez, for example, has put up successive CERAs of 3.04 and 3.24, which is tops in baseball. However, he is Greg Maddux's personal catcher, and that certainly has a lot to do with it. Anybody whose main job is catching Greg Maddux is going to have a low CERA.

CERA can be useful, however, when you're comparing teammates. In 1997, for example, left-handed-hitting Eddie Taubensee caught 407.1 innings for the Cincinnati Reds, while righty Joe Oliver caught 837. Knowing that Taubensee's CERA was 4.86, while Oliver's was 4.00, probably tells you that Taubensee doesn't call as good a game as Oliver. (The year before, Taubensee's CERA was 4.52, while Oliver's was 4.14. Not quite as large a difference, but still significant.)

So let's apply this methodology to Piazza and Johnson. In 1997, Piazza's CERA was 3.50. Piazza's backup was Tom Prince, who put up a 4.19 CERA in 260 innings. In 1996, Piazza led the NL in CERA (for a very good Dodger pitching staff) with a 3.31 CERA. Again his backup was primarily Tom Prince, who put up a 4.64 CERA in 178.1 innings.

Now maybe Prince is just horrible at calling the game; we can't tell for sure. We can say that Piazza was the best on his team at handling his pitchers.

In 1997, Charles Johnson had a 3.95 CERA; his backup, Gregg Zaun, had a 3.36 CERA in 356 innings. The year before, Johnson's CERA was 3.56, and his backups included Bob Natal (4.27 CERA in 255 innings), Joe Siddall (5.59 CERA in 116 innings), and Gregg Zaun (5.59 CERA in 74 innings).

Again, the contrast isn't quite as striking, but it's probably safe to conclude that Charles Johnson and Mike Piazza are both better than average at calling a game. Which, by the way, is consistent with scouting reports from people (like myself) who have watched both players. So call it even, and let's move on to the next aspect of catcher defense.

2. Catching pitches

Here, we do see a big difference between Piazza and Johnson. In 1997, Piazza allowed ten passed balls, which ranks near the bottom of major league regulars. Other contenders for the Butterfingers Award in '97 included the Yankees' Joe Girardi (eleven), the Cardinals' Mike Difelice (twelve), the Phillies' Mike Lieberthal (twelve). Topping the list were Boston's Scott Hatteberg and Bill Haselman — who caught knuckleballer Tim Wakefield — with seventeen passed balls each.

In '96, Piazza allowed twelve passed balls, which again ranked near the bottom in all of baseball.

Charles Johnson, on the other hand, is among the game's best at holding on to the ball. In 1,076 innings in 1997, he allowed just one passed ball; the year before, he allowed just five in 998 innings caught.

But this difference doesn't have much effect over the course of a season. Prorated out to the same number of innings, the Dodgers would save themselves seven extra bases by moving from Piazza to Johnson. Piazza's inability to hold on to those extra seven pitches, on average, would also cost his team one more out. (The law of averages suggests that about one of those seven passed balls would be on what would have been strike three.) Taking all this into account, the offensive side of the ledger is now thirty-four outs and eighty-six extra bases; the defensive side of the ledger is one out and seven extra bases.

3. Blocking the plate on throws to home

In all candor, I have no idea how one would measure this statistically.

I could quote putout totals, but factoring out which ones come on throws to the plate would be a nightmare. A catcher's ability to block the plate will also show up in the outfield assist totals of his teammates, but I'm reluctant to credit Piazza for Raul Mondesi's cannon of an arm.

In this area, I think there's nothing better — for the time being, anyhow — than the eyewitness and scouting reports of people who've watched both Piazza and Johnson. Most who do so generally give a slight edge to Piazza here, but since I'm arguing for Piazza and don't want to be accused of favoritism, I'm just going to call it a wash.

4. Fielding the position

Johnson gets the edge here. In 1997 he set a National League record by going all season without a single error behind the plate, while Piazza committed sixteen. The year before, the difference was insignificant; Piazza was charged with six while Johnson committed four, a difference of .003 in fielding percentage.

Johnson's stronger arm, unsurprisingly, gives him an advantage in throwing out runners on bunt attempts or swinging bunts. Over the past two years, Johnson has registered almost as many assists as Piazza (138 to 144) despite the fact that Piazza has caught nearly 400 more innings over that span.

Prorated out to a single season of equivalent playing time, Piazza would commit nine more errors than Johnson, while recording eight fewer assists. Again using league average figures, that translates to three outs and thirteen extra bases. (Errors by the catcher almost never involve turning a sure out into a runner on base; they're usually errant throws on attempted steals.)

Bringing the scorecard up to date, that's a total four outs and twenty extra bases prevented by Johnson so far.

5. Throwing arm

Finally, let's turn to the most visible difference between Piazza and Johnson: their throwing.

In 1996, Piazza had 189 base runners attempt to steal on his arm, and he threw out just thirty-four of those. That 18% success rate ranked him basically dead last in all of baseball — tied with then-Boston's Mike Stanley (who no longer works behind the plate), and behind such noted weak-armed backstops as Baltimore's Chris Hoiles (23%), Cincinnati's Eddie Taubensee (23%), and Montreal's Darrin Fletcher (20%).

In 1997, Piazza was quite a bit better from behind the plate, gunning down forty-three of 155 attempted thieves, for a 28% success rate. That ranked ahead of a bunch of regular starters — including Hoiles, Stanley, Taubensee, Fletcher, New York's Todd Hundley, Montreal's Chris Widger, Boston's Scott Hatteberg and Colorado's Kirt Manwaring.

During this same two-year period, Charles Johnson nailed ninety-six of 202 would-be base stealers, an impressive 47.5% success rate.

If Piazza had thrown out that percentage over the past two years, then instead of erasing seventy-seven runners, he would have nailed an astonishing 163. On a year-by-year basis, that comes out to forty-three additional outs. However, this number is highly skewed, since runners are much less likely to try to steal on catchers with strong arms. Piazza had 344 stolen base attempts over 1996 and '97; Johnson, just 202. While there is some value in intimidating a potential stealer into staying at first, it's not nearly as much of a bonus as recording an additional out.

Using stolen base attempts per-innings-caught rates, we can see that base stealers attempt to advance on Johnson's arm at roughly 2/3 the rate at which they run on Piazza. Johnson, therefore, should get credit for forty-three extra bases prevented and twenty-eight additional outs recorded.

Overall, Johnson's defense gets credit for thirty-two additional outs and sixty-three extra bases prevented. Keep in mind that this is basically the absolute most charitable case to be made for C.J. The difference between them as hitters is probably much greater than their 1997 figures suggest. In terms of defense, Johnson's miraculous 1997 errorless season wasn't to be repeated, and his error and passed ball totals were all much higher in '98 than the composite '96-'97 baseline used in this comparison. Piazza has also proven himself to be more durable and more capable of playing everyday than Charles Johnson. And finally, although we've called it a wash in some areas of the game that are difficult to quality, but reality probably gives a slight edge to Piazza.

Although we've given him the break wherever possible, Johnson still comes up short against Piazza. Let's do the math.

Dodgers pitchers faced 6,191 batters in 1997, allowing 1,325 hits and 546 walks. That means that opponents hit a combined .241/.313/.389

against Los Angeles. Giving the staff thirty-two extra outs and eliminating sixty-three total bases reduces the staff opponents' OBP by .005 and the staff opponents' SLG by .011.

The Dodgers hit .268/.330/.418 in 1997. Replace Piazza with Johnson, and the team loses .007 points of OBP and .015 points of SLG. This differential costs the Dodgers, on average, two wins over the course of a season.

Two wins is the amount by which the Dodgers fell short of the NL West title in '97. Perhaps this explains why, in the 1998 offseason, L.A. turned around and traded the defensive whiz — who had hit just .217 as a Dodger — for Todd Hundley.

One last note: Mike Piazza has played his entire career (excepting five games) for two teams who play in cavernous parks that are death to hitters. And his career OPS is *still* .971; that is far better than Yogi Berra or Johnny Bench (both .816) and they are usually considered the best-hitting catchers of all time. Even in the context of the periods in which they played, Piazza is a better hitter than Bench or Berra. Were I Piazza's agent, I would have advised him to sign a one-year contract with the Colorado Rockies, and let him cash in after hitting, oh, .400 with 70 home runs.

If that seems absurd, consider that through 1997, Piazza had hit .471 and averaged a homer every eight at-bats in Coors.

Mike Piazza *is* the greatest catcher of all time, although he never has been among the defensive greats. Catcher's defense is important, but it must be valued in its proper context, and for Piazza that context is offensive power which no other catcher has ever been able to sustain.

Every team wants a catcher who can hit like Piazza and throw like Charles Johnson, but that player doesn't exist. As always, player selection and roster building is a compromise, a judgment whether the things a player does well outweigh the things he does poorly. As at every other position, that judgment ought to be based as much as possible on verifiable facts, not on sentiment or myth or reputation.

THE MANAGER

Do Nothing?

Unlike that for many other sports — professional football in particular — the in-game strategy involved in baseball is fiendishly simple. This is one reason why a twelve-year-old can sit down at Strat-O-Matic or its modern computer equivalent and beat the snot out of even, say, a professional sportswriter.

This is not to say that there aren't amazing nuances and complexities to the game. The precise positioning of fielders, watching a player's footwork, knowing how many tenths of a second it takes the pitcher on the mound to deliver to the plate, and being able to translate that number into the number of strides the base runner can take away from first — these are all essentially invisible yet absolutely critical aspects of managing a baseball team.

That said, replace Joe Torre with the average twelve-year-old Strat player and my guess is that the Yankees still would have won the American League East in 1998. Give the same kid the undefeated 1972 Miami Dolphins of the NFL, on the other hand, and they probably would have gone winless.

This chapter focuses on the offensive strategies of strategic management. An effective manager will get his team to score more runs than you would reasonably expect from the sum total of the individual performances of the players.

I think sometimes we tend to forget this. Fans talk about managers being "unpredictable" or "exciting" or "shaking things up," but the whole point of the manager's moves on offense is to have the team be better off than if he had done nothing.

In that regard, several current major league managers could be better replaced with a shiny rock. Admittedly, the rock isn't going to out-maneuver the other team and make spectacular moves to win ball games. But it's not going to cost you runs, either. Sometimes doing nothing is exactly the best strategy. In the high-scoring modern version of pro baseball, games are won not by pecking away a run at a time but by scoring runs in bunches, and the way to get big innings is to stock your lineup with hitters who get on base and hit with power, and then sit back and let them do what they do best.

That's why almost any tactic that involves giving up an out is a bad idea in today's game. Scoring multiple runs in an inning becomes much harder when you've made the first out. If you want to score runs in bunches, you never give up that out. Most of the classic offensive tools, like the sacrifice bunt and the hit-and-run, are essentially one-run tactics derived from the dead ball era when a team had a good chance to win a game by scoring single runs in two or three innings.

The strategy of deliberately piecing together single-run innings by advancing runners on bunts, ground ball outs, and the like is sometimes known as "manufacturing runs." Sportscasters use the term with great admiration. The implication is that a manager whose team scratches out runs in this hands-on manner is somehow more clever and canny than the guy whose team scores bunches of runs without his intervention.

Or, to be more precise, without his *apparent* intervention. A big part of the manager's job is to get the maximum from his hitters, and that may mean subtle moves rather than obvious ones.

If the manager puts on the "take" sign with a weak hitter at the plate, a 3-1 count, and two outs, and that player walks, and the next batter hits a home run, then the manager has "manufactured" two runs for which he is unlikely ever to get credit.

If you're managing Roberto Alomar, a gifted hitter who nevertheless has a penchant for bunting in bizarre situations (such as the top of the first inning, with a speedy runner on first, and the team's number-three-spot hitter due up next), and you order Robby *not* to bunt, then you're contributing to the "manufacturing" of runs by forcing him to try to do what he does best, which is to hit the ball hard and get on base.

If you decide not to call for the hit-and-run with runners on first and second and nobody out, and those runners eventually score on a homer, you have "manufactured" runs (and have probably put your team in a good position to win the game).

It's a matter of taste, of course, but I do understand why some fans enjoy "little ball" tactics. If you're trying to really get into the game, it's fun to say, "Now, what Casey is thinking about here is whether to set the runners in motion, and whether that will open up a hole on the left side as the shortstop moves to cover second ..."

That's much more entertaining than saying, for the one-hundred-thousandth time: "The batter is going to look for a good pitch and try to hit the ball as hard and as far as he can."

But entertaining tactics which cost your team scoring opportunities will make game a lot less enjoyable in the long run. Because, whether you prefer 1-0 pitching duels or 13-12 slugfests; whether you enjoy Gashouse Gang-style aggressive base running or the sit-and-wait-for-three-run- homers approach, winning is always a lot more fun than losing.

Essentially, once a manager fills out his lineup card, he has eight different ways to influence how many runs his team scores.

1. Pinch hitting

I believe that, absent a drastic change in the rules of the game, the pinch hitter is almost — but not quite — a vanishing species.

The trend in recent years has been towards twelve- and thirteen-man pitching staffs. That leaves twelve position players on a team's twenty-five-man active roster. With nine everyday starters, a backup catcher and a utility infielder, that leaves just one more player on the bench.

One more player to be the top pinch hitter, outfield replacement, and pinch runner. Or, if you have a Troy O'Leary or Ryan Klesko — a player with a severe lefty-righty handicap, who therefore needs a platoon mate — that's essentially zero extra players.

(I imagine that most readers of this book are familiar with the concept of platoon splits, so I won't dwell on it here except to note right-handed hitters usually hit better against most left-handed pitchers than they do against righties; similarly, left-handed hitters tend to hit better against right-handed pitchers than against lefties. When a right-handed batter

164

stands in against a right-handed pitcher, the pitcher is said to have the platoon advantage.)

Sure, some teams still carry 11 pitchers, and, in the National League the DH slot is taken up by an extra hitter off the bench. Nevertheless, the trend is clear: as teams move more and more toward short-relief specialists, one-batter left-handed relievers, and Rule V draftee pitchers buried at the end of the bullpen, that leaves less flexibility off the bench to score runs.

Which makes it even more important to use one's pinch hitters effectively.

The diminishing size of the bench paves the way for another critical dilemma on a '90s baseball club. Namely, that teams are looking for more versatile bench players, but if a player is that good, chances are he ought to be starting.

Earl Weaver explained it best:

"For the bench, I look for a guy who can do a job when I want it done. Naturally, I'm looking for as many talents as possible in one player. But your all around players – those who can hit, run, and throw – are usually your regulars. On the bench you get guys with one excellent skill ... By matching your bench players' strengths to your starters' weaknesses, you can create a 'player' of All Star caliber from spare parts."

The best pinch hitters usually come from platoon partners. In a strict platoon situation, the manager will start the left-hander versus right handed pitchers, and then have a righty who plays the same position to start against lefties. Whoever starts, his partner is available off the bench.

A team can outsmart itself with lefty and righty platoon partners. Suppose you're managing the Boston Red Sox, and platooning Troy O'Leary and Jack Voigt in left field. The Mariners are starting now-traded lefty Randy Johnson, so you make out your lineup card with first baseman Mo Vaughn (a lefty) batting third, righty Nomar Garciaparra batting cleanup, and righty platoon outfielder Jack Voigt hitting fifth. In the eighth inning of a tie game, with two outs, Vaughn lines a deep double off of Johnson, and Seattle manager Lou Piniella goes to his bullpen for right hander Bobby Ayala.

When a relief pitcher is brought into the game, he must face at least one batter. On the other hand, a pinch hitter can simply "announce" for the hitter at the plate and be immediately pinch hit for in return; you can keep this up until you (very quickly) run out of bench players.

So Ayala must face Garciaparra, who walks on four pitches. That brings Voigt to the plate. Out in the bullpen, Seattle left-hander Paul Spoljaric has completed his warmup tosses and is ready to come in if necessary.

In this situation, the manager with the short bench almost always loses. If you pull the trigger and pinch hit O'Leary for Voigt, then manager Lou Piniella can counter with Spoljaric. Or you can leave Voigt in there against the righty Ayala, even though Voigt can't hit right-handers.

The "smart" manager may double pinch hit; he brings in O'Leary to force the pitching change, and then brings in a right-hander to face Spoljaric. But how smart is that, really? You've then burned your best pinch hitter (O'Leary) for nothing, and now you're left with your second-best right-handed hitter against the lefty Spoljaric. Particularly with a short bench, you may have just about exhausted all of your players.

Ideally, of course, Voigt would be able to hit right-handers, or you'd have a switch-hitter on the bench, or someone who hit well enough against pitchers throwing with either hand. But if you had any of those guys, why would you be platooning O'Leary and Voigt in the first place? The dilemma here is that a guy like O'Leary — who has a career .845 OPS against right-handers — (or the lesser-known Voigt, who has a career .916 OPS against lefties) is probably going to be one of the best bench players against the pitchers he can hit, but *only* against the pitchers he can hit. So on the one hand you want to set up platoons, but on the other, you can find yourself checkmated if you play lefty-righty against a team with a deep bullpen.

In these situations, it is critical that the team's second-best right-handed pinch hitter off the bench be able to crush lefties as well. Making this decision is easy; it means taking a utility infielder with less speed, or a backup catcher with a weaker arm, or foregoing a pinch runner. Sticking with the Red Sox theme, we'll call this guy Mike Stanley.

Now, in the above situation, if you have Stanley on your bench, who crushes left-handers, then you can safely pinch hit O'Leary for Voigt. Piniella knows that if he brings in Spoljaric, his lefty must pitch to at least one batter, and you can counter with Stanley.

But if you've signed a strong-armed defensive catcher instead, or a speedy utility infielder, then the threat isn't credible, and a smart opposing team can work around the only weapon on your bench.

So while pinch hitting is a tactical move within a game, it is really dictated by strategic decisions made during the off-season. And in many cases the thinking behind those decisions hasn't caught up with the new realities of the game. Far too often, a team finds itself pinch hitting with backup catchers and utility infielders. You just can't win that way. The key to effective pinch hitting is being able to get the right guy to the place at the right time, and the key to *that* is to have structured a bench in advance that makes it possible.

If I were running a team, I would keep two pinch-hit threats around: one all-around good hitter (or two platoon partners, like O'Leary and Voigt), and one lesser-regarded hitter with a high OBP, like Dave Magadan or F.P. Santangelo. This latter player may also serve other roles, like Santangelo, who can play any of seven defensive positions. I want the OBP-guy, not only to send up as a pinch hitter in cases where I'm outsmarted, but also for those situations when my light-hitting second baseman is leading off the bottom of the eighth in a one-run game. I don't want to waste my best pinch hitter with nobody on base, but I definitely want to get the weak hitter out of the game.

2. Pinch running

Consider the cost of this move. Not only do you usually take out a quality hitter, but you burn a replacement player, and unless he plays the same position as the man he replaced you have to bring in yet a *third* guy to play defense after the half-inning is over.

And what do you get for your three players? Not an extra run, or even an extra base. You get a runner on base who is faster than the guy he replaced. Sure, that may open up the possibility of stealing a base or running aggressively or hitting-and-running or any of a number of other strategies that rely on a fast base runner — but those are all risky strategies themselves! In other words, the pinch runner requires you to pay for the opportunity to take *another* risk.

And even if those gambles do pay off, the maximum benefit is one run.

Since the price you pay in pinch running is in players burned off the bench, there are only three times you can minimize that cost: in the ninth inning of a tie (or one-run-deficit) contest, in extra innings, or, in September, when the rosters have expanded. (Actually, managing in September is its own special category, but it's particularly applicable to pinch running.) Even here you run the risk that the strategy will fail to produce a run, the game will continue, and you'll be left with having to pinch hit for the pinch runner or defensive replacement some time later.

I should touch briefly on the short but strange career of Herb Washington, the game's first, and probably last, "designated pinch runner." Washington was the game's first professional runner. He never recorded a single at-bat or defensive appearance. He did, however, pinch run *ninety-two* times for Charlie Finley's World Series Champion 1974 Oakland A's.

Herb Washington was twenty-two years old. He held the world record for the sixty-yard dash, and was in tremendous physical condition. During spring training, Finley hired former six-time stolen base champ and ex-Dodger great Maury Wills to spend a week teaching Washington the fundamentals of base stealing.

But baseball — to repeat myself — is a very difficult game, even if you're a tremendous athlete, and Washington never really learned the art of stealing a base. In his ninety-two times on base for the A's, Herb Washington stole just twenty-nine bases, and was caught sixteen times. He scored twenty-nine runs, which would have to be viewed as a major disappointment. Indeed, in the playoffs, Washington made five appearances, stole no bases and scored no runs. He had zero impact, even though six of the nine games were decided by a single run.

If Washington had been a truly outstanding base runner, like former St. Louis Cardinals outfielder Vince Coleman, his career might have been different.

In 1986, Coleman had 139 hits and sixty walks, for a grand total of 199 times on base. I estimate that Coleman was on first base, with an opportunity to steal second, about 200 times that season. (There were undoubtedly times when Coleman walked or singled with a man on first, blocking him from any further steal attempts. On the other hand, there were also times when Coleman grounded into a fielder's choice, forcing the runner at second, therefore getting on base despite making an out.)

In those 200 opportunities, he stole 107 bases (most of them steals of second). He was caught just fourteen times, and scored ninety-four runs.

Approximately half the time, Coleman was able to steal second and put himself into scoring position, and slightly less than half the time, he was able to score a run for the Cardinals.

If Herb Washington had had Coleman's base stealing ability, he would have been 49-for-55 in stolen bases. (In fact, if he had had that kind of ability, he might have been used even more often.) Instead of being a net drag on his team, he would have been an asset.

I still doubt that Washington would have been worth a roster spot, but at least it would have made the question interesting. As it happened, Washington was invited back to the '75 A's, made another thirteen pinch running appearances, stole two bases and was caught once, and was released. The experiment was over.

3. Sacrifice bunt

The sac bunt is the ultimate "little ball" strategy. It has its roots in the dead ball era of professional baseball, when it was probably reasonable. It has survived because of the conventional wisdom that although a sacrifice decreases the chance that a team will score multiple runs in an inning, it does increase the probability that one run will score.

Phrased that way, you can understand why managers could rationally differ over how often to bunt. Is the manager essentially conservative, or a risk-taker? Should you give up a sure thing for a chance at the jackpot? It's Achilles' choice, the lottery and "Let's Make a Deal." It's the American Way.

But in today's baseball, it's a false dilemma. The fact is, over a long haul, sacrificing rarely increases a team's chances of scoring a run in an inning. But the cost in lost opportunities is real. In fact, with the changing game, that cost is greater than ever.

But many teams and managers have not caught on to this yet.

It works this way: as offense increases, the number of players hitting doubles, triples and home runs increases. The total number of extra-base hits rises as well. As this happens, "scoring position" starts at first base, rather than at second base. Moving a runner from first to second becomes less of an advantage, especially if big sluggers are due to hit. Of course, it's still always preferable to have a runner at second instead of at first; the question is whether that is worth giving up an out for a chance to gain the extra base. (Remember, sacrifices aren't always successful, so there's no guarantee of getting even an extra base from the out.)

Seemingly, the most obvious time to sacrifice is when your worst hitter
n the lineup is at the plate. Consider the following typical bottom-of-the-
order hitters in the American League of 1998:

.F	Rob Ducey, SEA	.240/.336/.410	5 HRs
3S	Mike Bordick, BAL	.260/.328/.411	13 HRs
*B	David Bell, CLE	.262/.306/.424	10 HRs
3S	Mike Caruso, CHI	.306/.331/.390	5 HRs
.F	Chad Curtis, NYY	.243/.355/.360	10 HRs
3S	Gary DiSarcina, ANA	.287/.321/.385	3 HRs
2B	Mike Benjamin, BOS	.272/.312/.372	4 HRs
3B	Fernando Tatis, TEX	.270/.303/.361	3 HRs
3S	Pat Meares, MIN	.260/.296/.368	9 HRs
3S	Alex Gonzalez, TOR	.239/.281/.361	13 HRs
3S	Deivi Cruz, DET	.260/.284/.355	5 HRs
3	A.J. Hinch, OAK	.231/.296/.341	9 HRs
3S	Mendy Lopez, KC	.243/.286/.325	1 HR
3S	Kevin Stocker, TB	.208/.282/.313	6 HRs

Those are, by and large, the worst hitters on their respective teams — and
even then, most of them have a touch of power, slugging .360 or better. Don't
get me wrong; .360 isn't an impressive slugging percentage, but it is a far cry
from, say, the 1970s, where teams from both leagues averaged a .360 slugging
percentage.

In other words, a team's worst hitter today has about as much power as the
average hitter twenty-five years ago. (And that's without delving into the
truly dead-ball year of 1968.) Today, the average player, including NL pitchers,
has about a .420 slugging percentage.

All this seems to suggest that the advantage of moving a runner from first
to second is likely not to be worth giving up an out — not even at the bottom
of the order, in the American League.

The best way to determine whether this is true is to look at the number of
runs that teams score in each of these situations, and see if there's any advantage to be gained from moving from one to the other. Fortunately, baseball
researcher Mike Emeigh has collected such data for the past two years, and his
information is in the public domain and available online, at:

http://www.geocities.com/Colosseum/Stadium/8957/index.htm.

We want to know:

- How likely a team is to score at least one run with a runner on first and no outs;
- How many runs that team is likely to score;
- How likely a team is to score at least one run with a runner on *second* and one out; and
- How many runs that team is likely to then score after giving up the out

What we find is somewhat shocking. For every team and every league, the expected run total drops dramatically when the team goes from "runner on first, nobody out" situations to "runner on second, one out" situations. This is exactly what we would expect; namely, that bunting a runner from first to second decreases the likelihood of a big inning, and thus reduces the total number of expected runs a team scores.

But we also find that bunting decreases the likelihood that a team will score *any* runs at all. In 1996, the average NL team scored at least one run 45.62% of the time that the team had a runner on first and nobody out. In situations with a runner on second and one out, that number dropped to just 41.90%. The same results happened the next year, as well as in the American League for both years:

League	NL 1996	NL 1997	AL 1996	AL 1997
Score one or more runs, without bunting	45.62%	44.19%	45.43%	44.67%
Average runs scored in that inning	.938	.898	1.011	.944
Score one or more runs, bunting to second	41.90%	42.67%	42.61%	41.78%
Average runs scored in that inning after bunting	.720	.714	.770	.706

In other words, sacrificing an out to gain an extra base makes a team worse off than it was before! Not only does the team score fewer total runs — by closing down the likelihood of a big inning — but the team has a decreased chance of scoring any runs at all.

So, should a team ever bunt?

Unpredictability is an advantage. The possibility that you're going to bunt orces the opposing team to play fielders in close, increasing the possibility of ιits on grounders through the infield. If you never bunt, other teams are going o catch on after a while, and adjust accordingly. So even the manager who :schews the bunt must, from time to time, drop one down anyway. And more- ιver, he's got to look really like he believes in it, too. Otherwise, the manager ιust concede an element of defensive strategy to his opponent.

Besides that intangible effect, there are two situations in which the bunt nay be useful:

One is when a team has a truly terrible hitter at the plate, in which case you ιan throw out "average" run-scoring, because the hitter at the plate is deci- ιively below average. If that hitter is going to be an automatic out anyway, it s generally in the manager's best interests to cut his losses and bunt. In the National League, bunting with the pitcher is usually the better move. In the American League, if you have a hitter at the plate so poor as to be compara- ιle to an NL pitcher, he probably shouldn't be in the lineup at all.

The other situation in which a bunt might be a smart move is with runners ιn first and second, in the ninth inning of a tie ballgame.

Throughout this section, I've been considering the textbook strategy of ιunting a runner from first to second with no outs. However, there is a ιigher percentage bunt situation when a team has runners on first *and* ιecond in a close game with a weak hitter due up. In those cases, a suc- ιessful bunt advances the runners to second and third in exchange for the ιut.

Take a look at the scoring chart, comparing "first and second, nobody ιut" situations with "second and third, one out":

League	NL 1996	NL 1997	AL 1996	AL 1997
Score one or more runs, without bunting	65.83%	63.47%	65.71%	67.64%
Average runs scored in that inning	1.572	1.493	1.663	1.613
Score one or more runs, bunting to second	67.05%	66.67%	66.96%	66.31%
Average runs scored in that inning after bunting	1.367	1.331	1.453	1.315

With the exception of the 1997 American League, these higher-percentage bunt situations do accomplish the classic justification: they give a team a slightly better chance to score at least one run, at the cost of scoring multiple runs.

Of course, in order to gain this scoring advantage, the bunt must be a good one. So far, I have simply presumed that all bunts are automatically successful, to show how poor a play the bunt is in virtually every situation — even when everything goes "right," the bunt almost always leaves a team worse off than before.

But the sac bunt isn't automatic. In fact, the standard success rate is generally about 75%. The number increases slightly if you look only at likely bunters; in 1997, for example, among major leaguers with at least ten bunt attempts — presumably the better bunters in the game — the average success rate was only 78%.

When a bunt goes wrong, a hitter may create a double play by bunting too hard or popping the ball up. Even if he just fouls off the pitch, the strike puts the hitter at a disadvantage in the count. Of course, if you're a real gambler and like to bunt with two strikes, you risk striking out by bunting through a pitch or by bunting foul. All of those negative consequences make even the bunt-to-second-and-third a poor play for most hitters.

But if you have a below-average hitter who is also a very good bunter at the plate, like Detroit's Deivi Cruz or Baltimore's Jeff Reboulet, and you only need to score one run, then the bunt to advance the runners to second and third is a slight improvement over letting a hitter swing away.

For all of the head-scratching and soul-searching I've done to try to justify this storied tradition of the game, I just can't come up with any other situations in which the bunt helps, rather than hurts, a team.

These situations are relatively rare, yet most teams' total number of attempted sacrifices is far higher. Most ML managers today are giving up potential runs, and costing their teams potential wins, by bunting too often and in the wrong situations.

If the Lords of Baseball eliminate the DH, raise the pitching mound, open up the strike zone, or any of a number of things which reduce scoring from five runs a game to three, then the sacrifice might become a more arguable strategy. But until that happens, it belongs on the shelf except in rare situations.

4. "Hidden sacrifices": The hit-and-run and others

Any play in which the offense is willing to give up an out, such as putting on a contact play, or instructing the batter to try for a fly ball to bring a man in from third — essentially, anything that deprives the batter of a chance to drive the ball hard or reach base on a walk — is, in effect, a sacrifice.

One of the most common occurs with a runner on second and nobody out. Frequently, a right-handed batter, who usually would be trying to pull the ball in the air with power, will instead alter his swing to create a ground ball to the right side of the infield. If he is successful, he moves the runner to third base, but in doing so he usually makes an out. He also costs himself a chance to drive in the run, to get on base by a walk and to hit with power; the better hitter he is, the greater the cost to his team's scoring chances.

Yet even today, a hitter who does this is rewarded with praise. Sportscasters and players and managers will say that "he did his job in moving the runner over."

Nonsense. His job is either to drive in the run or at least to get on base. Either will increase his team's chances of creating a big inning and winning the game. Making an out does neither.

Although it doesn't show up on the box score, this play is essentially a sacrifice — a "hidden sacrifice," if you will. It is a one-run tactic at best, a holdover from a time when outs were cheap and one run had real significance.

I include the hit-and-run in this category. Although it's not an automatic out, the odds of success are low, and most of the time the potential cost is unjustifiably high.

Teams usually try to hit-and-run when they have a smart base runner with above-average speed at first base, and a hitter at the plate who can put the ball in play. The runner watches the pitcher to make sure he delivers the ball to the plate, and takes off for second base. The opposing team's second baseman or shortstop (if the batter is left-handed) breaks to cover second base, and the batter at the plate swings at the pitch, trying to slap the ball through the hole created by the vacating defender.

When everything works right, the team at bat winds up with no outs and runners at first and third. In essence, the hit-and-run is an opportunity to advance the runner on first two bases, as well as put another runner on first.

The hit-and-run succeeds about one-third of the time. That's not nearly good enough when you consider that the hitter is giving up both the chance to hit the ball with power and a chance to reach base on a walk.

Part of the reason why the hit-and-run is such a low percentage play is that both the runner and the hitter must disregard their best instincts. The base runner *must* go on the next pitch, regardless of whether he has gotten a good jump, and the batter *must* swing at the pitch to protect the runner, regardless of whether it's a strike or a ball.

Here's what Earl Weaver had to say about the hit-and-run, in *Weaver on Strategy*:

"I don't have a hit-and-run sign, and I believe it's the worst play in baseball. First, the runner is going to second base at half speed, looking to see if the hitter makes contact. If the hitter fails to connect, 90 percent of the time that runner is thrown out stealing second. Also, the hitter is at a disadvantage because he knows he has to swing at any pitch in order to protect the runner. Odds are that he'll be going after a pitch that isn't a particularly good one to hit. It puts everyone at a disadvantage, and I don't think much of it ...

"I used to be a pretty good hit-and-run man when I played in the minors. I handled the bat well and could hit the ball to the right side of the infield. Nevertheless, I know that you often give the opposition an out on the hit-and-run play. That's because you can't trust the pitcher to throw a strike, so the hitter is often waving weakly at a ball that's off the plate. That usually results in a weak grounder that gets the runner to second, but the hitter is easily retired at first. Hell, you may as well bunt! Over the course of the season, only a few guys actually get hits on the hit-and-run play, because everything must go right for it to work."

Even teams which disdain the hit-and-run generally don't spurn it completely, as Weaver did. The reasoning is that if you have the bottom of the order due up, a fast runner on first, and a batter at the plate who makes good contact, keeps the ball on the ground, but isn't a good hitter — like Ozzie Guillen — then the hit-and-run seems to make sense.

In that scenario, managers reason, if there is a good probability of the guy making contact, and if there is a good chance that he'll hit it on the ground, then moving the runner (a) decreases chances of a double-play, and (b) might actually increase the chance of a hit since one of the middle infielders will be moving out of position to cover the bag at second.

What this train of logic leaves out, though, is that (c) on the hit-and-run, the batter at the plate *must* swing at the next pitch and attempt to put it into play, no matter what or where it is. Even Ozzie Guillen takes a pitch occasionally; moreover, when Guillen is down 0-2, he will try to fight off and foul pitches that are unhittable, rather than trying to slap them up the middle. On a hit-and-run, though, he must swing, and he must cut down on his swing and try to put the ball on the ground and up the middle. As a result, batting averages for the hit-and-run drop by something like three-fourths.

This factor is huge. The worse the hitter at the plate is, the smaller the effect, but, as Earl Weaver surmised, it is almost never small enough to be outweighed by the very small advantages of (a) plus (b).

Weaver also recognized that if the runner on first is fast enough to make it to second on a hit-and-run attempt, he ought to be trying to steal second outright. As a bonus, the straight steal often forces the hitter at the plate to be more patient, which is exactly what you want to do with someone like Ozzie Guillen.

(As a side note, I would add that it is always a losing strategy to play a hitter as poor as Ozzie Guillen in today's game of baseball. But that's probably obvious to you if you have read this far.)

5. Stealing bases

In recent years, teams have begun to focus on a player's stolen base success rate as opposed to just his total number of steals. It is commonly said that a player has to be successful anywhere from two-thirds to three-quarters of the time in order for his speed to help his team.

That's a handy benchmark, and better than just looking at a player's raw steal total, but it's still not precise enough to be very useful. Actually, the value of a given player's base running depends on his team's strengths and needs. On some teams, a player with an 80% success rate should be looking for opportunities to steal. On other teams, that same rate isn't good enough to justify a lot of steal attempts.

You can best understand this if you see the stolen base in terms of slugging and on-base percentage. A successful stolen base is a boost to SLG (because it adds a base) while being caught stealing lowers both SLB and OBP (because it creates an out). So stealing is a tradeoff, and over a season, the steal attempt basically is a way to increase SLG while lowering OBP.

Therefore, the teams which should try to steal most often are those with an "excess" of OBP: those who put large numbers of runners on base, but strand many of them due to poor slugging. On those teams, even a player who gets caught once every four or five attempts can add value with his running. But on a team with a high SLG, a player would have to be successful at least 90% of the time for the tradeoff to make sense.

Unfortunately, the common assumption is that if teams with great hitting shouldn't steal a lot, then teams with poor hitting should steal as often as possible, in order to "create scoring opportunities."

This is a fatal misconception. When teams are really having trouble scoring runs, it's usually because they're weak in both SLG and OBP. In that case the manager must be as conservative as possible when he does get runners on base, because he doesn't have any to waste.

Most big league clubs don't seem to grasp this, however, so periodically we get the silly spectacle of bad-hitting teams running themselves out of scoring opportunities by trying to steal as often as possible.

The prime example in the 1990s is the Kansas City Royals, with results that speak for themselves.

Again, these conclusions reflect the heightened scoring of the offense-crazy '90s. If we return to the days when even championship clubs slug less than .400, the stolen base will once again become a key offensive weapon in a team's arsenal.

6. Steals of third and double steals

I've put steals of third and double steals in their own category, not just because the plays are so much more rare, but because the throws involved by the catcher are very different from on the steal of second.

To the runner, the steal of third seems slightly easier than the steal of second, because the pitcher can't easily check a base runner directly behind him.

To the catcher, however, the throw to third is much easier because of the distances involved. From home to second base in a straight line is 127 feet, three inches, while home plate to third base is an even ninety feet. A catcher's throw to second which would arrive in four seconds (and probably fail to catch a fast runner) would arrive in under three seconds at third base, which is enough time to nail even Kenny Lofton. Shorter distances also allow the catcher to throw with greater accuracy.

Thus, the steal of third is successful, on average, about 20% of the time. Unless the runner is very good, it's almost never a worthwhile play.

The double steal of second and third operates the same way. If it is to be successful, the lead runner must pull off a straight steal of third. There's an additional risk because the trailing runner, if slow enough, can be nailed by a strong throw by the catcher to second instead of to third.

The double steal is really in the category of "trick" plays. Most managers employ it, on average, three to five times a year. (In the 1997 AL, for example, Lou Piniella attempted the double steal eight times, while several managers — including Johnny Oates of Texas and Toronto's Cito Gaston — tried it only once.)

The most extreme trick play is the sandlot first-and-third double steal. The runner at first either breaks for second and stops halfway, or takes a lead large enough to get picked off. At the same time — or before, if a left-hander is on the mound — the runner at third breaks for the plate at full speed. The object is to get the pitcher or catcher to throw to first or second base, where the trailing runner gets in a rundown. During the rundown, the runner at third races home. The play is almost always attempted with two outs and a weak hitter at the plate. Obviously, a lot can go wrong with it, and even when executed at the perfect time, it is still a low-success play.

The first-and-third double steal is a lot like the suicide squeeze, with one player giving himself up to buy time for the runner at third to cross home.

There's not much to say about these sorts of trick plays. They rarely succeed, and they're attempted generally just a few times a year. They're not intended to be used often, though they're the kind of play you need to execute every once in a while to remain unpredictable without seriously crippling your offense day in and day out.

7. Instructing the batter
Sometimes, the best play the manager can put on is the one fans rarely see: ordering the batter at the plate to swing away or to take the next pitch. Instructions to the hitter are valuable, not just on 3-0 when the next ball could put a runner on base, but also in terms of helping the hitter at the plate work a favorable count.

The average major leaguer, in 1997, hit .346/.470/.576 when ahead in the count, which is basically a typical MVP year from Ken Griffey or Barry Bonds. On the other hand, the average major leaguer hit .204/.211/.304 when down in the count and .187/.261/.285 with two strikes, which is more reminiscent of the average pitcher.

Now what manager wouldn't relish the opportunity to pinch hit Ken Griffey for his pitcher without any cost to the team whatsoever?

That's what flashing the "take" sign on 1-1 can do for a hitter. If the batter is a free swinger and would have waved at a pitch out of the zone, he drops to 1-2, where he's almost certain to be out. By putting on the "take" sign, the hitter is now ahead 2-1 in the count and can look for his pitch to drive.

Of course, if the pitch is across the plate, the hitter is now down 1-2 and at a big disadvantage. So the call is a gamble, but a gamble with a consistent payoff to the manager who knows how to pick his spots. It's one of the subtle elements that separate a good manager from a mediocre one.

8. Running aggressively

There a couple of kinds of aggressive running.

Every player ought to run hard, dig hard around the bases on two-out fly balls and run out even routine grounders.

That sort of aggressive running comes without cost; there is no downside to requiring a player to play hard, unless that player is injured and is being brought along slowly. With that exception, there is simply no excuse for a ballplayer who isn't "aggressive" in that sense.

But there is another sort of aggressive base running; it's the kind that waves in a slow runner rounding third against Raul Mondesi's arm, or that sends Mark Grace from first to third on a line single to right.

That sort of running often leads to base runners being criticized for getting thrown out on big plays. But it really is the manager who sets the tone for the risks his team takes on the base paths.

One complication is that fans like to see base runners take risks. So-called "station-to-station" baseball is often derided as predictable and boring.

I'll admit, the tactics that are appropriate for the modern game often aren't as flashy and unpredictable as those that grew out of the dead-ball decades. Is that a loss for us? Base stealing, suicide squeezes, hit-and-runs are undeniably fun to watch. And while I don't believe that the winning managers of that era were any more clever than their modern counterparts, their cleverness was more obvious and accessible to the fan.

But the real value of those tactics is that they were appropriate in their era. They were winning strategies. And they aren't any longer appropriate, not in today's game, though they have persisted for decades after they stopped being useful.

I do see signs that some teams and managers have grasped the realities of today's game, if only imperfectly.

For example, until around 1975, conventional wisdom held that the manager should bat his fastest player in the leadoff slot, and put the guy with the best "bat control" in the second spot in order to bunt or hit-and-run the leadoff man over if he got on.

That strategy in the art of lineup construction made sense in an era when scoring one run often meant the ball game, but it long outlived its usefulness and remained popular even into the '80s. Now we see it much less frequently; managers are catching on that the prime requirement for the top of the order is to get on base as often as possible to set up the big sluggers in the 3-4-5 slots.

As long as everybody in the sport clung to dead ball tactics and strategies, there was no penalty for failing to grasp the reality of the changing game. Now that some managers have begun to do it right, though, the old methods will become losing methods. And losing managers don't stay around long.

I believe that fans will adjust to the new realities as well. After all, winning is fun. Call me crazy, but if I were a Mariners' fan, I would much rather watch Ken Griffey hit a clutch two-out, two-run homer than see Joey Cora lay down a sacrifice bunt.

Defensive Strategy, Risk and `Little Ball'

Wh*hen his team is on the field, a manager can influence the game
five different ways to try to prevent runs from scoring. They are:

1. Relieving the pitcher
2. Making defensive substitutions
3. Ordering a particular pitch
4. Changing a fielder's positioning
5. Holding base runners

Mostly, these defensive strategies come at a lower cost than the high-
risk plays a team can employ when at bat. But that does not mean that
defensive strategies have no risk.

Going to the bullpen
Many of the changes in baseball that I've highlighted in this book are
evolutionary. They occur slowly, so that the game we watch today does-
n't seem much different than the game we watched ten or twenty years
ago. The increase in offense is one example. There were home runs in
1968; there are home runs today. Today we have more homers, but unless
you study the rights stats from year to year, the difference probably isn't
going to be apparent.

But the approach to relief pitching that we have seen over the last twenty-five years is not incremental: it is revolutionary. Even a casual fan can notice the difference, because it has brought about a change in the way the game is played from day to day.

In 1975, Catfish Hunter completed thirty of his thirty-nine starts, earning a decision in every game in which he pitched but two. Five pitchers completed twenty or more games. In 1975, Ferguson Jenkins gave up four runs a game, lost eighteen games, and still completed twenty-two of thirty-seven starts.

Compare that to 1997, when Montreal's Pedro Martinez led the NL with thirteen complete games. In the AL, it was even more stark, with co-leaders Roger Clemens and Pat Hentgen of Toronto completing just nine. And other than Clemens and Hentgen, no American Leaguer completed more than five games that year.

Twenty-five years ago, starters were expected to finish games. Today, a complete game is a rarity. Twenty-five years ago, the phrase "seven-inning pitcher" was an insult; today, it's a compliment.

Today, the most visible — and probably the most important — defensive action for a manager to take in today's game of baseball is deciding when to replace his pitcher, and with whom.

A manager really has two jobs when managing his relievers. First, he wants the most effective man possible. But, equally important, he must manage the bullpen so as to keep arms fresh and healthy.

This usually demands a balancing act, since the most effective pitchers will usually be the most often used — or overused.

The revolution in relief pitching has been driven in part by managers seeking platoon advantages. With most pitchers and hitters, the platoon effect is small, but significant. Individual matchups can occasionally turn around the advantage. Some lefties actually have more success getting out right-handers. Some right-handed hitters hit right-handed pitching better than they hit left-handed pitching.

The right-handed Eric Davis, for example, has hit .284/.368/.497 against lefties over the past five years, and an even-better .298/.379/.533 against lefties. Given that you have to rest Davis fairly frequently to keep him ready, most managers try to time it so that he's sitting down against a righty and playing where he has a "platoon advantage." But the manager's intuition is wrong here. Davis has always had a "reverse platoon split" and played better against right-handers than against lefties.

A good manager will recognize situations when the general rules don't apply. And that's true for pitchers, as well as batters. In 1998, the Texas Rangers had lefty Eric Gunderson and righty Xavier Hernandez pitching in middle relief. Against Gunderson, lefties hit .297/.331/.517; against Hernandez, lefties hit .213/.354/.338.

How often do you see teams bring in Xavier Hernandez instead of Eric Gunderson to pitch to Ken Griffey?

As I mentioned in the previous chapter, the defensive manager can always be outmaneuvered by the team at bat when he makes a pitching change, because the rules require a relief pitcher to face at least one batter, while the batter can be pitch-hit for at will.

So, going to the bullpen has several potential costs. Obviously, it leaves one fewer pitcher available for later, cutting down on a manager's options later in the game. Any given individual matchup might not create the advantage the manager expects. And the move opens up the possibility that the opposing manager will bring in a pinch hitter for a large platoon advantage that can't be trumped.

There's another cost to using relievers, and that has to do with how players hold up over the long haul of a 162-game season. Having a good bullpen is analogous to having a good bench; it's not just having one or two players who are extremely reliable, but making sure that the fourth and fifth (or sixth and seventh, on some teams) guys can contribute, too.

In recent years, those who track baseball statistics have begun to pay a bit of attention to relievers. It is now relatively easy, for example, to find out how many pitches a reliever threw yesterday, and how well that pitcher fared as his arm wore down. Of course, what a manager *does* with that information is another story. Consider the 1998 Baltimore Orioles, for example, who featured the frequently ineffective right-hander Terry Mathews in their bullpen. Mathews was cast in the role of long reliever for two reasons: he didn't throw overpoweringly hard, and he was the worst right-handed pitcher in the bullpen.

But even a cursory look at Mathews' numbers would have revealed how ill-suited he was for that role. For his career, in long relief outings Mathews' opponents hit .295/.377/.574 against him — nearly 200 points of OPS worse than in other situations.

Mathews clearly was most effective when he threw a minimum number of pitches. By using him in long relief, the Orioles virtually guaranteed that he would fail. Mathews struggled along to a 6.20 ERA before he was released. Had the Orioles limited Mathews to situations in which he was effective, I believe that he could have been an asset instead of a liability.

The Orioles were never going to be able to turn Terry Mathews into Mariano Rivera. But he could have been used much more sensibly. Nothing is more frustrating than watching a team use a player in such a way as to minimize his strengths and maximize his flaws.

Another long-term view of relief pitchers has to do with how frequently a pitcher is worked. Here, the manager's temptation is easy to understand: if you've got a player who's unquestionably effective, you want to use him as often as possible to get the job done. On the other hand, the harder a pitcher is worked throughout the year, the more likely he is to break down.

Consider the fates of the following relievers, all of whom pitched eighty or more effective relief innings in 1996. Note how many of them were unable to maintain their '96 levels over the next two years.

Pitcher	1996		1997		1998	
	IP	ERA	IP	ERA	IP	ERA
Toby Borland	90.2	4.07	3.1	13.50	9	5.00
Rafael Carmona	90.1	4.28	5.2	3.18	—	
Tony Castillo	95	3.60	62.1	4.91	27	8.00
Roberto Hernandez	84.2	1.91	80.2	2.45	71.1	4.04
Trevor Hoffman	88	2.25	81.1	2.66	73	1.48
Mike James	81	2.67	62.2	4.31	14	1.93
Richie Lewis	90.1	4.18	81.2	9.64	4.2	15.43
Barry Manuel	86	3.24	25.2	5.26	15.2	7.47
T.J. Mathews	83.2	3.01	74.2	3.01	72.2	4.58
Greg McMichael	86.2	3.22	87.2	2.98	68	4.10
Dave Mlicki	90	3.30	193.2	4.02	181.1	4.57
Mike Mohler	81	3.67	101.2	5.13	61	5.16
Robb Nen	83	1.95	74	3.89	88.2	1.52
Antonio Osuna	84	3.00	61.2	2.19	64.2	3.06
Mariano Rivera	107.2	2.09	71.2	1.88	61.1	1.91

Pitcher	1996 IP	1996 ERA	1997 IP	1997 ERA	1998 IP	1998 ERA
Mel Rojas	81	3.22	85.1	4.64	58	6.05
Ken Ryan	89	2.43	20.2	9.58	22.2	4.37
Jeff Shaw	104.2	2.49	94.2	2.38	85	2.12
Heathcliff Slocumb	83.1	3.02	75	5.16	67.2	5.32
Bob Wickman	95.2	4.42	95.2	2.73	82.1	3.72

My point isn't that eighty innings pitched is some kind of death toll for pitchers, but a manager does need to be aware of the long term every time he gets his pitchers throwing hard in the bullpen.

Let's take a closer look at one of the better pitchers on that above list, the Yankees' Mariano Rivera:

Year	G	IP	H	R	ER	HR	BB	K	W	L	SV	ERA	K/9	WHIP
1996	61	107.2	73	25	25	1	34	130	8	3	5	2.09	10.87	0.994
1997	66	71.2	65	17	15	5	20	68	6	4	43	1.88	8.54	1.186
1998	54	61.1	48	13	13	3	17	36	3	0	36	1.91	5.28	1.064

Obviously, Rivera is a terrific pitcher. But Rivera hasn't been quite as dominant since throwing 107 2/3 innings in 1996. He has suffered through arm injuries from time to time, hitting the DL in 1998.

Was it the innings pitched?

There's another aspect of using relief pitchers. Teams should track how often the relief pitcher gets up in the bullpen to loosen up, and number of warm-up tosses he throws. Although the first bullpen toss probably isn't thrown at full strength, the last few are.

Moreover, some managers will start a reliever throwing at the first sign of trouble, sit him back down if he's not needed, then get him back up throwing again an inning or two later. This may be even more tiring on a pitcher's arm. We don't have any way to know this, because, as far as I know, no team monitors usage in these situations. But take a look at the panicky manager who has always got two arms going in the pen. Study how often if his pitchers break down and lose their effectiveness. Even if his staff shows no obvious pattern of injury, he may find himself with a bullpen full of tired arms by mid-August.

186

Defensive substitutions

Conventional wisdom holds that the manager makes defensive substitutions in the late innings of close ball games. In this way, the manager gives the superior hitter three or four at-bats, and, when sitting on a lead with just a few outs left to go, brings in the better fielder to protect that lead.

I think conventional wisdom has it exactly right, for once. Ideally, the manager replaces a second-rate defensive player immediately after his last at-bat, and gets the best of both worlds.

I think this conventional wisdom would be effective in creating a sort of "defensive platoon." Here's how it would work: generally, even when a team has a light-hitting everyday shortstop (let's call him Deivi Cruz), that team will still often carry an equally light-hitting utility infielder who can also play shortstop (say, Billy Ripken). In terms of long-term development, the team wants Cruz to be the starter, but from game-to-game, there isn't really much difference between Deivi and Billy.

So what happens when Cruz comes to plate with runners on first and second and nobody out in the third inning? The manager generally gets to choose between the equally unappetizing options of allowing Cruz to swing away or instructing him to bunt.

Since you have a good defensive replacement, why not go to a pinch hitter? This gives you a chance to put a big inning on the board. Going to the bench early ensures that you'll get a platoon advantage (the opposing manager isn't going to take out an effective pitcher in the fifth inning just for platoon purposes, but he might in the seventh).

Yes, it uses up two players. But one was the utility infielder, who doesn't figure prominently into most games anyway, and the other was a pinch hitter in a key pinch hitting situation. With luck, you can limit the number of at-bats per game for Cruz and Ripken to two or three, and that's really the goal, isn't it?

Just a thought.

Calling pitches from the dugout

Managers don't usually call pitches from the dugout, but maybe they should. I believe that tracking individual pitches for hitters offers some possibilities of hidden advantages that a smart manager could exploit. Knowing that Paul O'Neill has swung at seventy-two left-handed sliders and missed seventy-one of them would sure be a good bit of info to have, wouldn't it?

You'd probably lean out of the dugout and signal "slider" to Ron Mahay, and maybe win a ball game if O'Neill strikes out.

I don't know that Paul O'Neill is 1-for-72 on left-handers' sliders, but I have no doubt that tracking individual pitches would uncover a lot of hidden advantages that a smart manager could exploit if he called some pitches from the dugout.

A laptop computer with a cellular modem would be a fine tool for tracking pitches. Finally, a real job for those bench coaches teams keep on the payroll. If you're really ambitious, hire a few part-time scouts to watch game broadcasts from around the country (nearly every big league game is televised these days) and let them track pitches and upload their data to the central database in the clubhouse.

What would that cost for a season? Maybe $250,000, tops? The price you pay for one forty-year-old with a 7.00 ERA that you sign to a non-roster invitation to spring training hoping he can squeeze one more year out of his dead arm?

I've asked a bunch of people why managers shouldn't track pitches and look for an edge by calling pitches from the dugout, and I've never gotten an answer better than the one your ten-year-old might give you for not wearing his helmet and knee pads while skateboarding: "It looks weird." Or, the slightly more-adult equivalent: "Calling pitches from the dugout might undermine the confidence of your players."

I'm not saying that the manager should call every pitch from the dugout; that probably *would* undermine confidence to a great degree. But calling the right pitch, at the right time, to save a ball game — why not, if you had the data to back up the calls?

The intentional walk is one time when today's managers today do call pitches from the dugout. (Another, of minor long-term significance, is the pitchout.) I know at least one scenario in which nearly all managers make the wrong call on intentional walks.

Consider the following:

It's a tie game, bottom of the ninth, with runners on second and third and two outs. At the plate is the number-eight hitter, the third baseman, who's hitting .260/.325/.425, with fifteen homers and sixty-five RBI. On deck is the ninth-place hitter, the shortstop, who's hitting .225/.300/.325, with three homers, twenty-five RBI.

Now, assuming that the shortstop doesn't have a big advantage in speed

188

and that there are no pinch hitters on the bench ready to come in, what's the proper call for the manager whose team is in the field?

Before you answer, remember that in this case, the opposing team needs to score only one run, and the defensive team needs to record one out.

Hint: those power numbers for the third baseman at the plate are a distraction. Whether he hits a single, a double, or a homer is irrelevant: anything off his bat that isn't an out is going to score the winning run. Now what are the odds that this happens? That's right, his batting average — 26%.

If you walk the third baseman, though, that loads the bases. Now, not only does a hit drive in the winning run, but so does a walk, a wild pitch, a hit batsman, anything. In that situation, what's important is the number-nine hitter's OBP — which is .300.

In other words, walking a much better hitter to get to a much worse one actually *increases* the chances that the winning run will score from 26% to 30%. And yet nearly every every big-league manager would go with the "by-the-book" play — and, possibly, cost his team the game.

Positioning fielders

In about thirty seconds after I log onto the Internet, I can pull up a defensive hit chart on ESPN's Web site that shows the location of *every* ball Al Martin has hit and where it has landed. Do you think that knowledge might help a manager in deciding where to deploy Barry Bonds?

Yet I believe that most managers either don't have this data, or disregard it if they do.

One common positioning decision is whether the corner infielders should guard the lines during extra innings. Everyone knows that if you guard the lines, you trade off extra-large holes in the infield for the opportunity to cut off potential doubles down the line.

Most managers make this decision based on the inning and the score. In the late innings, with the score close, they'll guard the lines. Otherwise, their instruct the corner infielders to "play normally."

This is, frankly, an idiotic approach. The right way to decide whether to guard the lines is to know how often the batter hits a ball down the lines.

Consider the following situation. You're managing the Texas Rangers, clinging to a one-run lead over the Chicago White Sox in the bottom of the ninth, with one out. Speedy second baseman Ray Durham is on first, and Frank Thomas is at the plate. Do you guard the lines?

A quick look at Thomas' hit chart shows that he rarely goes the other way down the first base line. So why move your first baseman a step or two to the left and increase the risk that Thomas will get a cheap single to prevent an almost nonexistent risk that he'll double to right?

Managers have to make these sorts of mental tradeoff decisions for themselves, but it's folly to do so without fully understanding the costs and benefits.

Holding runners on

Holding runners on first base comes at a real cost.

It takes the first baseman out of his optimal defensive position. And each snap throw to first base not only incurs the slight risk of a throwing error, but also takes a bit out of the pitcher's arm. These effects add up when a pitcher is putting twelve or thirteen men on base.

Yet most managers hold the runner at first, no matter whether he's a threat to steal.

I would hold runners much more selectively, particularly if my catcher had a strong, accurate throwing arm. If Russ Davis really thinks that an extra half-step will help him steal second against Rodriguez's arm, I'm more than happy to let him try. Even with a weak-armed catcher behind the plate, I would hold runners a lot less than most contemporary managers do.

Remember the way we looked at stealing bases, as a tradeoff of on-base percentage against slugging? Holding runners works the same way. In effect, by opening up a hole on the right side, you are cutting down the number of runners who advance by steals (which is to say, you're reducing your opponent's SLG) at a cost of allowing more runners to reach base (that is, you are increasing the opposing team's OBP). In today's game of big league baseball, giving a team extra OBP to reduce SLG is a really bad tradeoff. Stealing second just isn't that important, but having an extra man on first with Juan Gonzalez due up certainly is.

Just as "little ball" offensive strategies that run big risks to gain an extra base are, by and large, a waste of time in '90s baseball, so are "little ball" defensive strategies that are designed to prevent the extra base at the expense of shifting the defensive alignment all over the field, putting another runner on base, or opening up a big hole in the field.

17

Filling Out the Lineup Card

"The general idea is that a guy who can get on base and run makes a good lead-off hitter; a guy with good bat control, who can bunt and hit-and-run is a desirable second-place hitter; the RBI men bat third, fourth, and fifth ... and the weaker batters fill out the order."
— Tim McCarver, *Baseball for Brain Surgeons*

"**B**aseball is a game of firsts," says broadcaster and former catcher Tim McCarver. He notes that "the team that scores first wins two-thirds of the games." And sure enough, right there in the STATS 1998 Baseball Scoreboard, there's an essay entitled "How Important Is It to Score First?" calculating that, from 1986 through 1997, teams scoring first have won 66.4 percent of their games.

There are several ways to interpret that figure. To McCarver, it means that the first run is a huge psychological advantage. This explains why McCarver — and countless managers since the dawn of baseball — have set up their lineups in order to maximize the opportunities for employing "little ball" strategies designed to scratch a single run across the board, *first*.

192

And isn't this a winning strategy, as proven by the STATS essay? Not necessarily. If Juan Gonzalez hits a grand slam in top of the first inning and Texas goes on to score nine runs against Chris Haney, that counts as his "team scoring first." If Omar Vizquel singles home Kenny Lofton in the bottom of the eleventh of an 0-0 game in Cleveland, that also counts. Neither of those two scenarios seems to be particularly convincing evidence that Edgardo Alfonzo should bunt in the top of the first. At least, not to me.

So, following up on the STATS essay, I decided to take a look at the fortunes of teams which score the second run of the ball game, and then the third, and then the fourth, and so on. That way, Gonzalez's slam can be placed into its proper context (although it still doesn't help us much in scoreless ball games heading into the bottom of the ninth).

Over the past decade, teams scoring the second run of the game won more 70% of games — *regardless of whether they scored the first run*. Teams scoring the third also won more than 70%. As did those scoring the fourth and the fifth. In fact, that is true for the team scoring every run up to number nine.

In other words, the advantages of scoring first are even greater if you score more than a single run. Taken in this light, the strategy of playing for one run just to score the first run of the game seems less attractive. While "little ball" strategies may slightly improve the odds of scoring a single run in an inning, they severely *decrease* the chance that you'll score multiple runs. A team that gives up the opportunity to score the second and third and fourth runs of the game, in order to increase the chance of scoring the first, is almost certainly hurting itself.

That's baseball in the 1990s. And that's why contemporary managers ought to reject the time-honored strategy of setting lineups designed to score the mystical *first* run in exchange for a lineup designed to score the *most* runs.

The first-run, one-run approach is part of the rationale behind the traditional approach to lineup construction, in which the team's fastest player often hits first, followed by a hitter with good bat control, who can move the runner along on a bunt, hit-and-run or grounder to the right side.

The conventional wisdom on lineups is that you don't want to "waste your power" by hitting it at the top of the order, that your team's best hitter bats third and the next-best power threats hit fourth, fifth and so on.

The conventional wisdom — although it is changing — has a set of characteristics that players in each spot of the order are supposed to exhibit. But are these characteristics valid?

We know that the higher a player hits in the order, the more times he'll come to the plate. On average, a team's leadoff hitter(s) will accumulate 750 plate appearances over the course of a season, while the number nine slot will come to the plate 580 times. The full chart looks something like this:

Batting #1:   750 PA
Batting #2:   725 PA
Batting #3:   710 PA
Batting #4:   700 PA
Batting #5:   680 PA
Batting #6:   660 PA
Batting #7:   640 PA
Batting #8:   625 PA
Batting #9:   580 PA

In 1998, when St. Louis Cardinals' manager Tony LaRussa curiously began batting his pitcher eighth, few commentators mentioned the obvious cost, which is to give the worst hitter on the team another forty-five at-bats.

My thesis on lineup construction is fairly simple: you should bat your best hitter at the top of the order, your second-best hitter in the second spot, and so on. I wonder why this isn't standard. Why would any team not want its best hitter to come to the plate as often as possible?

Having said that, I have to add that lineup construction is a minor consideration in how many runs a team scores. I have run thousands of simulations to test lineup combinations. The variance in runs scored for a team employing the optimal lineup (in descending order of OPS), and the team employing the very worst order possible, was generally on the order of thirty runs or less. That's about three wins over the course of a season, and that's assuming extreme cases.

In 1996, Mike Hargrove would often bat Omar Vizquel second and Manny Ramirez seventh or eighth; that's about a hundred extra plate appearances that could have gone to a guy with a .950 OPS instead of a guy with a guy with a .715 OPS.

194

The Indians still scored a ton of runs, of course.

And that's part of the enduring lesson of Earl Weaver and other Hall of Fame managers. The most influence a manager can have is not in deciding whether to bat a player second or sixth, but in deciding *whether to play him at all.*

That said, here are some considerations in lineup construction.

Leading off

In the American League, it's possible to minimize the damage of your team's worst hitter. By batting him ninth all season, and pinch hitting for him whenever you have the opportunity, you can reduce that player's total plate appearances to about 450.

However, many teams persist in *leading off* their worst hitter, if he is also a base stealing threat. That is what the 1998 Tigers did with Brian Hunter, and what the 1998 Pirates did with Tony Womack, conforming to the conventional wisdom that you want your leadoff hitter to be a speedy guy who can put himself into scoring position.

Even if you really like the bunt, the hit-and-run, and other "little ball" strategies, you do really think they're worth giving 300 extra plate appearances to the worst hitter on the team?

But we've already talked about why baseball in the '90s makes it less important than ever to have a speedy guy at the top of the order. In 1998, the Seattle Mariners persisted in leading off their worst hitter, Joey Cora, because of his speed. Behind Cora in the lineup were Alex Rodriguez, Ken Griffey, and Edgar Martinez., a total of 250 extra-base hits, including 127 home runs.

Lou Piniella's decision to start Cora in the leadoff slot first came at a double cost. First was the risk of running him into an out in front of one of those extra-base hits. Even more damaging, though, were the scoring opportunities which the Mariners lost by not having a high-OBP hitter in front of all those extra-base hits.

Batting second

Traditionally, teams would reserve this spot for their best "bat control" guy, someone who puts the ball into play by not striking out, and who can bunt the leadoff man into scoring position if necessary. Tim McCarver gives the conventional explanation: "The plan is for the leadoff man to get on base and for the second batter to either take pitches so he can steal or move him along with a sacrifice bunt, productive out, or hit-and-run." McCarver's views of the game were shaped by the pitching-dominated 1960s. His reasoning is basically that teams should set up their lineups in order to use one-run strategies in the first and second innings. Gradually, as offense has increased, teams have started to learn that this doesn't make sense with all the big hits waiting at the heart of the order.

The RBI guys

Any manager who fills out the 3-4-5 slots by automatically filling it with his roster's three highest RBI producers is going at it all backwards.

At the risk of overkill, I'll repeat that there's really no such creature as a "good RBI man." Any decent hitter in the middle of a lineup with a high OBP is going to drive in plenty of runs, and if he does it by making outs he is actually hurting his team. The RBI total of a particular player is irrelevant: the only offensive stat that really matters to the outcome of a season is the number of runs the team scores overall.

And a "top-down" which gives maximum plate appearances to a team's best hitters will almost always score the most runs possible.

Don't just take my word for it. If you have a fairly reliable stats-based computer baseball program, load up your favorite team, plug in a "traditional" lineup, run a season, and note the team's total Runs Scored. Now plug in a "top-down" lineup in descending order of OPS, and run a season. Run the simulation twice. Run it ten times. Or, if you're like me, run it more than a thousand times.

You'll see that the team's overall total of runs scored increases with the top-down lineup. Yeah, you get some weird individual results, like Ken Griffey averaging around 80 RBI, but on the whole, the power Griffey "wastes" by having fewer men on base is made up by (a) having him come to the plate an extra fifty times, and (b) not having guys like Joey Cora and Roberto Kelly making outs in front of Edgar Martinez, Alex Rodriguez and Jay Buhner.

Two teams have seriously bucked conventional wisdom in the past few years with no harm to their offense. The 1997 Boston Red Sox lead off .306/.342/.534 Nomar Garciaparra and scored 851 runs; the 1996 Baltimore Orioles lead off .297/.396/.637 Brady Anderson and scored 949 runs. Both of those teams essentially employed a partial "top-down" lineup by batting their best hitter leadoff. And both scored a ton of runs.

The rest of the order

The #7 spot is really the ideal place for that speedy, slap-hitting weak hitter who used to leadoff. If there's only a small difference between the worst hitter and the second- and third-worst hitters on the team, then I'd bat the fastest guy of the three in the seven slot, so that I could put on all those fun "little ball" strategies with the *worst* hitters due up — which is when those strategies might actually make some sense.

Of course, if I were managing a team, I would try my best to avoid having hitters so bad that they make these strategies worthwhile!

Another tactic gaining in popularity these days is trying to alternate lefty and righty hitters, so that a team can't bring in specialty left-hander like Tony Fossas or Paul Assenmacher to shut down three or four left-handed hitters in a row. If you have essentially identical hitters for a couple of spots, you can gain a tiny advantage by alternating them lefty-righty this way. But it shouldn't come at the cost of batting weaker hitters ahead of good ones.

The pitcher

The pitcher should bat ninth. Period.

Sorry, Tony.

PART SIX

THE GM

What's He Worth?

"The game is so fundamentally unfair because its leaders have never figured out a legal way to stop the high rollers from keeping up with the other high rollers, never mind the middle-to-low rollers ... Baseball is in a tough spot. Everybody knows these kinds of contracts [like the one that paid Kevin Brown $105 million over seven years] are wrong, wrong, wrong — unless everybody can pay them. And nobody knows what to do about the teams that can't."
— Michael Knisley, *The Sporting News*, December 16, 1998

This chapter and the one that follows it are about money.

If you're a real baseball fan, your first instinct will be to start flipping past these pages to get back to "the good stuff." Sports fans are sick of hearing about money matters in sports. Money means disgustingly high salaries, strikes, lockouts, inflated ticket prices, the relocation of franchises.

Fans don't want to hear about money.

Yet big league baseball is a business as well as a sport, and money determines the quality of the game we love. You can't really understand major league baseball today unless you also understand how that business is run. Money, and how teams spend it, literally determines the won-loss record of your favorite team, although money alone doesn't buy success. To emphasize the truth of that statement, in the chapter after this I will discuss how the Baltimore Orioles managed to turn the highest payroll in baseball history into a sub-.500 season in 1998.

But here I'll deal more generally with how money influences the game played on the field. And the place to start is with salaries those outlandish, ridiculous salaries which most fans seem to resent.

Fortune magazine once estimated that Michael Jordan's career had a $10 billion impact on the U.S. economy. This meant that Jordan had encouraged ordinary consumers to purchase tickets to basketball games they otherwise wouldn't have attended, to purchase merchandise and memorabilia bearing his likeness, and to purchase products endorsed by Michael. And then there are spill-over effects. When all those new fans are at basketball games, chances are good that they're going to buy a hot dog or a beer, or maybe a T-shirt.

It all adds up to ten billion dollars.

That's an awful lot of money. (And it doesn't even touch on the effect of Jordan's *international* popularity.)

The *Washington Post* reported a private market research study showing that, in California, the *back* of Jordan's head is more recognizable than the *face* of President Bill Clinton. To paraphrase Joseph Heller, even if that study is a lie, it is a very impressive lie, and it speaks volumes about Jordan that such a claim can be repeated with a straight face.

So where does all the money go? Well, approximately $80 million per year went to Jordan — $35 million as his yearly salary from the Bulls, and another $45 million from other sources in endorsements.

Eighty million dollars. Was that a fair salary for Jordan to earn?

It depends on what you mean by the word "fair." One common argument — although, strangely enough, not one that's often applied to Michael Jordan — is that people ought to be paid based on some sort of subjective sense of the moral value of the work they perform. Jordan played a game for a living, and it's wrong that playing a game (and making commercials resulting from the popularity earned playing a game) can earn one person $80 million dollars a year, while an experienced and talented high school teacher might earn only $30,000. Isn't teaching our youth more important than playing a game?

I think this argument touches a nerve to some degree with almost everyone. Personally, I can't believe Lisa Kudrow gets $100,000 to airhead her way through each painful episode of "Friends," but I suppose that's another book entirely. The point is that, at some level, it just seems wrong to pay blinding amounts of money to someone who's doing something that, at its core, is kind of silly. For almost everyone, sports or music or television is a hobby, not a profession.

What this argument always misses is that the money created by Jordan or Kudrow has to go *somewhere*. If it doesn't go to the stars themselves, then where does it wind up?

That's right: in the hands of the stars' employers.

If Michael Jordan created $10 billion in wealth, and was paid $80 million for it, that left a staggering $9.92 billion completely unaccounted for. In order words, 99.2% of Jordan's value wound up in the hands of someone else — Jerry Reinsdorf, Nike, McDonald's, MCI, Warner Brothers, you name it.

All Jordan may have done was play a game, but all Jerry Reinsdorf did was *hire the guy* who played a game. Isn't that an extra order of magnitude of silliness? If we can't imagine paying millions to a guy to engage in a hobby, can we imagine paying billions to a guy who bankrolls that hobby?

My software company, Arbutus Sports Labs, is currently producing a baseball game. (Not a joke. Run to the store and buy it, if you can.) My goal in marketing "ASL Baseball" isn't to share the market with a bunch of other baseball programs; it's to make a product so good that nobody buys the others anymore. I stand to gain nothing if you plunk down forty or fifty bucks on "Hardball" or "Triple Play" or "Front Page" or any of the other competing products. Indeed, the more money you spend on them, the less likely you are to buy *my* product. I feel a little like Ross Perot, but this is a pretty good four-sentence summary of what capitalism is all about.

And in contrast, major league baseball *isn't* a very good example of capitalism in action. The Yankees' survival depends on the continued existence of other teams in the American League. The Dodgers' profitability isn't enhanced if Montreal and Milwaukee are pounded into oblivion. Competing teams in baseball need each other.

But there are problems when one team is more successful than another and thus generates more revenue. The more successful team can then reinvest more money into its business, signing more players and cementing its advantage over its competitors.

In theory, when this economic advantage is small, it can be offset by other rules that penalize the victor. For example, when a team signs a certain class of free agents, it forfeits a first-round draft pick, and the team from which the player was signed also earns an additional "supplemental" draft pick. Rules like these are supposed to help compensate a Montreal when its top star signs with the Dodgers.

However, this theory only works when the economic disparity is relatively small. In the current state of affairs, where teams draw grossly disproportionate shares of the total revenues generated, the rules simply aren't enough to rein in the enormous advantage of spending extra money.

This isn't to say that some teams aren't crying wolf. Some cities suffer from self-fulfilling prophecies. "Small-market baseball" has become perjorative shorthand for "can't afford to pay star players." So when owners complain that they're "small-market," they're running down their own product. And then they wonder why fans aren't showing up to the ballpark.

You know by now that I believe that teams tend to overvalue veteran players, and are too reluctant to use younger ones. Still, it's hard to win without some stars, which means that a severe imbalance is bad for both the sport and the business of big league baseball.

The solution, to me, is simple: redistribute some of the money from the Yankees to the Royals.

This is what the luxury tax was supposed to do. Unfortunately, it only helps the sport if the teams which receive the "tax" money actually use it to improve their rosters. But in 1998, teams aided by the luxury tax tended to pocket the money rather than reinvest it in their flagging teams. Montreal's payroll went *down* after it received its cash infusion. If you're George Steinbrenner or Peter Angelos, that's got to be maddening. It's one thing to recognize (grudgingly) that your deep pockets should aid a team having difficulty keeping its lineup together, it's quite another to write a check that goes to the CEO's sixth Bentley or new house in Carmel.

So, in the wake of the obvious failure of the luxury tax to solve issues of competitive balance, we're starting to see all sorts of creative ideas for how to "fix what's wrong with baseball." These ideas run the gamut from the patently unfair (salary caps) to the insignificant (changes in free agency and draft compensation) to the utterly absurd (realignment by economics).

The best idea is still actually to redistribute wealth in a meaningful way. Switching to the NFL system in which all media revenues are allocated equally among teams, rather than varying wildly on the size of the respective team's "media market," is a great start. Stipulating that all transfers must be spent on payroll increases is another.

Owners have a different proposal. Rather than share revenue, they want to cap salaries. I think this would be disastrous for the game of baseball. By and large, major league owners have been able to couch the salary cap issue as a question of fairness — "Is it right that Player X should be earning $10 million dollars per year?" The Michael Jordan discussion was about showing that yes, sometimes it *is* right, in the sense that the alternative is even worse.

But I'm not against the salary cap primarily because it would be unfair to the players. If there were a way to improve greatly the game of baseball at the expense of a little unfairness, I'd probably be for it. Maybe that's excessively harsh, but my interest is in seeing the best game possible on the field.

That's why I like free agency. The disadvantage to free agency is in heightened team turnover. But I can't imagine anything less interesting than baseball in the 1950s, when the New York Yankees won every year. In the 1990s, baseball has been more competitive than its detractors would lead you to believe. The "large-market" New York Yankees and the "small-market" Toronto Blue Jays have the same number of World Championships. So do the large-market Braves and the small-market Marlins. Heck, even the much-maligned Minnesota Twins have one of those elusive rings.

Another effect of free agency is that players are getting paid closer to what they deserve for their abilities. Funny how that works; often, the fairest option also is the one that's best for the game and for the fans.

But a salary cap would *not* be good for the game, because it would artificially depress salaries of veteran players. This would encourage teams to re-sign fading stars to fill backup roles, instead of opening up opportunities for young players. Already, as you can tell from this book, I think AAA players get the short end of the stick. A salary cap breaks off an even smaller piece.

204

Here's the way a salary cap works: the collective-bargaining agreement would stipulate that teams cannot spend more than a certain amount on player salaries. Every team would be forced to have the same budget. For discussion purposes, let's assume that cap is $50 million. Now suppose that the Blue Jays have $45 million committed in payroll for the next year, and Carlos Delgado is a free agent. The Jays *cannot* offer Delgado more than $5 million.

Presuming that players comparable to Delgado are making $10 million, there are really three options for Delgado's future: (1) there is a team or teams with an interest in Delgado and $10 million or more available under the cap; (2) there is a team or teams with an interest in Delgado and less than $10 million but more than $5 million available under the cap; and (3) there are no teams with an interest in Delgado and at least $5 million available under the cap.

Only under scenario (1) does Delgado get his full market value. In scenario (2), Delgado signs with another team for, say, $8 million, which is an offer that the Blue Jays are factually and legally prevented from matching. In scenario (3), Delgado re-signs (unhappily) with the Blue Jays for about half of his "real" value.

No matter how frequently (1) occurs and how infrequently (2) and (3) occur, the net effect of a salary cap is to reduce players' salaries.

What happens to fourth outfielders and utility infielders under the salary cap? In today's market, veteran players command three to five times the major league minimum; teams so greatly prefer veterans to rookies that they're willing to pay this differential for the supposed stability the veteran brings.

But that salary differential means that teams can make meaningful choices, and plug in a David Dellucci instead of a Luis Gonzalez, or an Aaron Ledesma instead of a Rich Amaral. And, as more teams realize that their minor leagues contain players who can contribute and help at the major league level, more opportunities open up for guys like Dellucci and Ledesma.

Institute a salary cap, and that salary differential disappears. Late in the off-season, when teams have just a few thousand dollars left under the cap, veterans will face "take it or leave it" offers near the major league minimum. Sure, some of them will leave it, but a great many more simply hold their nose and take it.

If a team can get a veteran for the exact same salary as a minor leaguer, it will almost never play the rookie. Oh, sure, top stars will get their shots. But the underappreciated contributors, the guys who are good enough to play but not good enough to dominate, will continue to toil away as AAA roster fodder unless and until some lucky break strikes. Fate does not favor the Indianapolis Indians.

Shouldn't fans want player salaries to be kept down? Don't rising salaries lead to increased ticket prices?

The truth is that rising salaries do not cause teams to raise ticket prices. Baseball owners, like most business owners, want to maximize revenue and minimize costs. They set ticket prices with that goal in mind. Now, a team's per-game costs are practically fixed; the incremental cost of each additional fan is negligible. So in effect, this means that teams set ticket prices in order to maximize total revenue.

Total revenue is, quite simply, attendance multiplied by ticket price.

Imagine that 3.1 million fans are willing to pay $10 per ticket to see an Indians game. At $12 per ticket, the number of willing customers drops to 2.5 million, and at $15 per ticket, the fan base drops to just under two million.

In this scenario, a rational team will set ticket prices at $10, because that brings in $31 million in revenue. At $12 or $15 a ticket, the team loses more than a million dollars from the optimal ticket price.

But if an extra hundred thousand fans would pay $12 per ticket, then the team will raise ticket prices from $10 to $12. Even though the absolute attendance drops from 3.1 million to 2.6 million, the team's total revenues increase because those paying customers are paying two bucks more a head.

Now what happens when a team's payroll is set to increase without changing the demand for the team? Imagine that Bartolo Colon is now eligible for arbitration, and his estimated salary will increase by $5 million.

Would a rational team raise ticket prices to cover Colon's salary increase? No. The optimal ticket price is still $12. It just happens that the Indians will now make a lower profit on those $12 tickets. This happens to businesses all the time; costs increase while demand for the product stays constant. Businesses *can't* pass these costs on to the consumer, because doing so would just create worse economic conditions.

Of course, when a team signs Albert Belle to a $13 million contract, the positive publicity and increased expectations for that team generate increased interest — and thus, more demand for tickets. This means that teams can raise ticket prices, because its fans are willing to pay more for them.

But it's silly to suggest that Belle's salary caused the increase. Even if Belle were forced to sign for half as much money — say, because of a salary cap — his impact on demand would still be *exactly the same*. (Fans aren't paying to see Albert Belle because he makes a big salary; they want to watch him play because he is Albert Belle, regardless of his salary.) So the team that signed Albert for $6.5 million a year would still raise ticket prices just as much. The only difference would be added profit to the team's stockholders.

Like the redistribution issue, blaming ticket prices on player salaries is a smokescreen designed to obscure the real issue of who ought to get what share of the money. After all, when was the last time a team that slashed payroll also cut ticket prices?

Even under the current collective bargaining agreement, which does an insufficient job of redistributing wealth, baseball is not in the dire straits that some claim it to be. Even when one player's salary can exceed another team's entire payroll, the lower-revenue team still can be competitive and successful.

How?

The rest of this chapter is a six-step plan for turning "small-market" franchises into competitive clubs. The plan is not simple, but somebody still should have pulled it off by now.

Stop running down the product

Imagine the CEO for Pepsi throwing a press conference in which he announced that, due to the number of consumers buying Coke, Pepsi was now forced to cut costs and use untreated river water instead of purified water in its beverages. Or imagine MCI claiming that, to cut expenses caused by AT&T's dominance, they would now randomly disconnect calls during off-peak hours. Or General Motors announcing that, because of poor sales, all GM cars will be made with substandard, shoddy components.

Wouldn't that just make matters worse for Pepsi, MCI and General Motors?

Yet that's the message the Milwaukee Brewers, Montreal Expos and Minnesota Twins send every day. "We can't compete with the Yankees, so we have to slash payroll," they cry. Is it any wonder that fans aren't excited about going to the ballpark? Who wants to pay for a product that the producers themselves don't believe is top quality?

Why aren't the Brewers aggressively marketing their product? In a blue-collar town, wouldn't fans appreciate a young, hard-working, blue-collar team? Fans like watching young players develop, even if they struggle a bit. Mariners' fans once had the pleasure of watching Ken Griffey hit .260 as an eighteen-year-old.

It's frustrating to watch a whiny, overpaid millionaire refuse to run out a ground ball. Similarly, it's exhilarating to watch a teenager covered from head to toe in dirt, dive head-over-heels to snag a hot shot up the middle. That's the kind of players that Milwaukee needs to sign and promote.

Of course, above everything else, it's more fun to watch a winner than a loser.

Build a winner

If you can't buy a winning team, develop one. This means that lower-revenue clubs must do a better job of drafting and developing young talent, and develop an eye for identifying bargains in the market. The Expos and Pirates already have (mostly) tried to implement this strategy, aggressively trading away players with little or no long-term future for younger players, particularly pitchers.

Having many millions to spend creates a margin for error when roster-building; franchises with lesser resources cannot afford to make mistakes in their talent acquisition, and they have to be brutal about cutting their losses. When they err, it must be on the side of youth.

For teams with big budgets, the conservative, play-it-safe approach is to sign the "proven" veteran player rather than working in a youngster. Teams with limited resources must take the opposite approach. For them, the inexpensive minor leaguer is the safe choice, since they can't afford a multimillion, multi-year mistake. When the Pirates faced a decision a couple of years ago on the popular, still somewhat useful veteran Jeff King, they had to bite the bullet and allow King to depart via free agency. They couldn't afford the risk of having King take a big nosedive in the middle of a multi-year contract.

(Pittsburgh pursued this strategy faithfully until 1997, and then completely reversed itself after 1998, acquiring an old, useless, expensive third baseman in Ed Sprague.)

Under the current rules, teams get the first six years of a player's career at below-market salaries. As I've shown from the chapter on career curves, those first six years often include the best years of a player's career; after he's eligible for free agency, it's usually all downhill.

Hold on to the very best players

Not all players enter the downside of the career curve after their first six seasons. Sometimes small-market teams develop a Jason Kendall or a Vladimir Guerrero or a Pedro Martinez, players who come up very young and play well early. Such exceptional players will still be reaching the peak of their careers when they become eligible for free agency.

Smaller-market teams should sign such players early to long deals: this way, Pittsburgh, Milwaukee, Montreal and the other smaller-revenue franchises have a chance at the kind of elite superstar around which winning teams can be built. This way a smart team can short-circuit a process that otherwise favors big-market clubs.

The Montreal Expos failed to do this with Pedro Martinez, at great cost to their credibility.

I believe that Montreal was correct in moving good-but-expensive veteran players like Delino DeShields, John Wetteland, Mel Rojas, Marquis Grissom and even Moises Alou. Most of those guys can be replaced by good minor leaguers. Billy McMillon may deliver only 75% of Alou's production, but if he does it at a fiftieth of the cost, then he's precisely what the team needs.

But Martinez was different, a great young pitcher who showed every promise of being an elite performer for years. A team must make every effort to keep these special players. Their decision to trade Martinez ended all pretense of being of cleverly competitive. Obviously, the Expos were looking at nothing more than cutting cost.

This is disheartening to fans. When a good young player comes up, Montreal fans know that he's going to be traded away soon after he develops. You can't build a team solely with youngster at the start of their careers.

As this book is being written, the Expos have found themselves with another extraordinary young star, Vlad Guerrero, whom they would never be able to afford on the open market. If they turn around and trade him, as they did with Martinez, it will be yet another black mark on baseball.

Put up or shut up

If a team is going to cry poverty, it should be willing to open up its financial accounts to an independent auditor who can make a reasonable determination of the team's financial status. Since Wayne Huizenga just sold the Florida Marlins for a handsome profit, it strains credulity to think that all of these organizations bottoming out in payroll are hemorrhaging money faster than the Russian economy. But sometimes the truth is stranger than fiction, and if that's the case, teams shouldn't be afraid to prove it.

Right now, there are a lot of rich but stupid teams. In 1998, several completely worthless players were signed for $3 million and $4 million per year. Good players earned twice that, and very good players earned twice again. Which were overpaid?

I believe the three- and four-million-dollar guys most hurt the teams with limited budgets. Why on earth would the Pittsburgh Pirates, supposedly strapped for every penny, sign the worst everyday third baseman in baseball, Ed Sprague, who hit .222/.280/.403?

Far better to pay twice as much money to someone who actually could have helped the team. Indeed, if the Pirates had passed on Sprague and traded Al Martin and Tony Womack, that would have let them take on the salary of a Denny Neagle.

Instead, the team is stuck with overpaid players who are *worse* than the guys waiting to take their jobs in the minor leagues. At third base, for example, the Bucs have a star-in-waiting in Aramis Ramirez. In 1998, when Sprague was busy hitting .222 for Toronto and Oakland, Ramirez hit .235/.296/.351. And Ramirez did it as a nineteen-year-old.

There's no question that Ramirez, for 1999, is a better player than Sprague. Yet the cash-short Pirates paid Sprague several million dollars. Why?

Take advantage of the rules

Inadequate though they may be, major league baseball still has rules in place designed to help the small-revenue team that loses players. The biggest example is the draft compensation system.

The rules for free agent compensations are as follows:

The departing team must offer the potential free agent salary arbitration. If the departing team does not offer arbitration, it gets nothing in compensation. This sounds stupid, but every year plenty of teams fail to offer arbitration to bona fide stars whom they know are going to sign elsewhere. The 1996 Orioles didn't offer arbitration to Kevin Brown. The Pirates didn't offer arbitration to Barry Bonds, for crying out loud.

(On the other side of the coin are teams which sign mediocre free agents who have been offered arbitration by their former teams; these acquiring teams are then sacrificing a first-round draft pick for a spot player, which is a terrible tradeoff.)

Assuming the departing team offers arbitration, compensation is based upon a player's statistical rankings with the ELIAS Sports Bureau. Mostly, those rankings reward full-time play, no matter how incompetent it is.

Once a team has offered arbitration to a "Type A" free agent, it receives two draft picks from any other team which signs that player. The picks are a "sandwich pick" between the first and second rounds of the draft, and another from the first to the fifth round, subject to a somewhat complex formula.

A team can pile up a lot of excess draft picks in this fashion. It's a great way to begin to restock the farm system.

However, many small-revenue teams are so budget-conscious that they refuse to offer their players arbitration, and thus receive nothing in return when those players walk via free agency. Usually the excuse is, "We didn't want to get stuck with his salary."

Let's blow that alibi out of the water. No team has ever been forced to take a player in arbitration that it didn't want to keep. That has *never* happened. Unless the player in question is a totally useless performer who has just put up a fluke of a big statistical season, there's no chance that his old team will be "stuck" with him. It doesn't happen. The demand for free agents is just too great.

So, small-market teams, if you're listening:

OFFER YOUR PLAYERS ARBITRATION.

Thank you.

Another rule that exists to benefit smaller revenue teams is the Rule Five draft.

The Rule Five draft prevents teams from stockpiling minor leaguers forever. It works like this: when a team signs a player eighteen years old or younger, the club gets four "free" years of his development before being forced to add him to their forty-man roster, or risk losing him. If the player is nineteen or older, that team gets three "free" years. At the end of a player's free years, he must be added to the team's forty-man roster. Otherwise, he is available to be drafted.

Teams draft in reverse order of standings, and can draft as many rounds as they like until their rosters are filled. If your forty-man roster is already full, you can't draft. Each player selected during the Rule Five draft is purchased for $50,000; that player must be kept on the drafting team's major league roster all season, or is offered back to his original team for $25,000.

It's a great way to pick up cheap talent. Yet, incomprehensibly, small-revenue teams rarely take advantage. They often head into the Rule Five draft with their forty-man rosters filled, with spots taken up by veteran utility infielders, fourth outfielders, right-handed relievers and other essentially interchangeable parts. How much sense does that make? If you're Minnesota, put those guys on waivers and draft some kids through Rule Five.

Who should you draft during Rule Five? Well, considering that most of the players available haven't advanced to double-A, it's clear that whomever you take is probably going to struggle in the major leagues. And since he must stay on the major league roster all year, you want to pick someone with whom you can minimize the damage he'll do to your team *this* year in order to keep him for the year afterwards.

So who fits this profile? Catchers. Good defensive infielders who can play a utility role. Accomplished hitters with defensive liabilities.

What's the worst type of player to draft? Pitchers, of course. (Few teams can afford to keep a pitcher on the twenty-five-man roster and not use him in some important spots.) Yet every year, more than half of the Rule 5 draftees are pitchers, and more than three-quarters of those get returned to their original team. That's $25,000, just flushed down the drain. Any team with an extra $25,000 burning a hole in its pocket that it just wants to throw away is welcome to mail it to me, care of the address in the front of the book.

Is a team likely to find the next Ken Griffey in the Rule Five draft? Of course not. But it's an opportunity to redistribute talent from the haves to the have-nots. And every year, teams crying poverty and unfairness refuse to take advantage of the rules designed to help them.

Be patient

A smart team — and particularly a smart, revenue-conscious team — will find a way to work in productive minor leaguers at minimum salary rather than overpay a veteran major leaguer to do the same job at ten times the rate.

I'm not suggesting that all minor leaguers are untapped jewels, waiting for the right opportunity to become big-time stars. Most of them aren't. But most *are* good enough to match the production of the veteran who's playing out the string at $3 million a year.

Going for the young bargains allows you to free up money to get players who can really improve a team. If you can get 85% of the production of a $5 million right fielder at a tiny fraction of the cost, you can use the money you've saved to replace a weakness elsewhere in the lineup.

But there's a catch. As much as I like young players, I have to admit that breaking in a rookie requires tremendous patience and a willingness to accept a year or two of production near the bottom of the scale. Andruw Jones hit .250 in 1997 and .210 for the first month of '98. In fact, most star players have had at least one season of struggle at the start of their big league careers. If a team is going to rely on youth, either by design or through financial necessity, it must be prepared to ride out the rough months without losing faith in its own judgment and the ultimate talent of its prospects.

Building a winner without the luxury of a huge budget is not easy, but it *can* be done.

The Root of All Mismanagement

"By matching your bench-players' strengths to your starters' weaknesses, you can create a 'player' of All-Star caliber from spare parts. In 1982, we used Benny Ayala, John Lowenstein and Gary Roenicke in left field. They combined to hit 37 homers, which is the same has having a Reggie Jackson in the batting order. Individually, Roenicke, Lowenstein or Ayala could never compare to Jackson, but when used against the pitchers they could hit, they collectively performed like a star."
— Earl Weaver, *Weaver on Strategy*

Sometimes the best way to learn how to do something is to learn how *not* to do it. A perfect object lesson in how not to build a roster is the 1998 Orioles, who sported the largest payroll in the history of the game and finished a miserable 79-83, nearly 20 games worse than the previous year's model. How could this happen? And, more important, how can other teams avoid repeating this colossal mistake?

Although the Orioles are a prosperous team owned principally by a very wealthy lawyer, I believe that the root of their problems is money. Or, to be more accurate, their mismanagement of money.

The "Cal Ripken Rule"

I believe that the overwhelming reason why the 1998 Orioles were so bad is the "Cal Ripken Rule."

I'm referring to the vow by Orioles owner Peter Angelos never to pay any free agent more than the $7 million per year of Ripken's contract. For a billion-dollar lawyer, this promise shows an appalling lack of understanding of even the most basic principles of (baseball) economics.

First, it fails to recognize that the price of talent in big league baseball is constantly in flux. Yet the Orioles capped their salary for individual players on the basis of a commitment they had made to Ripken six years earlier. Never mind that by 1998, Ripken's contract wasn't even among the twenty highest in the game.

The market blew past the Ripken Rule. In January of '96, the highest-paid player in baseball was Ken Griffey, at $8.5 million. Today — as this is written, anyhow — that honor goes to Kevin Brown at $15 million. So in less than three years, the market had gone up by almost 100%. In 1995, $7 million could buy you the best second baseman in baseball; by the end of '98, it wouldn't even buy you Al Leiter. By next year, $7 million may be the standard for middle relievers and utility infielders. Who knows?

The Highest Paid Player in Baseball

Player	Team	Date	Average Yearly Salary
K. Brown	LA	12-98	$15.0M
M. Piazza	NYN	10-98	$13.0M
P. Martinez	BOS	12-97	$12.5M
G. Maddux	ATL	8-97	$11.5M
B. Bonds	SF	2-97	$11.45M
A. Belle	CHA	11-96	$11.0M
K. Griffey	SEA	1-96	$8.5M
B. Bonds	SF	12-92	$7.29M
R. Sandberg	CHN	3-92	$7.1M
B. Bonilla	NYN	12-91	$5.8M
R. Clemens	BOS	2-91	$5.38M
J. Canseco	OAK	6-90	$4.7M
D. Mattingly	NYA	4-90	$3.86M
W. Clark	SF	1-90	$3.75M
D. Stewart	OAK	1-90	$3.55M

215

Even without inflation, the Ripken Rule essentially said, "The Orioles are not willing to add a player to this team who is better (i.e., demands more money) than Cal Ripken." This means that when the team had a player who *was* better than Ripken, it either let him go or tried to convince him to take sub-market rates (as they did with Mike Mussina). Although that approach may save some money, it can only hurt in the long run. By 1998 the Orioles — though massively popular — were forced into insisting that nearly every contract involve large amounts of deferred money.

Most important, an artificial salary cap forces a prosperous team to allocate its talent in strange ways. Teams with money feel that they must spend accordingly (in part to satisfy expectations of fans). But since the Ripken Rule prohibited the Orioles' front office from signing superstars, the Orioles spread around their wealth by signing expensive veterans of middling quality, who in many cases were only marginally better than what they could have picked up off the waiver wire or various AAA teams. They virtually ignored potentially useful players such as Troy O'Leary, Matt Stairs and Kirt Ojala.

These are the kinds of guys that Earl Weaver is alluding to in the quotation at the top of this chapter. Today's Matt Stairs is yesterday's John Lowenstein. As I explained in the last chapter, maximizing value for cost is critical for small-market teams. But, as Weaver notes, it's also an important factor even for teams that may lead the league in payroll.

When a team is willing to spend $75 million on the total player payroll, but the maximum individual salary is capped at $7 million, the front office will almost certainly end up paying big bucks for small and fleeting improvements.

This, in turn, clogs up the entire team with somewhat expensive, pretty good veteran players. For this there are two immediate negative consequences: "pretty good" veteran players get real old and real bad real fast, and "pretty good" players block minor leaguers who could be *very* good.

The result for the Orioles in 1998 was a roster of aging, declining and overpaid veterans. When these players faltered, the Orioles didn't attempt to replace them with younger players, but rather went on another shopping spree for — you guessed it — another set of aging veterans who were almost certain to decline in a hurry.

After all, why commit to a year of growing pains when the money is there to bring in a veteran to do a slightly better job than a youngster?

THE   GM

As this book went to print, the Orioles abrogated the Ripken Rule by extending a five-year contract to Albert Belle worth $13 million per year. But the damage done by the Rule is still in place. Of the nine everyday starters, eight are over thirty, and all have contracts in the multimillions.

Though it pains me to say it, the Orioles seems stuck in a cycle of mediocrity, perpetually trying to squeeze useful seasons from aging players whose peak years are far behind them.

The veterans' administration

The Orioles were especially vulnerable to the aging effects of the Ripken Rule because their management seems to reflexively favor older players and shun the idea of working in younger talent. For 1998, the team signed four free agents who were coming off poor 1997 seasons. Andno other club showed much interest. Each had been a good player in the past, but those productive seasons were well behind them, and each seemed clearly to be in the midst of a career-ending decline.

It was some of the most spectacular overvaluing of experience at the expense of talent that I have ever seen in the sport.

Here's what each of those free agents looked like at the time.

Player A: A 37-year-old, defensively challenged right fielder who finished 1997 ranked dead last among all major-league regular outfielders with a .234/.284/.399 batting line.

Player B: A 33-year-old shortstop coming off of a .245/.275/.337 campaign.

Player C: A 35-year-old right-handed starting pitcher who had just put up a 5.74 ERA in the best pitcher's park in the American league, given up 170 hits, walked 69 and struck out just 85 in 169 1/3 innings pitched.

Player D: A 34-year-old left-handed reliever coming off of a 3-8 season in which he blew 11 of 25 save opportunities and pitched to a 7.27 ERA.

These guys were, quite possibly, the four worst free agents in all of baseball. And the Orioles signed all of them.

Predictably, they all played terribly. Player A, Joe Carter, hit .247/.297/.424 before being mercifully shipped off to San Francisco for a sore-armed AAA pitcher. Player B, Ozzie Guillen, hit .063 before being outright released. Player C, Norm Charlton, pitched to a 6.94 ERA before being released. Of the four, only Player D, Doug Drabek, lasted the entire season with the Orioles. He went 6-11 with a 7.29 ERA.

Each of these players did *exactly* what one should have suspected, given heir age and their previous performance. I didn't go into full histories with he brief profiles above, but if you were to plot out their career curves, you vould see that 1997 wasn't some sort of fluke bad year from which you'd expect a bounce forward. Rather, it was part of a steady progression towards ock-bottom for four players at the very end of their careers.

And yet the Orioles, somehow, thought there was more to these guys than he numbers revealed.

Why? Perhaps because the Orioles were looking at the wrong numbers, and got mesmerized by Joe Carter's 102 RBI in 1997. Or perhaps they weren't ooking at the numbers at all, and were mesmerized by Norm Charlton's ninety-mph fastball and left arm. Whatever methodology was behind that thinking, it is clear they were wrong.

And it was clear at the time.

Any objective evaluation of Joe Carter would have placed him on about the same level as Pete Incaviglia. In descriptive terms, they're both big, slow, right-handed hitters who strike out a ton, can't field, hit for a low average, walk occasionally and smack a home run every now and again, mostly against left-handers.

In statistical terms, they're also awfully close. Joe Carter, at the time, was a .259/.310/.464 hitter. Pete Incaviglia's career line is .247/.313/.450.

At the time Carter was signed, he wasn't a *completely* useless player. He could still hit lefties a little. He's the kind of guy who might make a useful spare part on a team strapped for right-handed power off the bench. In short, he's in the same relative position as a Pete Incaviglia. But Carter got a guaranteed job worth 500 at-bats and $3.5 million.

The Orioles spent more than $10 million on those four free agents. With that money, they could have signed a true superstar. Instead, they spread it around to four guys who made the team worse.

The winner's curse

If you turn back to the salary chart earlier in this chapter, you'll notice that, in many cases, the highest paid player in baseball wasn't the actual best player in baseball at the time he signed his contract (or ever). Sure, Bonds and Griffey are on that list, but so is Mattingly, three years past his prime, and Bobby Bonilla, and Will Clark, and, of course, Kevin Brown.

Clark and Bonilla and Brown all were good players, but how is i possible that these merely good players could make more money thar the actual best players in the sport?

George Washington University Law professor Charles B. Crave describes a game he conducts in his "Legal Negotiating" course in hi book *Effective Legal Negotiation and Settlement*. As an exercise, Professor Craver auctions off a one-dollar bill to the highest bidder. The twist on the auction is that not only does the winning bidder pay his bid (and receive the dollar), but the *second-highest* bidder also forfeits his bid as well, and gets nothing in return. The professor starts the bidding at fifty cents, with subsequent bids required to be a minimum of five cents higher.

The students are of course willing to offer any amount less than a dol lar in order to win a dollar, so the bidding escalates to fifty-five, sixty sixty-five cents, and all the way to ninety-five cents. At ninety-five cents the next bid submitted is $1. This brings the process to a temporary hal — and, incidentally, brings the professor a profit of ninety-five cents, since he collects the two highest bids and needs to turn over only one dollar.

Professor Craver then reminds the losing ninety-five cent bidder tha he or she can reduce his or her *overall* loss by bidding $1.05. Even though bidding more than a dollar for a dollar seems irrational, by "winning" with a $1.05 bid, the student is able to go from losing ninety-five cents to losing a mere nickel.

Once the bid is $1.05, the runner-up must now choose between losing a full dollar, or bidding $1.10 and losing a mere ten cents. And once the bid is $1.10, the just-outbid participant must choose between losing $1.0! and losing fifteen cents. And so on. The bids continue to escalate until one of the two remaining participants bails out, usually around $1.75, though sometimes the bids go as high as three dollars or more.

Here's how Professor Craver explains what has just happened:

"The purpose of this seemingly frivolous exercise is to graphically demonstrate how easily auction participants may become *psychologically entrapped* by the process itself. They initially believe they will make a prof it from the transaction. They quickly discover, however, that they mus accept a loss. The only question concerns the amount of their ultimate deficit."

When teams pursue free agents, they're playing a version of Craver's auction game. The bidding escalates for a player's services, and the hometown papers begin to cover the fact that their team is interested in spending money on a particular player. This generates expectations of a "victory" in terms of signing a free agent.

Like the two top bidders chasing after the one-dollar bill, two teams competing for the same free agent often find out that they're both losers, after all. The "winning" team succeeds in signing the player only after offering a price that no other team thinks is rational. And the "losing" team, having built up expectations with fans, often takes the amount of its last bid and offers it to another free agent, who it signs by offering a price that no other team thinks is rational.

A good example of "winner's curse" occurred during the 1998 off season, when Baltimore and Pittsburgh engaged in competition for the services of 34-year-old outfielder/third baseman B.J. Surhoff. Ultimately, the Pirates' bid forced the Orioles to offer nearly $20 million to Surhoff over four years, which was a level beyond which Pittsburgh was willing to go. The Pirates then turned around and spent several million dollars on Ed Sprague.

Both teams wound up losers. The Orioles got the better player — but at what price? The Pirates spent a lot less money, but in doing so deliberately blocked an outstanding prospect and threw away several million dollars on an awful player.

In 1997, the Orioles experienced "winner's curse" repeatedly: they tried to sign Paul Molitor and failed; they tried to sign Willie Banks and failed; they failed again and again until few players were left in the free agent pool. Then, in order to secure "victories," the Orioles went out and paid far more than any other team was willing to pay for Carter, Drabek, Guillen and Charlton.

Craver's advice?

"Before individuals commence negotiations, they should establish appropriate bargaining limits ... Unless they obtain information that objectively induces them to alter their preliminary assessments, they should be prepared to terminate their participation in the negotiation process as soon as it becomes apparent that they cannot obtain beneficial solutions through that means. If they instead continue to negotiate in a desperate effort to achieve any agreement, they are almost certain to experience 'winner's curse.'"

I couldn't have said it better myself.

PART SEVEN

THE VIEW FROM THE CHEAP SEATS

The Hall of Fame

Most baseball fans have two competing impulses on the Hall of Fame. We want our hometown and childhood heroes to be included with baseball's all-time elite. But we certainly don't want somebody else's marginal candidate bringing down the quality of the institution.

Of course, one fan's marginal candidate is another fan's hometown hero. This is probably why Hall of Fame debates tend to be so animated and passionate, and why they produce such strong emotional reactions whenever a fringe candidate is elected (or not elected).

Are there reasonable, objective criteria for what makes a Hall of Famer? One approach is logical and orderly. The Hall of Fame is an existing institution. There are existing Hall of Famers. All we have to do is look at the guys who are in the Hall of Fame, and from there, we can extrapolate the criteria for what makes a Hall of Famer. In essence, we follow precedent: if a player's career looks like that of other Hall of Famer players, he's in. If not, he's out. To elect a player who looks markedly different from the rest of the occupants at Cooperstown, you have to make a new rule. And to keep a guy out who otherwise appears to have Hall of Fame credentials, you have to do the same thing in reverse.

A good example of the "precedent" theory in action is Dave Kingman. He finished with 442 home runs. Every other eligible player with 442

224

home runs is in the Hall of Fame, and a bunch of power hitters with a lot *fewer* home runs are also in. So why not King Kong?

Some people have reasoned that Kingman's absence from the Hall somehow downgrades home runs as a qualification. That's silly. Home runs are still important. But we have to look at the total value of a player. Kingman hit a lot of home runs that helped his teams. Practically nothing else he did helped his teams, and plenty of things he did hurt them immensely. On balance, Kingman's strength (hitting homers) — great though it was — was solidly outweighed by his weaknesses (hitting for average, drawing walks, hitting for doubles and triples, speed and defense).

No player with one outstanding skill and six lousy ones should be in the Hall of Fame. Kingman doesn't belong; neither does Vince Coleman or Jack Tobin or Mark Belanger.

The problem with the "precedent" approach is that we also know that there are some mistakes in the Hall of Fame. (We often disagree as to who these mistakes are, but we can all agree that they're out there.) In order that these players not skew our reasoning, we have to admit candidly that their selection was a mistake.

Lawyers, incidentally, do this all the time. Nobody cites the *Dred Scott* decision as precedent. We recognize that sometimes human beings make mistakes and sometimes those mistakes get carved into stone. We can't take down Chick Hafey's plaque at Cooperstown , but we can make sure that no more Chick Hafeys get in, and one way to do that is not to use Chick Hafey as a rationale for admitting our marginally qualified Hometown Heroes.

And with the changing game of baseball, to apply precedent, we have to get more and more creative. As offense levels continue to skyrocket, the merely above-average of the '90s start looking a lot like the All-Time Greats of the '60s.

Faithfully we can pay homage to the code of the Hall of Fame only if we correctly place our modern heroes in their proper context. We must make sure we do not elect the merely above-average.

That brings us to Don Mattingly (and, later in this chapter, to Joe Carter). Both of these players will be eligible for the Hall within the next several years, and I don't think that either should be there.

First, Don Mattingly.

We all know that some achievements are typical of Hall of Fame players. Batters with 200-hit seasons, guys with career .300 averages, or 500 homers, or 3,000 hits, and so on. Baseball researcher Bill James has conducted an exhaustive comparison of all the players in the Hall of Fame and determine what statistical characteristics they share. From that research, he compiled a list of questions which he calls the "Hall of Fame Monitor." The Monitor is an objective yardstick to compare a current player to players already in the Hall.

The Monitor does not reflect James' opinions, or mine, about whether a player *ought* to be elected to the Hall, it only looks at the criteria that past voters have used.

For example, James discovered that most of the middle infielders in the Hall of Fame have played on several championship teams. Accordingly, the Monitor awards more points to a shortstop who played on a team that won the World Series (say, Jeff Blauser) than to a player who was both Rookie of the Year and the league leader in home runs. Objectively, I would say that this is silly. But the Monitor is designed to reward players with points for doing the sorts of things that the voters (members of the baseball Writers' Association of America) have rewarded in the past.

The Monitor awards points for proven Hall of Fame milestones. Once a player has around 100 points, he becomes a likely Hall of Famer; above 130, he's a near-lock. (For the full system, I recommend James' book *The Politics of Glory.*)

Using James' Hall of Fame Monitor, here's how Don Mattingly scores:

1. Batting average. Mattingly has one season in which he hit .352, and five others above .300 in 100 or more games. He just misses credit for 1994, in which he hit .304 in ninety-seven games. That's a total of seventeen points. (No, the Monitor does not put batting average into context across ERAs. But neither do most voters — hence, Chick Hafey.)

2. Big seasons. Mattingly has three seasons with 200 or more hits, two in which he scored 100 or more runs, and five during which drove in 100 or more runs. That's thirty-six more points, for a total of fifty-three.

3. Homers. Mattingly hit thirty homers on three different occasions, lodging six more points, bringing his total up to fifty-nine.

226

4. Doubles. Mattingly had two seasons above forty-five doubles and six more with thirty-five or more. That's ten more points, for a grand total of sixty-nine.

5. Awards. Mattingly gets eight points for his 1985 MVP Award. Additionally, he earns eighteen points for appearing in six consecutive All-Star games from 1984 to 1989, and one point for each of his nine Gold Gloves. That's a whopping thirty-five points for awards, bringing Mattingly's total to 104.

6. Championships. No points for Mattingly.

7. Black ink. Mattingly gets six points for leading the league in batting average in 1984 with .343, four points for leading the league in RBI in 1985 with 145, four points for twice leading the league in hits, and three points for leading the league in doubles on three occasions. That's seventeen more points, bringing Mattingly to 121.

8. Career milestones. Mattingly finished with 2,153 hits, earning four more points, bringing his total to 125.

9. Career average. Mattingly's lifetime average of .307 earns him 8 more points, bringing his total to 133.

10. Positional adjustment. Don Mattingly gets nothing for playing first base.

(The highest Monitor score for an active player is the Baltimore Orioles' Cal Ripken, who currently rates a 202 and will probably finish with 234 points.)

So, according to traditional Hall of Fame standards, Don Mattingly will almost certainly be elected. Is this really a proper interpretation of precedent? Or, put another way, given that we think it's likely that Mattingly will get in, we can now ask the harder question of whether he *ought* to get in.

Looking at the accomplishment list generated by the Monitor, there are really two broad arguments in favor of Mattingly: (1) Don Mattingly had a high batting average and three tremendous seasons at the plate, and (2) Don Mattingly was honored frequently by the baseball cognoscenti of his day, with numerous All-Star Game appearances, Gold Gloves and even an MVP trophy.

To that list, I'll add a third reason that Mattingly gets a lot of Hall of Fame attention: he was a very popular player for the New York Yankees.

Should those three arguments be enough to put someone in the Hall of Fame?

Let's dig deeper to find the principles behind the precedents. Broadly speaking, other Hall of Famers have been elected because of both their dominance and their longevity. And dominance is relative. A shortstop who hits .270/.340/.450 may be dominating. An outfielder who hits .300/.375/.525 may not be, even though the second player is clearly a better hitter than the first.

Dominance and longevity are the two characteristics of the players whom we identify as Inner Circle, no-doubt-about-it Hall of Famers — guys like Babe Ruth, Ted Williams, Ty Cobb, Mike Schmidt and so forth. Those guys are, of course, easy cases.

The harder cases come in balancing between players who were outstanding, but in a shorter career, or those who were very good for a very long time. Historically, the Hall of Fame has preferred the former to the latter; that's why Sandy Koufax is a no-brainer but Bert Blyleven has drawn little support.

The Monitor, for the most part, doesn't look at the player's career as a whole — instead it focuses on individual season milestones. In other words, accurately reflecting Hall voting patterns, it favors dominance over longevity. But since both are important, let's look at Don Mattingly's career statistics:

YRS	G	AB	R	H	2B	3B	HR	RBI	BB	SB	CS	AVG/	OBP/	SLG	OPS
14	1785	7003	1007	2153	442	20	222	1099	588	14	9	.307/	.358/	.471	.829

Clearly, in terms of overall career value, Don Mattingly isn't within a light-year of the Hall of Fame. When ranked against the all-time greats, he shows up on exactly two leader boards. His .307 career batting average ranks ninety-ninth all-time, just ahead of Joe Vosmik. And his 442 career doubles tie him with Dick Bartell for sixty-fourth place all time.

Neither Vosmik nor Bartell is in the Hall of Fame.

And that's it for Mattingly. To even crack the top 100 in any other statistical category, Mattingly would have needed to play more than 400 more games, compile more than 1,000 more at-bats, score 265 more runs, lodge another 200 hits, hit forty more homers, draw 375 more walks, drive in eighty-six more runs, and raise his OPS by thirty-seven points.

In terms of overall career value, Don Mattingly matches up quite well with another far less-celebrated contemporary, Danny Tartabull. Like Mattingly, Tartabull is hanging around the very bottom rungs of the top 100 All-Time leaderboards — he's ninety-ninth all-time in OPS and one hundred in home runs.

Here are Tartabull's career numbers:

YRS	G	AB	R	H	2B	3B	HR	RBI	BB	SB	CS	AVG/	OBP/	SLG	OPS
13	1403	5004	754	1366	289	22	262	925	764	37	30	.273/	.368/	.497	.865

Tartabull's career doesn't exactly mirror Mattingly's; Mattingly had a higher average, more doubles and played for a longer time, while Tartabull had more walks and home runs, and much higher rates of overall production and driving in runners. But Mattingly and Tartabull were comparable in terms of overall value. Tartabull was a superior hitter, but Mattingly played longer and was a superior defender, albeit at a position where defense isn't considered particularly important.

One could make arguments either way for preferring Tartabull to Mattingly, and that's precisely my point: it's not clear that one is significantly better than the other.

Yet. at the risk of wagering on the stunningly obvious, I'd bet a ham sandwich that Danny Tartabull's Hall of Fame vote total taps out at zero.

So what separates Mattingly from Tartabull? Several things, including career path, intangibles, defense and differing skill sets. The question is whether those differences are enough to put Mattingly in the Hall of Fame.

Career path

Even though Mattingly and Tartabull put up similar career numbers, the way each one got there was quite different. Tartabull was amazingly consistent. Mattingly had several great seasons but otherwise was barely better than average, and sometimes worse than that.

Tartabull had just one year in which he led any league in anything
— 1991, when he led the AL in slugging percentage with .593. His batting average didn't vary much from year to year — he hit .270, .309,
.274, .268, .268, .316, .266, .250, .256, .236 and .254 for his career. Scan
through Tartabull's home runs totals, and you find pretty much the
same boring consistency: 25, 34, 26, 18, 15, 31, 25, 31, 19, 8 and 27. RBI?
96, 101, 102, 62, 60, 100, 85, 102, 67, 35, 101.

In other words, for the most part, Tartabull chugged along at a
.270/.370/.500 pace, hitting about twenty-seven home runs and driving in around 100 runs per season. He never came close to being the
best at anything at any given time, but over his career he was consistently very good, year after year.

On the other hand, the bulk of Mattingly's career numbers come
from a few tremendous peak seasons. In 1984, he hit .343/.381/.537,
with 44 doubles, twenty-three homers, and 110 RBI. The next season,
his MVP year of 1985, he hit .324/.371/.567, with forty-eight doubles,
thirty-five homers and 145 RBI. And the year after that was an even
better season with the stick: .352/.394/.573, with 53 doubles, thirty-
one HR, and 113 RBI. In those three seasons, he led the AL in hits
twice, in doubles three times, in total bases twice, in RBI, batting average and slugging percentage once each.

(I should point out that Mattingly's 1987 was superficially similar to
those three superb seasons of '84-'86: .327/.378/.559. But in 1987,
offense levels jumped more than twenty points of OPS across the
board, so Mattingly's numbers actually declined. Again, context is
everything.)

And after 1987, Mattingly's career could be described charitably as
mediocre. He would never again lead the league in any statistical category. His batting average remained around .300 — three seasons
above that line, and five below it — but ranged from .256 to .311, never
again close to the .352 he had hit in 1986. His power dropped from thirty homers to as low as five; from fifty doubles to as low as sixteen;
from 388 total bases to around 200. A first baseman who routinely hits
.290/.330/.400 isn't just below average, he's awful.

But during his career peak, from 1984 to 1986, he was arguably the
best hitter in baseball. That should count for something. Is it enough to
get him into the Hall of Fame? Not for me.

Intangibles

At the risk of being labeled a Yankee-hater, I'll go double-or-nothing on the ham sandwich wager and bet that if Don Mattingly had been the first baseman for, say, the Montreal Expos from 1983 to 1995, then the demand for Don Mattingly's induction into the Hall of Fame would be comparable to that for Danny Tartabull.

Mattingly didn't play for Montreal, though. He played for the New York Yankees, and along the way he acquired an aura of leadership that seems to give him a big edge in the "intangibles" department.

Having been a Yankee adds a lot to a player's Hall of Fame resumé. The Yankees are baseball's most storied franchise, and they play in baseball's biggest media market. New York is the sports media center of the universe, meaning that Yankee players are the subject of more discussion and more analysis and more hype than players on any other team. Furthermore, the Yankees and the Mets are the home town team of most of the important figures in national sports media — the network sports anchors and commentators and those of (Connecticut-based) ESPN.

To play in the pinstripes automatically adds glamour and lustre to a player's career, and if he plays well, he's the subject of more adoring attention than he would get anywhere else.

For most of the non-Yankee fans reading this book, I'm just repeating the obvious.

To Yankee fans — and, by default, to millions of fans around the country whose opinions were shaped by New York-based media types — Don Mattingly was "Donnie Baseball." He was said to have "embodied baseball in his soul." He was the Yankees' clubhouse leader. Furthermore, the Yankees traditionally have had at least one marquee player every year who embodied the franchise, and during much of Mattingly's career he was that player, with a lineage going back through Mantle, DiMaggio, Gehrig and Ruth. He was *special*.

Even if you accept these claims at face value, there's still one problem with giving Mattingly credit for being the Yankees' team leader: Mattingly didn't lead the team anywhere.

During the career of "Donnie Baseball," the Yankees finished third, third, second, second, fourth, fifth, fifth, last, fifth, tied for fourth, second, and second. Their lone postseason berth — as a wildcard team that lost in five games to the Mariners — came in the last year of Mattingly's career.

The very next year after Mattingly retired, the Yankees won 92 games, the AL East and the World Series. The year after that, the Yanks made the playoffs again. The year after that was 1998, in which I shouldn't have to remind you that the Yankees set a record for total wins in a year with 125 en route to another World Series title.

When you play for fourteen years, and the team wins nothing, and then the instant you retire the team wins two World Championships in three years, well, it's awfully hard to argue that the team missed your leadership.

Obviously, Mattingly's popularity is beyond dispute. But "popularity" isn't the same as "leadership."

Fielding

An edge here to Mattingly, but it's of minor value. Virtually no players are in the Hall of Fame primarily because of their fielding, and certainly no first baseman has ever been elected for that reason.

Mattingly's fielding was highly praised during his career, but I wonder how much of that was the Pinstripe Effect in full bloom. Even though he has nine Gold Gloves, I'm not convinced that Mattingly was "the best defensive first baseman of all time" (as he was sometimes touted). I'm not sure that he was the best defensive first baseman in *New York* for most of his career, given the Mets' Keith Hernandez.

But even if it were true, I can't see that it would be significant enough to put Mattingly into the Hall of Fame. If his numbers were otherwise borderline; if he'd had six or seven top seasons instead of three; if his dropoff had been less severe; if any of those things made him more deserving on the merits, then perhaps his defense would be enough to push him over the top.

The counter-argument, from those who argue by analogy, is usually Ozzie Smith, who will be inducted into the Hall of Fame around the same time that Mattingly starts getting serious consideration. If Ozzie can get in on the basis of a decent bat for his position and superlative defense, why not Donnie?

The answers are numerous: (1) Over the course of their careers, Ozzie was probably a better hitter for a shortstop than Mattingly was for a first baseman, even though the numbers on the surface might suggest otherwise; (2) Ozzie was, in all likelihood, the best defensive shortstop of all

232

time, and Mattingly wasn't the best defensive first baseman of any time; and (3) defense at shortstop is only about a million times more important than defense at first.

His defense doesn't get Don Mattingly into the Hall of Fame — not if I'm casting the ballot. Don Mattingly's only claim to the Hall is three superb years as a hitter, and that's not good enough.

In fact, the Mattingly vote will be a good test of the Monitor, which predicts that he is a near lock. If BBWAA voters do not vote in Mattingly, it will be a sign that voters have become more sophisticated, and that the Monitor's criteria will have to be revised.

However, if Mattingly *is* voted into the Hall, then a lot of players are going to be shafted during the next ten to twenty years, because there simply isn't enough room in the Hall for every player whose qualifications will be equal to Don Mattingly's.

Joe Carter is another widely touted but marginal Hall of Fame candidate. This is his career line:

YRS	G	AB	R	H	2B	3B	HR	RBI	BB	SB	CS	AVG/	OBP/	SLG	OPS
17	2189	8422	1170	2184	432	53	396	1445	527	231	66	.259/	.306/	.464	.770

Since I have denied Mattingly his Cooperstown niche, it probably comes as no surprise that I think Carter should have to pay to even visit the Hall of Fame.

Let's get Carter's qualifications out of the way up front. His RBI total of 1445 ranks forty-second of all time, just above Gorgeous George Davis, and just below Jim Rice. And that rank will have dropped by the time Carter is eligible.

Carter's home run total of 396 ranks twenty-eighth, sandwiched between two non-Hall of Famers, Dale Murphy and Graig Nettles. (In all fairness, I should add that neither Murphy nor Nettles would be a disgrace to the Hall if admitted, and Murphy is still under consideration by the voters.)

His 432 doubles tie him with non-Hall of Famer Tim Wallach for seventy-sixth place. (Tim Wallach, I shouldn't have to tell you, *would* be a disgrace if somehow selected to the Hall of Fame. Of course, you never know what the Veteran's Committee will do.)

And that's all.

Despite Carter's higher career totals than Mattingly, he has many fewer individual milestones. The Hall of Fame Monitor rates him an 85, which isn't even a borderline candidate.

So what are the arguments in favor of Carter? Essentially, I think there are three:

1. He was a big-time RBI man;
2. He hit a really famous home run during the World Series; and
3. He once had a 30-30 season, and finished with 396 homers and 231 steals (this latter total doesn't put him anywhere near the top 100 all-time).

None of these arguments is particularly persuasive, at least not in the face of Carter's lifetime .770 OPS. The RBI, I guess, will carry the most weight with the BBWAA voters. But to be honest, for a "big-time RBI man," Carter didn't really have all that impressive a career. In sixteen seasons, he led the league in RBI exactly once, in 1986, when he had 121 with Cleveland. He has a lot of seasons with 100 or more RBI — ten, to be precise — but 100 RBI in the 1990s is simply no big deal. In 1998, *forty-two* players had at least 100 RBI. That's a long way cry from 1971, when only four managed to knock in 100 or more.

Context, context, context.

Finally, it should be added that Carter compiled his RBI in perhaps the least impressive fashion: for much of his career, he was a relatively poor hitter in the middle of good lineups with guys who got on base a lot, so he got a ton of RBI opportunities. He drove in many of those runners by making outs. As ESPN's Rob Neyer once put it, "Four men in the entire history of baseball have driven in 100-plus runs while posting a sub-.700 OPS, and Joe Carter is two of them."

Carter's speed/power combination is just another variant of the Dave Kingman question. The issue is not whether a player has a single exceptional skill or even a rare combination of two skills. What really counts is how much, overall, the player contributed to his teams. Carter's speed plus Carter's power just isn't enough to make up for his lifetime .259 average, poor walk rates, relatively weak slugging percentage, and the fact that he played the outfield (where high offensive production is expected).

This leaves us with the 1993 World Series. It was a great home run, but if that's what counts, I vote for Kirk Gibson.

21

Fantasy Baseball: Getting Unreal

I'm no Rotisserie expert. I've played in a grand total of one fantasy league, in 1998. On the other hand, I won that league rather handily, so I *do* have a perfect record at the time I write this. My experience is with a draft-style league rather than an auction-style, but the general principles are similar for both.

I wouldn't presume to write a full treatment on how to draft, trade and win in fantasy baseball. There are entire books dedicated to this subject by people who've played fantasy baseball for more years than I've been alive. But just as in real baseball, fantasy baseball suffers from its own "conventional wisdom" that often leads people to make wrong decisions — and presents the opportunity for you to make the right ones.

Here are some guidelines to being a winner in fantasy baseball.

None of these principles are a substitute for doing good basic research on the players. But if you take a critical eye into the draft, you'll find opportunities that others miss.

Accumulate the most points

This is going to sound absurdly simple, but the biggest thing to remember about the difference between fantasy baseball and real baseball is that the objective of a real baseball team is to win ball games. The object of a fantasy team is to *score points*, and that's it.

In my league, I finished with almost twice as many points as a team featuring Mark McGwire and his 70 home runs, Mike Piazza, Juan Gonzalez, and Jeff Bagwell. Those were probably four of the ten best players in baseball, and any real team with those four players in the lineup would almost certainly be polishing its World Series rings by now.

But fantasy baseball isn't real baseball, and in most leagues four players — even four super-stud players — can't carry you to the top. When averaged into nineteen other guys, even Mark McGwire doesn't add up to much more than eighth place if the other guys are stiffs.

Had this team owner put as much effort into drafting his supporting cast as he did in drafting and trading for his front-line players, he might have won the league.

A corollary of this very simple rule is to know your scoring categories. Our league, for example, uses the custom category of doubles plus triples. So it came as a shock to me to see players drafting off of third-party publications and cheat sheets, because *none of these publications ranked players by doubles and triples!*

Frank Thomas went with the sixth pick overall in our draft last year. I wouldn't have bet on Thomas' awful year — and I wouldn't bet on it happening again in 1999, either — but this was a silly pick for our league. Frank Thomas hits for good extra-base power, but he is not an elite hitter when it comes to doubles and triples.

This means that Thomas, who dominates every other category except stolen bases, isn't quite as valuable in our league as he would be in another. I had Thomas ranked below Edgar Martinez, who hits for average, hits home runs, scores runs, knocks in RBI, *and* hits a bunch of doubles.

There is no way on earth I'd draft Edgar Martinez ahead of Frank Thomas in a real baseball league, but this is fantasy. The object isn't to win, it's to score points.

Don't fixate on the recent past

As I prepared for my first year of Roto ball, I read most of the major publications devoted to the fantasy game. I was astonished to see how much weight the fantasy publications gave to a player's immediate previous season. Not surprisingly, perhaps, the other players in the league had adopted this same mentality, which allowed me to pick up an amazing steal.

Virtually every publication which forecast the draft in the '98 season had A-Rod ranked a low first-rounder, number 10 or so, based on his 1997 season:

G	AB	R	H	2B	3B	HR	RBI	BB	K	SB	CS	AVG	OBP	SLG
141	587	100	176	40	3	23	84	41	99	29	6	.300/	.350/	.496

If you were projecting for 1998 based primarily on 1997, then you probably wouldn't have had A-Rod in the top five, either. But the outlook is different when you consider Rodriguez's only other big league season.

	G	AB	R	H	2B	3B	HR	RBI	BB	K	SB	CS	AVG	OBP	SLG
1996	146	601	141	215	54	1	36	123	59	104	15	4	.358/	.414/	.631
1997	141	587	100	176	40	3	23	84	41	99	29	6	.300/	.350/	.496

And all of a sudden, instead of projecting twenty-five homers and a .300 average with 100 runs scored, you set your sights a bit higher, especially when you consider his age (22).

In our league, I drew the fourth drafting position. There were two players kept as franchisers, so I had, in effect, the sixth draft pick overall.

I had had Rodriguez rated as my number one pick. I couldn't believe it when he wasn't franchised, and I couldn't believe it when he was available when the draft order got to me.

I snapped him up.

This was only possible because the other players in the league had become fixated on his slight decline in '97 and had managed to persuade themselves that it represented his true level. I knew that at age twenty-two, Rodriguez was more likely to improve in '98 — and he did.

This myopia works the other way, too. I have found that when a player has a career season, virtually all fantasy baseball publications project him to repeat or at least approach those numbers again, even if that peak was way out of line with everything he had done before.

Playing it my way, you will miss some breakthroughs, I'll admit. I never would have drafted Damion Easley in 1998. Here was a guy whose previous career high until 1997– in six seasons of mostly part-time duty — was six home runs, forty-one runs, thirty-five RBI, and nine stolen bases.

238

In 1997, he hit .264/.362/.471, launched twenty-two homers, scored ninety-seven runs, drove in seventy-two, stole twenty-eight bases, with thirty-seven doubles and three triples. This was at age twenty-eight. So I passed on him in '98, figuring that one year way out of line with the rest of his career had to be a fluke. Easley, of course, promptly bettered just about every one of his numbers from the previous year. Oops.

Whenever you're dealing with 300 players, you're bound to see a few strange career curves. In general, though, solid fundamentals will make you a winner.

Replacement, average values and positional scarcity

After you've generated reasonable projections for all of the players available in your league's draft, you need to come up with a system for comparing value across players.

I project only the maximum number that can be drafted. If we have twelve teams, each with one shortstop and one middle infielder, then I draw up projections for exactly twenty-four shortstops.

The shortstop rated number 25 then becomes my "replacement-level" shortstop. I know that if I draft a shortstop and he's sent back to the minors or he breaks his leg or falls into a tiger pit or something, I can always get a player at least as good as this number-25 guy.

The other thing I do is take the average production of every hitter and pitcher on my list. (I also calculate standard deviations, but I'm real geeky.) Then, I assign a point value to each player based on how he stands in relation to the average player.

Most of my outfielders will have a higher value, overall, than most of my shortstops. I'll return to this in a moment. But in effect, assigning an overall value this way allows me to compare any player to: (1) the player I could get in the very last round if I pass on this guy, and (2) the average production that every team is going to get from its hitters.

This method would be helpful to a real-life GM as well. It would allow him to put a true value on anomalies like a slugging second basemen by comparing his production to that of the "replacement level" player.

Actually, I think that all big league GMs and their assistants should be required to play in a Rotisserie league; if you can't beat a bunch of amateurs playing a much simplified version of baseball, how are you going to succeed at the Real Thing?

One lesson that many GMs need to learn — but which every smart fantasy player knows — is positional scarcity. Good players are harder to find at some positions than at others.

To understand what is "good," look to the bottom echelons across different positions. If you are in a mixed league that drafts a total of sixty outfielders and twenty-five shortstops, compare the outfielders you rank as numbers fifty-five through sixty against the shortstops you rank from twenty to twenty-five.

You'll learn a lot that way. Most magazines and books and players plan their draft from Round One on down; they plot out the best players and then work in the next best, and then hold their nose and dive in for the worst ones. I do the opposite. I start out with pick number 23 and figure out who I would be willing to accept in that spot. Last year, that dead-last spot got me Jason Giambi. Another team selected Matt Walbeck(!) with their last pick.

That, in a nutshell, is positional scarcity.

A word of caution: some leagues minimize the effects of positional scarcity by drafting from a pool of teams equal to the number of owners while still requiring you to field five starting outfielders. Since real teams play only three outfielders on a regular basis, your "expert" fantasy team is now arbitrarily forced to draft five outfielders, pinch hitters, defensive replacements and other seldom-used spare parts. The sixtieth-best outfielder in an AL-only league is just as bad as the worst catchers and shortstops. In such leagues, positional scarcity may be harder to calculate, and may not exist at all.

Understand opportunity costs

When I project players, I draw big thick lines between relatively comparable classes at each position. For example, if you rank the available shortstops in your draft as: Alex Rodriguez, Nomar Garciaparra, Derek Jeter, Omar Vizquel, Miguel Tejada, Mike Caruso, Royce Clayton, etc. — then you want to put a big divider between Garciaparra and Jeter, between Jeter and Vizquel, and between Tejada and Caruso (or however you see the classes break down).

Suppose in your first round, A-Rod, Garciaparra and Jeter are all picked. (This isn't much of a stretch.) Do you then turn around and take Vizquel in the second round, in order to secure a shortstop? Of course not.

240

Vizquel is roughly comparable to Tejada; if you pass on Vizquel now and he is taken before your next round, you can still get a guy almost as good.

One of the more stupid mistakes I made in my draft was panicking as I watched a lot of closers get taken in the fourth round. I then spent my fourth-round pick on Mark Wohlers, which would have been a total disaster if I hadn't traded him before he completely self-destructed.

Drafting Wohlers in the fourth round was an idiotic move, not because he had an unexpectedly awful season, but because he was virtually identical to a bunch of players who were drafted a lot lower. Troy Percival lasted another five or six rounds, and I had him and Wohlers ranked roughly equal.

Yet I chose to forego a quality player I could have gotten with that fourth-round pick — Jason Kendall, Scott Rolen, Ray Lankford and David Cone all went after Wohlers. Stupid, stupid, stupid.

Play poker

Going hand-in-hand with the principle of opportunity cost is the fact that you are drafting against human beings, not against a computer projection system. You need to figure out what the other guys are thinking and how they value players.

I had Vladimir Guerrero rated as about the twenty-fifth-best player overall last year, but I waited until the thirteenth round to draft him because I noticed that my competitors were shying away from young players, particularly young guys on lousy teams. I probably could have waited even longer than that, but the thought of losing Guerrero was too painful. I *did* lose out on Ben Grieve, by overestimating how long I could wait to sneak him through.

Playing poker isn't always about sneaking a bargain through in the later rounds. If you're in a league where six guys grossly overvalue starting pitching, you'll have to over-value at least one pitcher yourself — or resign yourself to not getting a good starter.

This is all part of why draft day is so much fun. You can plan and strategize all you want, but ultimately, those battle plans will hinge upon how your enemies plan *their* strategies.

"Playing poker" extends far beyond the actual draft. Just like Bud Selig shouldn't run down baseball and his Brewers whenever he opens his mouth, you should *always* talk about your team as though you've drafted according to divine inspiration. Never let your fellow owners pick up on your mistakes and disappointments; talk up your players as though you planned it that way.

I did that after I drafted Chipper Jones in the second round — probably too high — and, when he had fifteen home runs by early May, I traded him with a straight face to a guy who assumed he would hit forty-five. I think this was possible only because I talked about Chipper as if he *was* going to hit forty-five.

Don't watch TV before your draft

For a week or more before your draft, you should *not* watch SportsCenter or read *Baseball Weekly* or any other up-to-the-minute sports publication. You shouldn't watch any spring training games, either. And more than anything, you shouldn't draft anyone from your hometown team unless it's a player most fans dislike.

I say this somewhat tongue-in-cheek, but the general principle is valid. When you're making baseball decisions, you shouldn't get caught up in emotions or the heat of the moment. This is why scouts ought to judge real baseball talent from the armchairs first and the field second. We're humans. We love human-interest stories. It's hard to resist when Peter Gammons calls a fringe prospect a "can't-miss-superstar," or a rookie you've always liked hits .587 in March, or when Chris Myers interviews a beloved veteran who's been "training harder than ever" for the upcoming season.

I promise you that if you make your decisions based upon all of these "intangible" factors, and you throw out the hard work you've done in preparation just because someone has strung together thirty decent at-bats in spring training, you'll be sorry.

The Last Word

The book you are holding in your hands grew out of a series of arguments that began in the early 1990s. Back then, I was just a kid in college, a die-hard Orioles fan who found the Internet a fruitful place to discuss my opinions and insights about my favorite team.

I like to think that I was a pretty well-informed fan back then. Then, as now, I read just about everything about baseball that I could get my hands on. I went to as many games as my college budget would allow, and watched the rest on TV or listened on the radio. I could recite Craig Worthington's RBI totals or rattle off Jeff Ballard's record and ERA off the top of my head.

But I had never seriously questioned the things that team management espoused, never turned a critical eye towards the newspapers, never scratched my head and wondered whether the TV broadcaster or radio call-in show host might be completely wrong. Oh, sure, I disagreed with grand pronouncements from time to time, but when something was presented to me as a fact, I simply presumed that I wasn't being lied to.

So when all the local sportswriters tabbed Juan Bell as a top-notch prospect, then by golly, he must be. If it was all right to trade Eddie Murray because he was a malcontent and a poor influence in the clubhouse, then that must be gospel truth. If the Orioles weren't going to notice Murray's absence because they had a hotshot slugger named Jim Traber, well, you get the idea.

I quickly learned a harsh lesson in expressing one's opinions on the Net. Unlike writing an op-ed piece (or a book), it will simply not do to be *mostly* right in a message posted to thousands, each of whom has the ability to write you back. It doesn't help to please *almost* everybody in your audience. In a message that's 95% correct, you will almost immediately get a slew of responses assailing that remaining 5%. It doesn't matter whether the rest of it was brilliant; you get no extra credit for being right about a bunch of other things if you're wrong about something else.

Similarly, if your message pleases 1,000 people and annoys ten, it will be the ten malcontents who respond, not the thousand members of your silent majority.

And, of course, in those days, I was neither 95% right nor appealing to all but a cranky minority. I was absolutely dead wrong. When I said, "Bill Ripken is a tough out" — that was indefensible. He simply *wasn't* a tough out, and the fact that he made a ton of outs (by having a low on-base percentage) was a pretty good indicator of that fact. When I said "Craig Worthington is the kind of player you want up there in the clutch" — that, too, was indefensible.

This all seemed drastically unfair to me. After all, I hadn't made up these pithy assessments of various players. I was merely repeating the assessments that others, unquestioned experts in the field, had made as if they were fact.

They weren't fact. Not even close.

And so I learned that sometimes journalists are just as fallible as the rest of us. I learned that a reporter doesn't have a clear view of a team's strength and weaknesses simply because he interviews Brian Holton in the locker room. I learned that sometimes teams lie to the press, and that *always* teams exaggerate and shade the truth.

And I learned that sometimes the professionals, the guys who get paid six and seven figures to know better, just aren't that smart. When Boston Red Sox GM Lou Gorman traded Jeff Bagwell to the Astros for thirty-nine-year-old journeyman left-hander Larry Andersen on the last day of August in 1990, there was nary a peep in the mainstream media. Red Sox press releases touted Gorman's "stretch drive acquisition" to shore up the bullpen. At the time, Red Sox officials viewed Bagwell as a defensively challenged third baseman with moderate, gap power. And what's the loss of one fringe prospect compared to winning the American League East?

In fact, the only place I saw anything negative about this trade was on the Internet, where howls arose. Heck, there are still howls: log onto rec.sport.baseball and post a message even mildly favorable to Lou Gorman, and I promise you that you'll earn no shortage of angry replies.

In hindsight, of course, everyone believes that Bagwell-for-Andersen was an idiotic trade. The Red Sox gave up an almost immediate MVP candidate for one month of a lousy left-hander. But at the time, the self-styled baseball "experts" didn't raise their arms in protest. They were simply unquestionably, unimaginably wrong. Only a few well-informed fans were unquestionably right — the people who had bothered to look at the facts and understand them and ask, "Are things really the way the experts tell us?"

A deal doesn't have to be Bagwell-for-Andersen bad to still be bad. In 1997, the Baltimore Orioles acquired Todd Zeile and Pete Incaviglia from the Philadelphia Phillies to bolster their team for the stretch run. Originally, the deal Orioles GM Pat Gillick had struck with the Phillies was that the O's would part with top prospect Calvin Maduro and throw in a player to be named later.

The teams had agreed that the PTBNL would be twenty-nine-year-old journeyman AAA player Don Florence. Florence was what the teams would affectionately call "roster filler." Neither side viewed him as a prospect, and he wasn't a major-league-caliber pitcher.

Unfortunately, Gillick hadn't bothered to check with his own AAA team before placing Florence on the PTBNL list. If he had, he would have found out that the Red Wings *released* Florence several days previously.

So the Phillies then received the other player on their list, 24-year-old right-hander Garrett Stephenson.

In 1997, Don Florence was out of baseball. In 1997, here's what Garrett Stephenson did for the Phillies:

G	GS	CG	IP	H	ER	R	HR	BB	K	W-L	ERA
20	18	2	117.0	104	45	41	11	38	81	8-6	3.15

That's probably a five-million-dollar pitching performance. And the

Phillies got him for nothing, because the Orioles' GM had made an administrative oversight. Stephenson wasn't a factor in the Phillies' 1998 season, and he may never pitch that well again. But the fact remains that he added a tremendous amount of value to the Phillies for that one year — and he was only a Phillie because Gillick wasn't smart enough to make a phone call before closing a deal.

If you or I made an "administrative oversight" that cost your company a five million dollar asset, how long do you think we'd remain employees?

But Pat Gillick wasn't excoriated or roundly criticized or even *marginally corrected* by anyone in the local Baltimore press or any national media sources. Not even when he pulled a similar boner a year later, "accidentally" releasing a player during spring training who suffered a serious arm injury. No, Gillick was hailed as a "genius," and there were columns mourning his passing when he retired from baseball after 1998.

Those are your experts.

Right now, you have an opportunity to be a free rider on the widespread ignorance of others. It's not quite so widespread anymore; you'd have a tough time convincing today's GMs to trade their Jeff Bagwell for your Larry Andersen. But there are still gaps between what people *ought* to know about baseball, and what they *do* know. By simply not believing everything you've read or been told; by simply desiring to find out the truth for yourself, you can make yourself an expert. And you can outperform the so-called experts handily.

The window of opportunity is closing, however. For the good of baseball, teams are learning, little by little, that the old ways don't work any more — and that perhaps, they never did.

In the late 1980s and the early 1990s, the New York Yankees were the equivalent of today's Baltimore Orioles. The team had the largest budget in baseball, was very active in the free agent market, and threw around enormous salaries that dwarfed other teams' ability to pay. Oh, and the Yankees were terrible. From 1989 to 1992, the Yankees finished every season with a losing record, ranging from fifth to seventh place in the AL East, an average of about nineteen games out of first.

They bottomed out in 1990, finishing dead last, with a 67-95 record. That year, the Yankees had a team .300 OBP, which was also dead last in the AL. The next year, their team OBP rose slightly, to .316 — which was still twelfth in the American League — and the Yankees won four more games. The year after that, team OBP rose another few points, to .328, and the Yankees won an additional five games.

In 1993, the Yankees acquired Wade Boggs and his career .416 on-base percentage at the top of the order, among others. Team OBP shot up from .328 to .356. The Yankees went from having the eighth-best on-base percentage in the league having the second-best. And they went from being a 76-86 team in fifth place to being an 88-74 team in second place.

Since that time, the Yankees have been among the top three teams in the league in on-base percentage, and they haven't had a losing season since. In 1998, when the Yankees were 114-48, their .364 team OBP was tops in baseball.

Yankees GM Brian Cashman has spoken about the organization's shift in philosophy towards promoting, acquiring and teaching the value of getting on base. He specifically mentions the acquisition of Wade Boggs as opening the eyes of the Yankees.

It certainly has brought home the victories.

I hope that this book has opened your eyes in much the same way that Wade Boggs opened them for the Yankees. If you're a fan, maybe you'll know just a little bit more than you did before sitting down with *Off Base*. And if you're a professional, perhaps some of the object lessons I've tried to discuss will leave a lasting impact. And for those of you who have to have a crib sheet, here are my last words to you:

- The single most important thing you can know about a player is his age. Players follow a career path, and their age when playing is the critical key to placing performance into its proper context.

- Minor league performance is meaningful, when understood properly. How a player actually performs is more important than what a scout thinks he *looks* like.

- Most people use statistics incorrectly. Know what a statistic is and how relevant it is to the performance you want to measure before placing your faith in numbers. The two most important statistics are a player's on base percentage (OBP) and his slugging percentage (SLG). By adding them together and dividing by ten, you get a neat scale that corresponds to how schoolchildren get graded on a test; an A+ is 100; an A, 92; a B, 85; a C, 75; a D, 65; and anything below 60 as a failing grade. It's not perfect, but it's a good way of getting a handle on how good a hitter someone is at a quick glance.

- Most people don't understand the way baseball in the 1990s differs from baseball in the '60s, '70s and '80s. Those differences can turn otherwise valid strategies into sure-fire losers, and cause us to over-rate today's hitters and under-rate today's pitchers.

- Most "experts" aren't any smarter and don't have any greater access to information than you do.

I'm still a long way from knowing it all about baseball, and I still believe that being forced to justify yourself to each and every reader is the best test of knowledge. So if you're mad as hell at this book and you can't take it any more, feel free to email me at **offbase99@hotmail.com**.

INDEX

250

254